Madcap Family
Book 6

Sheriff Morgan

Pamela Torrey

Dedication

This book is dedicated to anyone that has been mistreated or abused. Domestic violence is an epidemic.
Don't hide the abuse. Tell! Let people help you!
Don't become another statistic.

While reading this book, there may be some triggers. Some scenes that may be uncomfortable. I just want you to be aware of that.

I want to thank Drew Hays for his amazing photo that I used for the cover of Book 6. His work is amazing!

About Author is at the back of this book.

Other books in this series should be read in order.

Madcap Family
Madcap Family Book 2
Madcap Family Book 3
Madcap Family Book 4
Madcap Family Book 5
Madcap Family Book 6, Sheriff Morgan

October 1st, the night that Stella gave birth to Grace and Hannah.

Episode 1, Freak Storm

Morgan could not believe the level of crazy going on. Why, when a freak storm hit, did people not stay home?

Morgan could not fathom why there was a blizzard in October in the first place. Morgan wasn't sure where he heard the saying, *If you don't like the weather in Michigan, just wait five minutes.*

Morgan was parked by the North Star Café, on M-37.

An SUV flew past Morgan, heading for Fremont, they had to be doing eighty!

Morgan hit his flashers and siren, he roared up on the vehicle, scanning the guy's plate.

Morgan did a double take.

That's Alden's SUV! His mind registered.

Alden pulled over.

Morgan jumped out heading for the driver's side window.

Alden rolled down his window.

"No time to talk Morgan! Stella's in labor! She's going to drop these girls out right here! How about a police escort?"

Alden looked frantic, his eyes wild and panicked.

1

Morgan glanced inside the vehicle; he shifted his flashlight around. Stella wasn't in the front seat, he moved to look in the back, no Stella there either.

"Alden? I'm not seeing Stella... where did you stash her? In the way back?" Morgan asked with a big grin.

Alden frowned. Alden turned his head; he realized that Stella wasn't next to him. He glanced in the back, the suitcase was back there, but no Stella.

Alden started to shake. He slapped the palm of his hand to his forehead. He turned his head to look at Morgan; he tried to talk, but nothing came out.

"Alden? Did you jump in your car, and race towards the hospital, without your very pregnant wife?" Morgan grinned with glee.

"Morgan! I can't breathe! Help me! I think I'm dying!"

Alden gasped while grabbing his throat and face.

Morgan rolled his eyes and opened Alden's door.

"Dude! You know you have panic attacks!

"No! This time I'm dying, for sure! I swear my cheeks are numb!" Alden exclaimed.

"Dude! You are gripping your face! Let go! That's why your face is numb!"

Alden let go of his face.

"Ok... yes... that is better." Alden replied.

Morgan shook his head.

"I'll give you a police escort home, Alden."

"Thanks man! I'm much calmer, but I need to get home! Her contractions were so close together!" Alden huffed.

"You probably shouldn't have left without her, man. Never going to live that one down. I thought your "vasectomy failing" was hilarious! Impregnating your wife "twice" with twins was also outrageous! But this stunt? Whooee! You are a, DEAD MAN WALKING Alden!"

Alden dropped his forehead onto the steering wheel.

"My father is never going to let this go! Never!"

"Pop was at your house?" Morgan asked in awe.

"Yes! I must go Morgan! She probably already had them!" Alden exclaimed.

"Maybe if you missed the birth, would that really be so bad? You always pass out Alden."

Alden glared at Morgan.

"Some friend you are Morgan! Sure! Hit me when I'm already digging my own grave!"

"I'll turn my car around and get in front of you, Alden."

"Okay."

Morgan turned to get in his car. Another car came straight at him, it almost clipped him. The car was moving fast; faster than Alden had been moving! Morgan couldn't figure out how the car squeezed between him and his police car. Granted, the car was small, but it was too close by far!

Morgan turned to tell Alden he was on his own; Alden waved at him to go and get the bad guy.

Morgan once again hit his flashers and siren. Morgan's features turned grim when he realized that the dare devil did not appear to be pulling over.

Morgan was about to call for backup when he saw brake lights. The small car pulled over slowly, easing off the road, as best it could.

Morgan got out of his car. He unsnapped his service revolver, while sweeping his flashlight. His dash cam was recording, as well as his body cam, didn't pay to be too careful these days.

Morgan saw the window ease down. Morgan stepped up to the window. Inside, he saw a woman with long blond hair. When she looked towards him, he was shocked to see blood on her face.

Morgan lowered his flashlight a bit.

"Could you turn on your interior lights ma'am?"

When the woman tried to wriggle around to do as he asked, he saw metal glint from his flashlight. Morgan raised his gun and flashlight, his finger laid flat along the trigger guard, so he didn't accidentally shoot.

"Wait!" The woman cried out.

"I'm just trying to reach the interior light switch! My left wrist is cuffed to the steering wheel, off to the right side of the wheel. I can't use my left hand. I was trying to reach it with my right!"

Morgan's flashlight picked up the handcuff. He lowered his gun, flicked the safety switch back into place, holstering his side-arm.

Morgan opened the driver's door and flipped on the interior lights. Morgan could see her much better now. If he looked beyond the blood and the dirt, he could see that she was a very beautiful woman, a very beautiful, pregnant woman!

Morgan glanced in the back, there wasn't anything in the vehicle. No suitcase, she didn't seem to have a purse.

"What's your name?" Morgan asked.

The woman looked frightened.

"I'd rather not say." She whispered.

Morgan titled his head, slightly.

"Do you have any form of identification on you?"

The woman still looked frightened.

"No... I don't have anything."

Morgan sighed.

"Listen, I'm not going to arrest you... not yet anyway, but I need to take you to the hospital so you can be assessed."

The woman turned towards him quickly.

"Couldn't you just turn your head and let me go? Please! I need to keep going!" She started crying.

Morgan couldn't stand to see a woman cry; it ripped him apart every time.

"From what I can see, you have no money, no belongings, no purse, and your tank is empty. How far do you think you are going to get?"

Morgan squatted down next to her.

"How about I uncuff your left wrist; it looks bad. Your wrist needs medical attention. Would you like to tell me why you are cuffed to the steering wheel?"

Her expression could only be described as stubborn.

"I have nothing to say."

Morgan stood up, he leaned into the car, unlocking the cuff. The woman only had about five seconds of freedom. Morgan pulled her out of the car, he cuffed her wrists in the front, so he didn't hurt her wrist further. He tried to be as gentle as possible, but she still made an exclamation of pain.

Morgan led her to the squad car.

"But! I thought you weren't going to arrest me! Why are you doing this?" She cried.

"As of now, I have no idea who you are, or why you are cuffed to a steering wheel. You have no identification, and you have obvious wounds that need attention. Plus, you are pregnant! I would think that you would want to make sure the baby is alright."

The woman was now sobbing uncontrollably.

"Please, if you don't let me go... he is going to find me!" She sobbed.

Morgan deposited her in the back of his car. He called a tow truck to take the car to the impound station. Morgan cranked the wheel, heading towards the hospital in Fremont.

Morgan eyed the sobbing woman in the back of his car.

"I can't help you if you don't let me. I don't know what is going on in your life, but you must trust someone, trust me."

The woman slumped back; defeat written all over her.

"I tried that once, trust that is, look where that got me. Plus, there are two things in this life I don't trust, cops and lawyers."

Morgan grinned a bit.

"I can honestly say ma'am, I don't have a whole lot of trust in lawyers myself, and one of my best friends is a lawyer, go figure! But to lump me and my kind in with them... I'm feeling a bit wounded." Morgan joked.

Morgan felt a bit reassured when the woman let out an involuntary giggle.

Episode 2, Stella Meets the Mystery Woman

Morgan waited in the entryway. The hospital was so full they had people lying on gurneys everywhere.

The staff pushed his mystery lady out into the hallway.

A member of the hospital staff stopped next to the gurney.

"Hello dear, my name is Mildred. Can you tell me your name dear?"

Morgan's eyes shot towards the beautiful blonde.

His mystery lady scowled; her eyes went to evil slits.

"Janey... call me Janey."

Morgan arched an eyebrow.

The elderly staff member typed in Janey.

"Your last name?"

"Doe... buck. Yep, it's Doebuck."

Morgan snickered at the stunned look on Mildred's face. She turned towards Morgan, looking flummoxed.

"What do I do about that, Sheriff Dun?"

"I'll get back to you if she decides to confess her true name."

His mystery lady scowled at him.

"What makes you think that *Janey Doebuck is not* my real name?" *Janey* grumbled.

"If *Janey Doebuck*, is your real name... then, my name is *George Clooney.*"

Janey turned towards Morgan.

"You sort of look like *Clooney,* in a weird sort of way... bigger... and... meaner!"

Morgan chuckled.

"So, you think I'm a hotter, bigger, meaner, *Clooney?*" Morgan asked.

Janey made a sound of disgust.

"I never said you were hotter! Just bigger and meaner! You are mean because you could have let me go!"

Morgan shook his head no.

"Just doing my job... *Janey Doebuck*." Morgan tried to look stern, but he just couldn't pull it off. Morgan doubled over snickering.

Morgan turned towards Mildred.

"Thank you, Mildred."

"We will get to her as quickly as we can, sheriff. This storm brought out the crazies tonight... I mean... this morning. What time is it?" Mildred asked.

Morgan glanced at his watch.

"It's 5 am. I need a coffee for sure, but I can't leave her." Morgan groaned.

"I'll get you a coffee Morgan." Alden said from behind him.

Morgan spun around to see Alden walking in with a big grin on his face.

Morgan watched as the ambulance team unloaded Stella.

Morgan's jaw dropped seeing Stella being wheeled in, holding two beautiful baby girls. They both had dark swirling hair. That was about all he could see because they were wrapped up so nicely.

Stella grinned at Morgan.

"I heard you had to pull over this madman. All I can say is that I am so glad that I wasn't in that car with him. I probably would have had them on the side of the road."

Stella, made exaggerated, side-eyes, directed at Alden.

Stella went on to say, "Morgan, you know I would have been delivering those babies on my own. Because this guy would have been passed out cold!" Stella exclaimed.

Alden scowled.

Stella giggled.

"Pop delivered the twins, Morgan." Stella announced.

Morgan's face said it all. Morgan let out a whoop of laughter.

"Are you kidding me? Pop, delivered the girls?" Morgan asked.

Morgan looked at Alden.

"Dude! Where were you? You didn't make it home in time?"

Alden blushed to the roots of his hairline.

"I made it home!" Alden declared.

"He passed out! He woke up in time to see his girls come into this world." Stella said with a grin.

"I passed out because I saw my dad, sitting johnny-on-the-spot, in front of my woman's lady parts! Threw me into shock, I tell yah!" Alden declared.

Morgan patted Alden on the back.

"So, now for the rest of your life Alden, you will have to hear how your dad, YOUR DAD Alden! Delivered those girls!" Morgan laughed.

The ambulance guys laughed along with them, then asked where they should park Stella.

"We are beyond full but someone from the birthing floor is headed down to get them. Park her across from the mystery lady." The nurse stated.

Stella looked curious, as they slid her across the aisle, next to a filthy, bloody woman.

"Mystery lady? I admit I'm intrigued." Stella stated.

Stella noted that the woman was probably a stunner under the blood and dirt. The woman's hair was so blonde it was almost white.

The woman glanced at Stella and her two darlings, she smiled hesitantly.

"Twins? Oh my! How wonderful!"

Stella grinned.

"Well, I am now the proud mother of eight children, and this is my second set of twins. My first set are boys, these two, are Grace and Hannah."

Morgan watched the two get on like gangbusters; he figured babies brought everyone together.

"This is... my first child." The mystery woman said quietly. "I can't imagine having eight children." She went on to say.

Stella noted that the young woman's wrist was handcuffed to the gurney.

Stella glared at Morgan.

"What on earth Morgan! Do you see this poor woman's wrist? It looks like it needs medical attention immediately!" Stella exclaimed.

Morgan gaped at Stella.

"I didn't do that to her wrist! It was like that when I found her." Morgan explained in a rush.

"Well! Put that cuff on her other wrist! That looks painful! Have you no sense at all? Besides, she doesn't look like a criminal to me! Personally, I think she looks harmless!" Stella totally used her MOM voice.

Morgan unhooked the cuff, he felt guilty when the woman yelped. Morgan had to lean over her to clip the cuff to her right wrist.

Morgan ended up eye-to-eye with her. Her eyes were deep blue, the color of sapphires. Morgan froze, he realized that her skin was milky white under all that dirt and blood. Her lips were lush and full, he had the craziest, almost uncontrollable urge, to kiss her.

Morgan shot up and away from her. He was sure his face was on fire; he cleared his throat.

"How about that coffee, Alden? I could use a cup of strong coffee right now." Morgan's voice was usually very deep; he was sure it sounded a couple of octaves different, more soprano.

Alden eyed Morgan, he then, glanced at the woman on the gurney.

"She doesn't look like a criminal Morgan, more like the victim of a crime! What you got her cuffed like that for?" Alden looked disapproving, as well as suspicious.

Morgan seemed to shrug, he almost caught himself looking at the floor in shame, but then he reminded himself that he was just doing his job.

Alden shook his head.

"Why don't you come with me Morgan, the coffee station is right there. It is only about twelve feet away. I doubt she's going to get away! Plus, we can let these two ladies have a chat." Alden said.

Morgan eyed the coffee station, he nodded. He would still be able to see her, not hear their conversation but he would be able to keep his eye on her. He also thought that maybe Stella could get something out of her. People confided in Stella, she was kind and it showed.

"Good! Now that they are gone, why don't you tell me what you are doing here. What's your name? My name is Stella."

The woman seemed to hesitate.

"Just call me... London."

"London? How pretty. So, London, what brings you to our neck of the woods?"

London sighed.

"It's a long story and not a very pretty one either. I'd rather talk about your girls."

Stella smiled.

"Grace is on my right, and Hannah is on my left."

London eyed the two girls.

"They look identical! How can you tell them apart?"

"Grace has a string wrapped around her wrist; she came out first. My oldest boy AJ, put the string on her. AJ wanted to make sure that they didn't get mixed up."

"How old is he, your AJ, I mean?"

"He is fifteen! I can't believe my husband's "vasectomy failed" and I'm a mama to these two beauties." Stella crowed.

"Wow! So, tell me about your kids." London encouraged.

"We named AJ after his daddy, Alden James, Benjamin is next. Ben is named after my dad. Caleb and David are my twin boys, Elijah is my youngest boy, and then my Francine! Franny was my one and only girl until we had Grace and Hannah."

London gasped.

"Wait! You named your kids in alphabetical order? How amazing!"

Stella giggled.

"Caleb and David became the turning point. When they came along, we decided to pick a C and D name. We picked an E name for our last boy. Then, I finally got my baby girl Francine. I had to come up with an F name, I just had too! My Franny is fierce, bold, and beautiful. She is the only one in our family with hair like flame, streaks of different colors of fire. Not orange fire, but deep dark, warm reds. Franny's eyes are pale blue, they pop right out of her face!"

"She sounds lovely." London sighed.

"When you get away from that gorgeous hunk of a sheriff you come on over for dinner. We would love to have you."

London's eyes filled with tears.

"Oh honey, don't cry." Stella crooned.

London shook with the force of her feelings.

"Stella, you don't even know me... for all you know I could be a serial killer." London sighed.

Stella chuckled.

"If you are a serial killer, then I'm a bank robber. I'm a very good judge of character, always have been. You look like a lady in distress to me, someone that needs a nice, warm hug. Truth is London, you look like you need a vacation."

London laughed out loud; she hadn't laughed in so long that it felt... unnatural.

Morgan and Alden heard London laughing, they looked towards the women.

Morgan looked curious; Alden just grinned.

"I'm just so tired. Tired of being tired. Tired of running. You seem so nice... I'm not used to... nice." London gulped.

Stella murmured sympathetically.

"Morgan is a man you can trust London. He's the best man I know, other than my husband. He's so smoking hot that when he looks at me with those turquoise eyes... I forget I'm married, almost. I have never seen eyes that color! Morgan may be the youngest Sheriff I've ever known, and I'm sure he won the election by a landslide because every woman in the county voted for him. The truth is... he's the best sheriff we've ever had. When I think of honor, integrity, and strength, that's Morgan."

Stella winked and whispered.

"Admit it, you think he's gorgeous."

London eyed the men. They stood in the hallway, just outside the coffee room. London looked the sheriff over, she had to admit that he was very good looking.

Dark hair, black as night. It curled slightly, she figured he probably hated his hair, but she had the oddest urge to run her fingers through it, to see if it was as soft as it looked.

London realized that he had to be six-four, broad shoulders, all-in-all, very handsome.

"He's a man... just like any other man. The outside package can be great, but the inside... well... not interested."

Stella looked sad.

"I'm sorry some man hurt you... but what about the baby? Where's the father?"

A nurse from the baby floor stepped up to Stella's gurney.

Stella was still waiting for an answer.

"This baby doesn't have a father. I will never let that man anywhere near my baby." London said with conviction.

Stella nodded.

"If you really feel that way London... then, I believe you. You must have your reasons. Just know that in our town, you never have to be alone. We help each other, we are here for one another. You need help? You got it."

Stella asked the nurse to write down her phone number to give to London.

London took the scrap of paper.

The nurse wheeled Stella away.

Morgan wandered back towards London.

Just as Stella's gurney was being rolled onto the elevator, she yelled out a final goodbye.

"Bye London! You call me, you hear?"

Morgan's eyes shot towards his mystery lady.

"Your name is London?"

London wasn't listening, she was staring at her scrap of paper. Tears tracked down her face, her shoulders shook with fatigue.

Morgan leaned over London again, he uncuffed her right wrist.

London glanced up at him.

"Why did you do that?" She asked.

"I've decided to trust you, in the hopes that you will decide to trust me. Stella seems to like you and Alden chewed me out for treating you like a criminal. He yelled at me so much... I started to squirm."

Morgan stuck his hand out to shake London's hand.

"Hi, let's start over. My name is Morgan, just Morgan. I'm not the sheriff right now. Just a new friend. What do you say?"

London peered at the hand that was in front of her. She hesitated.

What if she decided to trust this man and he... hurt her?

London glanced up, into Morgan's face.

He looked sincere, and kind, but she had seen that before... how quickly things changed. But she had no money, no car, nothing.

London nodded, she tried to hide her fear. London placed her right hand in his. London's hand all but disappeared, his hand swallowed hers.

London gulped yanking her hand away.

"I'll... do my best to... try... to trust you. I can only hope that you are being sincere."

Morgan smiled softly at London; London felt her heart speed up a bit.

Oh no! Not happening!

London scowled at Morgan.

"You are in my bubble! Back up buddy!" London leaned back as far as she could, to put some distance between them.

Morgan chuckled, but he backed up.

There was a loud crash, Morgan whipped his head towards the commotion.

London looked nervous.

Morgan patted her good hand.

"I'm going to trust you to stay put... looks like the nurses have a drunk on their hands. I'll be right back."

Morgan raced to help.

Episode 3, We Still Seem to Have Trust Issues!

Morgan stood outside, the wind was wild, the snow coming down so hard that seeing was impossible.

I never should have trusted her! Now, she's probably out there somewhere, in the cold! She's going to freeze to death!

Morgan looked around, listening for any cries of distress but all he could hear was the howling wind.

Morgan got to his car, he sat there, wondering what his next move was. *If he called it in, he would have to write up a report. But if he didn't call it in... what were the chances of finding her in this freak storm?*

Morgan's cell buzzed; he sighed while reaching for it.

"Hey sheriff Mildred here, we have a lady here, she's crying and asking for you. Where did you go? We are keeping her overnight, to give her fluids, and keep an eye on the baby."

"Wait! She, is still in the hospital? When I went back, she was gone!" Morgan exclaimed.

"Sheriff! She had to pee! Pregnant women pee! We ran some tests on her. Could you please just get your butt in here and calm her down! This can't be good for the baby!"

Morgan hung up his phone, feeling all kinds of a fool. When he saw the empty gurney, he just assumed she ran.

Morgan raced back into the hospital.

Mildred waved at him vigorously.

"Oh, thank goodness you are back! That girl is not a happy camper! Room fourteen, Sheriff."

Morgan charged down the hallway to room fourteen. Morgan could hear someone crying.

Morgan flew into the room. London took one look at him and opened her arms wide.

Morgan sat on the edge of the bed, taking London in his arms. He didn't want to even think about the fact that this woman felt so right in his arms.

"I thought you left me! I didn't know what to do!"

"I thought you left London. I was outside looking for you, not knowing what to do either."

London leaned back; she snickered a little.

"They took me for an x-ray. Plus, I had to pee! Pregnant women pee a lot don't yah know!" London exclaimed.

Morgan turned a bit red, then he looked down at her wrist. She had a pink cast on her left wrist.

"Your wrist is... is it broke?" Morgan questioned.

Morgan was beyond upset! He cuffed that wrist twice!

"Yes, it's not a complete break but it is cracked. Yay me! I get to wear this cast for six weeks. I sure hope I have it off by the time the baby is born."

Morgan looked flummoxed.

"Uh... when exactly is your baby due to be born?"

London's face flamed.

"I'm not sure, exactly."

Morgan went still.

"What do you mean you don't know?" Morgan made sure to keep his voice soft and soothing.

London looked down.

"I haven't been to an OB doctor… yet." She whispered.

Morgan surged to his feet.

"Did the doctor check the baby over yet? What exactly have they done for you here?"

London glanced up.

"They did vitals, and then an x-ray. The doc is keeping me overnight because I'm dehydrated. Dehydration can throw me into labor, he says."

Morgan's eyes widened.

"Are you having pains?"

London shrugged a little, then, she nodded yes.

"I wasn't… but I am having some twinges, now."

Morgan was about to charge out of the room to find the doctor, but the Doc came strolling in.

Dr. Wills is a tall man, in his fifties, with white hair and twinkling blue eyes. His eyebrows are still dark, it is a good look for him.

Morgan shook hands with Dr. Wills.

"Hey doc, I know you are keeping her, but she just told me she is having pains! What are you planning on doing about that?" Morgan practically shouted.

Dr. Wills arched one dark eyebrow.

"You almost sound like a panicky, expectant father, there Morgan." Doc chuckled.

Morgan scowled, he crossed his arms, looking a bit fierce.

"Of course, I'm not the father! She's a... friend."

Dr. Wills turned towards London.

"I must say Miss London, to have Morgan as a friend and champion, you could do no better."

London's gaze travelled between the two men.

She said nothing.

"Could you leave the room Morgan? I'm going to need to examine my patient."

Morgan nodded, leaving the room.

Morgan waited outside the door.

Doc stepped out, closing the door behind him.

Doc and Morgan sat down in a couple of chairs, slightly down the hall.

Doc sighed.

Morgan immediately went on red alert.

"Why the sigh doc?"

"I asked my patient if I could share my medical concerns with only you... she finally agreed."

"Is she okay?"

Doc shook his head.

"No, she is very much not okay. She is being moved upstairs to the OB floor. She's dehydrated, malnourished, and trying to go into labor. If you hadn't gotten to her, she probably would have been in serious trouble, out on the side of the road somewhere. On top of that, by examination and questioning her, I believe she is about six months into her pregnancy. When we do an ultrasound, we will have a more accurate due date for her. Why hasn't she had any OB treatment? That... I can only take a guess at."

Dr. Wills was always an easy-going guy but right now, he looked grim.

Morgan frowned; he had to admit that he was feeling kind of sick inside.

Doc went on to say, "I asked her if she had ever had any broken bones before... she gave me a fairly long list, Morgan." Doc said grimly.

Morgan felt the air rush out of his lungs, he sucked in a deep breath and wanted to punch something. Morgan was always cool under pressure but not today.

"She's a little slip of nothing! You are telling me that some... animal, out there, hurt her repeatedly?"

Doc patted Morgan's arm.

"You are in law enforcement Morgan; this cannot be the first time that you have seen domestic violence."

"Of course not!" Morgan exclaimed.

Morgan shook his head, frowning.

"But... she is so delicate; it seems unimaginable that anyone would want to hurt her." Morgan stated.

"There are some crazies in this world, Morgan. She will be staying up on the OB floor for a few days. She needs fluids, good food and a whole lot of rest. We also have people she can talk to; that is... if, she will talk."

Doc said goodbye, heading to his next patient.

Morgan stood up as the nurses wheeled London out of her room.

London looked around the nurses, spotting Morgan.

London seemed to relax when her eyes fell on him.

Morgan smiled, walking beside her gurney as they headed for the elevator.

When they got to the OB floor, the nurses eased London's bed to a halt.

Morgan could hear Alden and Stella talking.

Morgan glanced into their room.

Alden was holding one beautiful baby; Stella was holding the other.

Stella looked up.

"Hey Morgan! Where is my London!" Stella demanded to know.

Morgan grinned.

"Your London? Seems to me, all you care about is London! I took her to jail! She's a master criminal with a list of priors as long as my arm!" Morgan huffed.

Stella rolled her eyes.

"Seriously Morgan! Where did you put my new bestie?"

"I'm out here Stella! They are trying to figure out where to put me!" London yelled.

Stella's jaw dropped open.

"I'm in the ward! There are four beds here! For the love of goodness bring her in here, please!" Stella yelled.

One of the nurses popped into the room.

"Uh, but I thought she was under arrest? She would need to be isolated."

Alden surged to his feet in outrage. Alden frowned fiercely, pointing his finger at Morgan.

"You arrested her, Morgan? I thought I knew you man! What charges Morgan? Explain yourself, Morgan! Don't worry London, I will get you the best lawyer ever!" Alden's entire body trembled with aggression.

Morgan rolled both eyes so far, he should have fallen backwards.

London could be heard... giggling... in the hallway.

Morgan spun around, eyeing London, in awe.

London's smile vanished.

Morgan smiled widely at her.

London just gaped at him, looking hesitant.

Morgan turned towards the nurse.

"London is not under arrest." Morgan stated quietly.

The nurse turned towards Stella.

"But Mrs. Westman, you gave birth to twins! We thought you might need extra rest! Although, why you wanted to be in the ward, I can't fathom."

"I have a very large family. I chose the ward so we can all fit! They all visit at once; we get it over with in one fell swoop! So, bring London on in here! There is plenty of room in here with me."

So, nurse Mary wheeled London into the room. She parked her next to Stella. Stella was by the window, London, closest to the door.

An old battle-axe of a nurse, sailed into the room. She frowned at London fiercely, yanking the curtain shut between the two women.

Stella, Alden, and Morgan could not believe what that woman had just done to London!

The old, cranky nurse sailed back out as fast as she showed up.

The other nurse, named Mary, stopped at the foot of Stella's bed.

"Is it ok if I open the curtain? I'm so sorry Louise acted like that." Mary said.

"Yes, please, and keep that woman out of my room!" Stella demanded.

When Mary slid the curtain open, they could all see what Louise's actions had done to London.

London was curled on her right side, crying.

Morgan and Alden looked stressed.

Stella talked softly to London.

"London, pay no attention to Nurszilla. Besides, I heard the nurses saying they were bringing someone up that was trying to go into labor. I was worried that it was you. The best thing for you to do is to roll over onto your left side. I don't know why, but for some reason, being on your left really works." Stella stated.

Mary agreed with Stella.

"I'll make sure that Louise... doesn't bother you again." Stella whispered.

London sighed, she rolled over onto her left, looking exhausted.

London's eyes filled with tears. Her eyes were so heavy, she couldn't fight sleep anymore.

"Ok... and... thank you, Stella." London whispered.

Stella eyed London, she chewed on her thumb nail. Stella looked at London like she was a lost puppy that needed saving.

Alden caressed Stella's cheek.

"You get some rest too sweetheart. We have eight children woman, but even I can see that you would wrap that girl up in one of your special Stella hugs, and carry her on home, forever!"

Stella's eyes were also closing, she yawned.

"You know me so well Alden. I love you. You guys go on home, I'm beat."

Stella rolled to her side, and promptly fell asleep.

Morgan and Alden slipped out, closing the door softly.

The guys looked towards the nurses' station where they heard raised voices.

Morgan strolled over to Nurszilla.

"First, lower your voices, those two just fell asleep."

Nurszilla scowled at Morgan.

"You do not tell me what to do Morgan Dun! You may be the sheriff, but you don't get to come in here and throw your weight around!"

"Listen lady. That woman in there, she has been beaten, I'm sure many times. Too many of her bones have been broken, who knows how many times over. Who knows what else has been done to her? We don't know, because she's too afraid to talk. Can you find even one ounce of sympathy for that woman?"

Nurszilla froze.

"I... I... just thought she was a criminal! I had no idea!"

The nurse looked beyond upset.

Morgan noted that her name on her badge was, indeed, *Louise.*

Louise seemed much more subdued.

Louise seemed to hesitate.

"My sister... she was put in intensive care, because her husband was an alcoholic and an abuser. You have my word that I do understand, and I am so very sorry. I will be extremely kind to her, from here on out."

Morgan calmed down, hearing her words.

Morgan was quick to forgive.

"I believe you ma'am. In fact, I think that you will, indeed, be the perfect nurse for her. Thank you. I'm trusting you to take good care of them both, ok?"

Louise smiled.

"You have my word Sheriff Dun. I want you to know that I will be apologizing to that young lady. If I'm in the wrong, I admit it. It's been an extremely awful day and night but that is no excuse for my behavior."

Morgan shook hands with the nurses, then turned to leave.

"I'll walk out with you Morgan; I'm headed home myself." Alden said.

The men left the hospital.

They both went their separate ways, home to their beds.

When Morgan drifted off, the last thing he remembered was a small woman, beautiful but broken. He could see her lying on her side, curled in on herself.

Morgan could only hope London would begin to trust him.

Episode 4, Suspicious Nature.

"Look Sheriff! We don't know her name! We don't know anything about her! How are we supposed to bill this?"

Twenty-four hours later Morgan was standing in front of a very frustrated hospital employee.

"Tell me you are not badgering this woman for information!" Morgan exclaimed.

Mrs. Town huffed.

"Look it is my job to make sure that this stuff gets taken care of! While I do sympathize with this... London woman... the bills must be paid."

Dr. Wills wandered up.

"Are you harassing my staff, Morgan?" Doc grinned.

Morgan crossed his arms, he looked like a solid, unmovable wall.

"When can she be discharged Doc?" Morgan growled.

Doc looked shocked.

"Well, I was hoping she would be here for at least a week. What is the problem, here?"

Mrs. Town turned towards Doc.

"She won't give us any information! I don't know how to bill this!"

"Set her free Doc, I'll take a vacation. She can recuperate at my place. I'll pay the bill."

Mrs. Town gaped at Morgan.

Doc rubbed his chin in thought.

"She would have to be on IV's, we can have a nurse stop in and change the fluids out. Her labor has stopped but it won't stay stopped if you keep questioning her Mrs. Town."

Mrs. Town looked offended.

"I am only doing my job, Dr. Wills!"

"Itemize the bill, please. Give it to me and I will have it paid before she leaves the hospital." Morgan declared.

Doc nodded.

"Okay, I can entrust her to you Morgan but I'm not releasing her until tomorrow. I will need to see her at my clinic in three days."

Doc walked in one direction, Mrs. Town stuck her nose in the air, storming off in the opposite direction.

Morgan chuckled stepping onto the elevator.

When the doors slid open, Morgan got the shock of a lifetime.

London was standing, with her back to the elevator doors. Nurse Mary was pleading with London to get back into bed.

London didn't see the doors open because she was frantically, repeatedly, pressing the elevator button.

"No! I'm leaving! You can't stop me!"
London screamed.

Morgan swooped down on London like a
bird of prey.

One second London was standing on her
own two feet. The next second, she was scooped
up into a strong pair of arms.

London screamed; she fought but Morgan
kept walking.

"Stope that screaming or you will upset
Stella and the twins. You wouldn't want that,
would you?" Morgan asked calmly.

Stella and the girls were London's weak
spot. Morgan had that all figured out, and he
wasn't afraid to use that information for his own
benefit.

London stopped struggling.

Nurse Mary fretted, running ahead to fix
London's sheets.

Stella was out of bed, moving slowly, she
was determined to get to London.

"See what you did, London? You got Stella
all upset! She was getting out of bed to come
after you. Do you feel guilty, at all, about that?"
Morgan admonished.

London sagged.

London crossed her arms while looking very
much like a mule.

London got quiet, remembering her left wrist being cuffed. London seemed to drift off. Her eyes went vacant, she looked off to her left. London closed her eyes; she inhaled deeply through her nose. Then, she exhaled slowly out through her mouth.

Morgan stepped forward but Stella waved him away.

Stella eased down till she was sitting on the side of London's bed. Stella talked softly to London, while she held her hand.

Morgan didn't think that her words made much sense, but it seemed to calm London down.

London opened her eyes.

London's eyes tracked to Stella. When London realized that Stella was within reaching distance, London leaned her head on Stella's chest. She looked like a child in need of comfort.

Stella stroked her hair, talking softly.

London fell asleep against Stella.

Morgan eased London back, pulling her covers over her.

Then, Morgan took Stella by the arm, putting her back to bed also.

"Morgan? You think she's ever going to be, ok?" Stella asked.

"It's going to take time Stella... but I just don't know. I'm going to go put in for a vacation. She's being discharged tomorrow. I'm taking her home with me. I admit, I'm nervous about this, but until we know what is going on with her, I don't see any other alternative. I have a very bad feeling that her troubles are not over. This feeling I get, I never ignore it, Stella, not ever." Morgan stated grimly.

"If anyone can help her Morgan, it's you. I'm going home tomorrow too. Please bring her over to my house in a couple of weeks, promise me Morgan." Stella pleaded.

"You have my word on that, Stella."

Morgan headed out to make some calls and fill out some paperwork. Morgan would need to bring his second in command, up to speed.

Morgan had plenty of vacation time built up. He planned on sticking close to London until he could get this all sorted out. Morgan was determined to find out who she was running from.

London wouldn't be able to move forward until she faced her past.

After he went to his office he would go home and get her room ready. Morgan knew she was going to throw a fit, but her choices were slim-to-none.

Morgan stepped outside.

Yesterday there was a blizzard; today, sunshine and warmth.

Morgan shrugged.

That's Michigan for you. He thought.

Episode 5, Wall of Westman's

Morgan strolled down the hallway to Stella and London's room. Nurse Mary and Nurse Louise stood in the doorway grinning from ear-to-ear.

Morgan stopped.

"Hello ladies, what on earth is going on here?" He asked.

Louise patted Morgan on the arm.

"I'm pretty sure that every Westman known-to-man is in that room. I now see why Stella chose to be placed in the ward."

Morgan nodded.

Morgan stepped forward. AJ shook his hand, then Ben. Caleb and David grinned at him and waved. Elijah had a camera in his hand, he was acting like a professional with that thing. Francine took center stage. Franny had one of the girls in her arms, she looked down on that baby with adoration.

"Mama! You did so good! They are so pretty they make my heart hurt!"

Franny kissed her baby sister on the forehead. She handed that one to her daddy and reached for the other.

When baby number two was placed in her arms, she sighed like her life was complete.

Morgan grinned.

Even at the age of six, Franny tells anyone that will listen, that when she grows up, she's going to be a doctor. Sitting in the center of the Westman's she is like a flame, a burning sun in their center. Her features, one hundred percent Westman, her hair and eyes she supposedly got from her great, great, great aunt.

Pop and Grandma Nettie arrived. Everyone parted like the *Red Sea,* allowing the couple to get to the bed.

Nettie sat down next to Francine she stroked her hair lovingly.

Francine looked up at her grandma.

"Look at her grandma, isn't she the most beautiful thing you have ever seen?"

Grandma's eyes were focused on Francine.

"Yes, the most beautiful thing in the whole world."

Franny tilted her head.

"Grandma! You aren't even looking at her!"

Nettie cupped Francine's cheek.

"I'm looking at you darling, you are so amazing. Did I tell you that you are my favorite, oldest granddaughter?"

Franny rolled her eyes.

"Grandma Nettie, I am your ONLY oldest granddaughter."

Nettie chuckled.

"But you are still my favorite oldest!"

"Look at the babies' grandma, they are perfection!" Francine exclaimed.

Grandma looked down.

"Oh my! She is beyond beautiful!"

"Here mom, hold this one." Alden said. "They are a match set." He went on to say.

Nettie held Grace; Franny held Hannah.

Grandma Nettie looked up.

"They take my breath away!"

Pop cleared his throat.

"I have an announcement to make."

All eyes turned towards Pop.

"Some of you may not know this... but I delivered these two beauties, in a raging storm! My poor wife had a cast on her arm, she was all but useless! Alden walked in and promptly fainted! But I stayed cool under pressure! I caught those babies when they popped out!"

Pop waved his arms around while shrugging.

"You women talk about how difficult childbirth is… huh… I just don't see it that way. All-in-all, those girls were born quick!" Pop exclaimed.

London giggled, she put her hand over her mouth to try to stifle the sound, but it had to be set free. London's hand dropped and her beautiful laughter filled the room.

Morgan couldn't take his eyes off her.

Every other female in the room, talked at once, at Pop!

"You don't know what you are talking about old man! I had to give birth to our almost twelve-pound baby by myself! Where were you again?" Nettie questioned.

Pop's eyeballs practically fell out, they were so wide.

"I've given birth to eight children Pop! It doesn't feel good!" Stella chimed in.

Stella's sister Annie patted Pop on the shoulder.

"That last part Pop, you probably shouldn't have gone there, just sayin."

Stella was still glaring at Pop, she started unbuttoning her shirt.

"I think I'll give the girls a snack!" Stella said, in a very snarky manner.

Pop's eyes went wide with horror, he tried to run away, but there were too many Westman's in the way.

Pop turned fast, bouncing off the wall of Westman's. Pop tried to wriggle between them but there was no getting past them.

"Don't you be whipping those out with me in the room! You just hold on a second! What is this? A nudist colony?" Pop questioned.

No one moved, they all crossed their arms, creating an even stronger barrier.

Pop, realizing that he couldn't get out that way dropped to all fours.

Nettie laughed evilly.

"But dear, YOU delivered those girls SINGLE HANDED, I was ALL BUT USELESS you said... and remember... you LOOKED at Stella's LADY PARTS!"

Pop glanced back at Nettie, still on all fours, his mouth open.

"Don't remind me of what I saw! It was not natural! Not natural at all!" Pop exclaimed.

Alden chuckled. "Dad, you do know that what Stella went through is called *Natural Childbirth.*"

Pop gaped at his son but then slammed his eyes shut, again. Pop crawled forward but the men kept stepping in his way; the men stood their ground. Stella stopped opening her blouse, but Pop didn't realize that. Pop had his eyes shut tight, while trying to crawl forward.

"Is this family for real?" London giggled.

Morgan eased closer to London. When he sat down next to her, she didn't seem to mind. Morgan figured she was too focused on his crazy friends.

Nettie smiled at London.

"This is as real as it gets darlin. By the way, welcome to the family!" Nettie exclaimed.

London's jaw dropped.

"I'm family?" She whispered, in awe.

Nettie nodded, everyone nodded, while smiling at her.

London got misty-eyed, her smile a bit watery.

Alden bent down, hauling his father to his feet.

"Her blouse is not even open, Dad!"

Pop turned to look at Stella.

"Daughter in-law, you are beyond evil!"

Pop shrugged, then smiled.

"But I like it." He chuckled.

Episode 6, Lactating?

Morgan stood in Stella and London's room. Morgan knew he was staring at London, but the truth was, he couldn't seem to look away.

Plus, he was keeping his eyes trained on London, so he was careful NOT to stare at Stella.

London was cleaned up and ready to go.

Stella took down London's sizes, she sent Grandma Nettie and her sister Annie shopping. London had bags and bags of stuff that had to be carried out.

London had a shirt on as blue as her eyes, she paired her shirt with leggings, and slip-on shoes.

Stella glanced from London to Morgan, back and forth.

Stella smiled a secretive smile, an all-knowing smile.

"You two do realize that I'm still right here, don't you?" Stella asked.

Morgan and London blushed, simultaneously.

London blushed because she got caught checking out Morgan.

Morgan blushed because he was avoiding looking towards Stella... she was... so... swollen today.

"Ok, we must go... you ready London? Say goodbye to your gal-pal. We must get going!" Morgan exclaimed.

Stella looked confused while she hugged London goodbye.

"Morgan? Sometimes, you act so weird. What is your problem today? You won't even look at me... "

Stella's voice trailed off, then an evil grin spread across her face.

Morgan saw that grin, then he quickly looked away.

"Let's go, London! I'll grab the bags!" Morgan rushed.

"Hold on just a second big guy." Stella said.

Morgan froze, he closed his eyes, he just knew she wasn't going to let this go!

"Are you by any chance avoiding... looking at me? Why is that I wonder?" Stella teased.

Morgan glared at Stella, his eyes staying focused in the corner behind Stella's head.

Morgan was so relieved when Alden walked in to pick up his wife.

Alden slapped Morgan on the back, said hi, then turned towards his wife.

"Whoa babe! Your milk came in! Whooee! You walk in a "B" cup and leave a "D," or is it an

"E?" Is that a real size? "E," I mean?" Alden laughed while gently hugging his wife.

"Hi honey, pretty sure these things are Double Ds." Stella complained.

Alden shook his head back and forth.

"You always did lactate like a champ."

London looked a bit disturbed.

"I didn't want to say anything, but... when I opened my eyes today and saw that you had... grown? I admit I am quite curious. This is my first baby, am I going to swell up like that?"

Morgan blushed, again.

"Maybe you two could talk on the phone about this? We should go, London." Morgan whispered.

Stella grinned.

"Have a seat for just a quick second Morgan. I'm going to educate London on the wonders of breast feeding."

Morgan groaned; Alden laughed.

London sat back down.

"You see London..." Stella started to say.

"I am going to take these bags to the car! You women get to saying what needs to be said. When I get back up here, you all better be done!" Morgan growled.

Stella rolled her eyes.

London copied her.

Alden grabbed some bags.

"I'll help you man, but don't worry I'll fill you in on the way down to the car. I wouldn't want you to miss out on some of the interesting facts about breast feeding, dude!"

"You wouldn't!" Morgan exclaimed.

"Oh, I would! Payback dude!"

"For what? What could I ever, have possibly done to you, Alden?" Morgan sputtered.

"You pulled me over; I almost missed the birth of my twin girls. When Stella teased me about passing out, you didn't have my back, DUDE!"

Morgan shrugged, he tried to hide a smile.

"But it's so funny when you pass out like you do! I've never seen a guy pass out as much as you do, Alden."

"I have low blood sugar!" Alden insisted.

"Have you been tested for that Alden, or do you just like throwing that diagnosis around?" Morgan grinned.

Alden frowned; he had a very determined look on his face.

"As I was saying Morgan, when the baby suckles, it stimulates the breast...

"Aw man! Stop! I thought we were friends!"

Morgan charged out of the room, Alden hot on his heels, still spouting off facts about breast feeding, *and how important the mother's antibodies are for the babies...*

Morgan all but roared, while stabbing the elevator button.

"If I say I'm sorry, will you stop?" Morgan pleaded.

"I would love that!" Alden exclaimed; while grinning from ear-to-ear, rocking back and forth on his heels.

Morgan gritted his teeth.

"I'm sorry!" He growled, while grinding his molars.

"See! That wasn't so hard, was it? You're not gonna hit me are yah? Because I know, that would be considered assault. Don't make me call your pal, Jonas. Just think about it! You get arrested! Jonas becomes our Sheriff! You end up living above my garage! A pariah! A drunk that never showers."

"Are you quite finished Alden? Because I'm usually a pretty, calm guy, but I'm feeling the need to punch... something." Morgan's eyes glittered dangerously.

"My work here is done. I accept your apology. You said it sooo pretty! I will never forget it!" Alden had his face right up in Morgan's face.

Morgan placed his big, giant hand over Alden's grinning face and shoved.

Morgan stepped into the elevator, crowding the doorway. Alden's mouth dropped open; shock written all over his face.

As the elevator doors closed, Morgan smiled.

"I'm pretty sure you and I should avoid being together in this itty-bitty box together. I may not be able to control myself, DUDE!" Morgan taunted.

The elevator doors shut.

Alden doubled over laughing.

"Man! I love that guy!" Alden said out loud.

Alden took to the stairs, moving fast!

He planned on beating Morgan to the first floor!

As he charged down the stairs his laugh could only be classified as juvenile.

Episode 7, Home Sweet, Home

Morgan pulled up in front of his farmhouse. Morgan picked up the old house cheap when the market turned into a buyer's market.

Morgan's house has three stories. At the very top level is the attic. The attic window faces the front of the house. Its decorative window tends to catch people's attention. Morgan loves the swing on the front porch, he tends to sit outside, quite often, after dinner. The house, pale yellow, with white trim, sported flower boxes at every window.

London stepped out of the car.

London glanced at Morgan.

Morgan caught her looking at him.

"What? Is there something wrong?" Morgan asked.

"I guess... I wasn't expecting... this." London said.

Morgan smiled.

"What were you expecting?"

"I'm not sure, but not this perfectly beautiful farmhouse that should be in a magazine!" London exclaimed.

"I take it, you like my home?"

"Like is not a strong enough word."

"Come on, if you love the outside; wait until you see the inside." Morgan stated.

London practically speed walked inside.

When you enter through the front door, the foyer is huge and open. The stairs leading to the next floor are the main focal point and beyond stunning. To the left is the living room. It is very large. It has floor to ceiling windows; the room looks comfortable but stylish.

The dining room is to the right of the foyer, and behind that, is the kitchen.

London back tracked. Behind the stairs is a half-bath, beyond that a room that Morgan must use as an office. Off to the right of his office, another door. When she peeked into it, she realized that you could get to the kitchen from that way, as well. It was one giant circle; a lot of older houses were set up like that.

"There is another half-bath when you first come in the house from the back. There is a mud room, then the bathroom. Laundry facilities are in that bathroom. There is a washer and dryer upstairs as well, linen closet is in that room. There are four bedrooms total; two bedrooms on the left and two across the hall from them." Morgan explained.

"You live here, all by yourself?" London asked.

Morgan nodded.

"I saw this place and fell in love with the bones of it."

"The bones?"

"They just don't make houses like this anymore."

London heard the love and appreciation that this man had for his home.

"Who did the renovations? I assume it took some work to get it to look this wonderful?"

"I did most of it, but Alden and his boys helped, his brother in-law Tom jumped in. Pop directed, a lot!"

London grinned.

"I bet he did!"

"Come on, I'll show you where you are going to sleep."

Morgan led London up the stairs.

London ran her hand along the old banister, it was smooth to the touch.

When they reached the second floor, London saw a door immediately to the right.

"That's a bathroom. Down this way on the left is a closet, the second room was a bedroom, and a third bedroom after that, but I opened them up to make that my master bedroom. I have my own bathroom; you don't have to worry about sharing. The next door after mine is your room."

Morgan opened the door to her room.

London gasped.

The bed was against the back wall. It was a queen-size sleigh bed. The furniture in the room matched the bed.

The room was cream colored with touches of sage green.

Morgan opened a door, showing London her personal bath.

London was overwhelmed with the beauty of this place.

"You can use all the water you wish. I have solar panels out back, with floor to ceiling back up batteries. I put in a state of the art, top of the line, furnace. This place is insulated from top to bottom. I didn't want to give up the tall ceilings. I went crazy while insulating. Alden swears there is so much insulation in my attic crawl space that the house should cave in."

London was very quiet.

Morgan looked nervous.

"You, okay, London?"

London looked up.

"I've never seen a house so beautiful. You..."

London was about to say something, but she hesitated.

"What? What were you going to say?" Morgan asked.

"You built this home... and this is a home, Morgan. You hope to have a family, kids, a wife someday? You did all of this for her didn't you?"

Morgan looked around; he thought about what London said.

Morgan turned slowly, looking at his home with fresh eyes.

"I guess... I did. I mean, I'm in no rush to get married, but I never realized that that is what I was doing." Morgan said softly.

"She is one fortunate lady, Morgan; the one that wins your heart."

London set down some of her things.

Morgan seemed to wake up.

"Oh! Sorry! I've kept you standing here! You are supposed to be resting. I'll bring in all your stuff. You take a nap, while I cook dinner."

"I can help! I'm not an invalid Morgan."

"No way! You take a nap, doctors' orders, not mine. Besides I put dinner in the crock pot, it'll be done in a couple of hours."

"I could sleep. I feel like I've been sleeping and sleeping but I just want more. I'm just thankful that Dr. Wills changed his mind about the, in-home, IV's!" London exclaimed.

"About that, he said no IV's if you drink lots of fluids. I plan to push the fluids like a boss." Morgan assured her.

London chuckled as she got into bed.

"I am very sure that you will Morgan."

Morgan turned to leave.

"Morgan... thank you... for helping me." London whispered.

"You are very welcome, sleep well."
Morgan shut the door.

Episode 8, London's Past

London tried to run, she kept tripping and falling. She knew he was close! She could hear his evil laugh. He loved dragging out her terror, she knew if he caught her, he would beat her. Last time he caught her, he cut her.

London glanced back, it was so dark, he stopped in front of a window. The moon's light showed him clearly. London saw a knife glint in the moonlight. He resembled an angel, with his beautiful blonde looks, but his insides, rotten, evil.

"I know you're there. This time... you will never run from me again! I'll make sure of it!"

When he surged forward to grab her, she screamed the longest, most piercing scream she could manage. She could feel him on top of her, she fought like a wildcat, scratching and punching.

"London! Wake up! London! It's me, Morgan!"

London opened her eyes; she was pinned to the bed. Morgan had both her arms flat against the bed. Morgan was sitting on the side of the bed; he was breathing hard. London saw scratches on his face, he had blood running down his cheek, towards his chin.

London's eyes opened wide; horror crossed her face.

London started to sob, she felt weak from her dream, unable to even try to move.

Morgan lifted his hands away from her.

"You had a bad dream, London. Just a dream." He murmured. "He can't get you here. You are safe with me."

On Morgan went, talking in a reassuring voice.

London finally sat up; she cupped his cheek.

"I hurt you. I'm so sorry Morgan. We need to clean this! Please let me clean you up!" She begged.

Morgan smiled softly.

"I won't stop you if you want to, but I've had my share of bad days, in the injury department."

London looked disturbed by that revelation.

Together they went to the bathroom; Morgan pulled out the first-aid kit.

"Here you go." Morgan said.

Morgan sat back down on the bed so London could reach him.

London washed his wounds, she fretted about how to put a dressing on it.

"Let's leave it open to the air. You got the bleeding to stop, it should heal up quickly."

London fretted but she nodded.

Morgan put everything away, he placed his hand on her low back, escorting her down to dinner.

When they were seated, London looked at her meal. Roast beef, red potatoes, and baby carrots; it smelled wonderful.

"Do you like roast?" Morgan asked.

London looked up.

"I do but... I'm feeling a bit sick... from my dream... could I wait a bit to eat?" London asked.

"London you do not have to ask me for permission to eat or not eat. You can do whatever you want, while you are here."

London looked relieved.

London wandered outside. She spotted the swing on the front porch. London sat down. Looking around, London realized that the farm was very isolated.

Morgan wandered out.

"Mind if I join you?" He asked.

London nodded, patting the seat next to her.

Morgan sat down.

They were silent for a while, they listened to the sounds of nature, soaking up the beauty around them.

"You must tell me London." Morgan whispered. "You must tell me everything. I can't keep you safe unless I know what I'm dealing with here." Morgan's tone was kind but firm.

London looked a bit panicky, but she knew she had to trust someone.

London gulped, she didn't know what to do with her hands, so she gripped them together, tightly.

"I met Trent my fourth year of college... he seemed like... perfection. From his golden curls to his toes, his manner, and the way he treated me... he treated me like a princess."

Morgan waited; he didn't rush her.

"Looking back, I realize that he swept me off my feet; everything happened so fast! Trent insisted that we get married. He said that we would finish our last year of college together. He bought me the biggest diamond I'd ever seen."

Morgan glanced at her finger.

"I sold it, to run." London explained.

"It was too gaudy anyway, not my taste, at all." London stated.

Morgan grinned.

"After we were married, he started to change. Just little things, controlling things. One day I walked into the kitchen to find the refrigerator and all the cupboards locked. He even controlled how much I ate and drank. I have no family Morgan, I'm all alone in this world. I was always shy, quiet, happy to sit and read a book."

London sighed.

"I was the perfect target for him, I see that now."

London went quiet. She squirmed a bit, her hands shook.

Morgan held out his hand.

"You can take my hand in comfort or not, you have choices London. If you don't want to take my hand, that's ok, too."

A tear broke free, sliding down London's cheek.

London took his hand.

Holding Morgan's hand seemed to calm her down a bit; she felt anchored, secure.

"Trent moved us into a penthouse. The entire top floor was ours. I had no idea Trent was that rich! I was at Harvard on scholarship, he was there because he was filthy rich."

"You went to Harvard?" Morgan was impressed.

"I never graduated. Shortly after we married, Trent told me that he wanted a stay-at-home wife. So, I stayed at home. Whatever he told me to do, I did it. The first time he hit me… I thought I deserved it."

Morgan tried not to react, but he felt himself stiffen up.

"Trent told me what to wear, he allowed me to go shopping but he gave me deadlines. I was two minutes late one day because the traffic was so bad. I was explaining that to him. That was the first bad beating that he gave me."

"I should have gone to the hospital, but he wouldn't allow it."

London glanced at Morgan, he looked grim.

"You okay big guy?" London questioned.

Morgan huffed out a small laugh.

"You are asking me if I'm, okay? Please tell me this guy's last name so I can take care of business."

London froze.

"I'm telling you my story, so you know what you are getting yourself into. Know this, Morgan; he cannot know where I am!" London exclaimed.

"Keep going, I won't pressure you for his name, yet."

"Trent would beat me unconscious and then he would…he would…want to make up with me... even if I didn't want to." London's voice was so low that Morgan had to strain to hear her.

Morgan's gaze shot to London.

"He raped you?"

"He says it's not rape, if we are married."

"Years ago, that may have been the law, but that's not the law anymore." Morgan assured her.

"Trent was determined to get me pregnant. Trent beat me up every time the pregnancy stick showed that I wasn't pregnant. When I got away the first time, an agency hid me, it was a shelter. I was hidden for a long time; they helped me get my divorce. I thought I was finally free of him, but he found me."

Morgan tried to remain still, he tried not to react, but he had a feeling that the worst part of her story was to come.

"He grabbed me at a park. He tied me up with zip ties, I had duct tape on my mouth. We drove for hours; he loved the fact that I was terrified. I hyperventilated and passed out. When I woke up the duct tape was removed."

"He took me to the middle of nowhere, to a place called Monowi, Nebraska. When I tell you this place is remote... that just doesn't describe it. Trent owns a ghost town, I think only one person resides in the town, a caretaker. Trent dragged me into the woods, all I remember seeing was a sign that said, *Hold Up! Entering Outlaw Territory.* Come to find out it was an abandoned ski lift; they call it *Devils Nest.*"

London hesitated. "Like I said, he took me into the woods... and... after he finished with me... he pulled out a shovel. He started digging, he was laughing like a maniac. What he didn't know was that I had gotten into the habit of carrying a small knife. It was tucked in my right sock; thank goodness it was still there! He was so busy talking to himself that he didn't see me cut those ties. I ran for the car. I got in that car, just in the nick of time and locked the doors. Trent threatened me and raged at me."

Morgan sucked in a breath, waiting.

"I got away. I drove away wearing only a long shirt and my socks. I left him there with my grave almost completely dug. I kept running. I never stopped. I ditched his car, sold my ring, and held onto every dime. I bought a beater car, paid cash for it and kept my foot on the gas pedal. I started feeling sick, I thought it was because I wasn't sleeping well. I bought a pregnancy test. When it came back positive... I cried for days. Just think, if he would have been standing there, seeing that positive sign, he probably would have praised me that day."

Morgan finally asked a question.

"When I found you, you had a broken wrist, and you had bruises and blood on you. How did that happen?"

"He found me! I was on the outskirts of Fremont, in a little town called Holton. I was coming out of a small tavern. I think it was called *Dave's Tavern and Grill;* he grabbed me! He put me in my car, in the passenger seat. When he clapped that cuff on my wrist, I thought for sure I was dead."

London hesitated.

"When he realized that I was pregnant, I think he decided to let me live, but I fought him. That's why I was a bit bloody and that's how my wrist got messed up. I fought harder than I've ever fought in my life! The driver's door was still open, he fell out of the car, because I kicked him hard. I slid into the driver's seat, slammed the door, and locked it just as he pulled on the door handle. I raced away with my left wrist still cuffed. I saw a car come up behind me. I knew it was him! When the car got up alongside me, it slowed down. We were level with each other. He was smiling at me; he swerved his car into mine bumping my car. I floored the gas pedal. He caught up to me on a massive curve, he slammed his car into my car so hard that I lost control. I drove down into a ditch. I bumped my head. I think I got knocked out for a second. When I opened my eyes, he was by my window. The doors were still locked, he still couldn't get me, but he started pounding on the window. My wrist was killing me, I could feel the blood sliding down my face but all I could think about was getting away! He was so close to my car that I…" London started to giggle.

"What? He was so close to your car… what?" Morgan really wanted London to finish what she was saying, but London was laughing, he was sure, hysterically.

"I pulled forward and he screamed. My car was parked on his foot!" London fell against Morgan, laughing and wheezing.

Morgan shouted with laughter.

"What did you do?"

London's face turned viscous.

"I stayed put! I let him feel the weight of that tire. I popped the car into park and revved the engine."

London eyed Morgan, he saw a bit of fire in her eyes, he liked it.

London's eyes twinkled with glee.

"His eyes went wide, he pleaded with me to move the car. I revved the engine some more, put it in drive and peeled out of there. Did I hurt him? Oh yes!" London said with great satisfaction.

Morgan gaped at London.

"I wish you would have told me this sooner! I bet he had to get medical attention! He was probably at the same hospital we were at! I might be able to track him down and arrest him!"

London shook her head.

"You don't get it Morgan. He's a lawyer, he would find a way to get off. He knows about the baby. He won't rest until he gets his hands on this baby. I think... he's insane!"

Morgan went still.

"What is his name London?"

London sighed.

"Trenton William Forester the third. He's one of THE Foresters, Morgan."

Morgan whistled long and loud.

"Whooeee! I wish you had led with that, but it doesn't matter. He's an abuser, a rapist, a kidnapper, and a stalker. The man dug your grave! He is going down! I don't care who his daddy is, or who his grandpa is. Now that I have a name, I can quietly get my guys on this, do some digging and bring this loser to justice."

"But Morgan! He will know where I am! He will come for me, that is a given! You can't protect me from him; his family is too powerful."

"London, you must trust me. I have friends, people I can count on. This house has security cameras, you need to use a code to get inside. My plan is he won't find you here but if he does, I got this."

London smiled at Morgan.

"There is a big part of me that wants to lean on you and accept your help, but there is another part of me that wants to hijack your car and race off into the night."

Morgan roared with laughter.

"Well, now that I know your evil plan, I'll be sure to hide all my car keys. I probably better hide the lawn mower keys too! Just to be on the safe side."

London snickered.

"I don't know about you Morgan but unburdening my soul has perked up my appetite. Let's go eat some of that wonderful dinner you made tonight."

Morgan stood up and stuck his hand out to London.

"You can take my hand only if you wish. My hand is here to help you, comfort you, and haul your big ol pregnant butt up. You can choose to ignore my hand. You have choices London."

Morgan twinkled at London.

London twinkled back and took his hand.

"You had me at "help," but did you have to bring up the part about my big ol butt? Pregnant women are sensitive you know." London made a sad face, sticking her lip out.

"Aww, let's eat, you'll feel better. I just hope all your food doesn't head straight to your butt!"

Morgan opened the door wide, for London to get through.

She sailed past him, giving him the stink eye.

"Opening that door pretty wide, Morgan!"

"Kidding! Your butt is amazing!"

London gasped and turned around quickly.

Morgan ran straight into her.

Morgan couldn't help it; he slid his hands around her low back.

London's eyes were as big as saucers.

Morgan was a bit encouraged that she didn't immediately pull away, but she did pull away. Morgan let her go with an easy-going smile on his face.

Morgan intended to make some calls after they ate. He had a name; he knew what he was up against.

Morgan always got his man.

As they faced each other to eat, Morgan asked London one more question.

"What were you going to Harvard for, exactly?"

London gaped at Morgan.

"Law... I was studying to become a lawyer."

Morgan tried not to smile.

The smile won.

London tried to glare at Morgan.

The smile won.

They both sat back laughing so hard that they couldn't eat.

Episode 9, First Kiss

Morgan woke up in the middle of the night. What caught his attention, he wasn't sure. Morgan listened intently but he didn't hear footsteps, nothing.

Morgan shrugged.

Just as Morgan started to turn over, he heard... breathing!

Morgan shot straight up in bed, he turned and saw... London?

Morgan was stunned!

Morgan could see from the moonlight that London was asleep. She was curled up on her side, facing him.

Was she scared in the middle of the night? Maybe she had another bad dream? What to do. Morgan wondered.

Morgan lay down, he was on his side, facing her.

She is so beautiful! But I have a job to do. I must keep my head on straight. I can't get distracted. Distraction could get her killed.

London wiggled a bit; she slowly opened her eyes.

London's eyes went wide, she screamed.

Morgan slapped his hands across his face to protect himself from her nails.

Morgan felt London lean away from him, he peeked out between his fingers.

London was breathing hard.

"What are you doing in here Morgan? I thought I could trust you! How dare you climb into my bed in the middle of the night! You sir, are for sure, IN MY BUBBLE!"

Morgan removed his hands, he eased himself up onto one elbow.

"Woman! This is my bed!" Morgan huffed in outrage.

London's rage changed to confusion.

London glanced around. From what she could see... she... was... in his bed!

"How? When? I don't understand!" London exclaimed.

Morgan decided to give her a taste of her own medicine.

"What are you doing here, London? I thought my virtue was safe around you!"

Morgan yanked the covers to his chin, looking like an outraged, Victorian Virgin.

"I thought I could trust you! How dare you climb into my bed in the middle of the night!" Morgan stuck his nose in the air. "I'm not that kind of guy, yah hussy."

London gaped at Morgan. London's lips twitched, then she full on smiled. London slapped the side of the bed while roaring.

"Morgan, how did I get in here?" She gasped with laughter.

London continued.

"The last thing I remember, I went downstairs to get a drink. I came back up and the little light that is supposed to turn on, when you walk towards it, didn't come on. I counted two doors!"

"Three doors London, three not two."

"What?"

"Remember the closet door? You counted wrong."

"Well! Call me embarrassed!" London exclaimed.

Morgan laughed.

"I guess I should go back to my room, then." London whispered.

Morgan eyed London.

"Before you go... maybe... since you're here." Morgan mumbled.

London eyed Morgan.

"What? What do yah mean, *"Since I'm here!"* London said, fiercely.

"Don't go crazy and scratch my face all up again. I was just wondering... if maybe... I could have a good night kiss?" Morgan sounded hesitant and hopeful, all at the same time.

London thought about that.

"I don't know..."

"I tell you what, I'll just stay right here, and you can do the kissing. I won't move a single muscle."

"You promise?"

"Scouts honor!"

Morgan held completely still.

London slowly leaned towards him; she stopped a couple of times, but then she wiggled closer. London placed her hand on his chest, she slanted her face slightly, her lips met his briefly, she pulled back quickly and stared at him.

Morgan smiled.

"You okay, London?"

"I... uh... let me try again." London whispered.

"Only, if you insist." Morgan stated.

London grinned.

"You are such a nerd! You promise you won't move?"

"You have my word, London."

London seemed a bit bolder this time, her lips met his with a bit more conviction.

Morgan had to lock every muscle in his body, to keep his promise.

When London didn't pull away immediately, Morgan groaned.

London pulled away, worry on her face.

"I'm sorry London! I didn't move... but it felt so good."

"It did? I admit... I liked kissing you."

"You're killing me woman! I think you need to go back to bed!" Morgan roared.

London looked disturbed.

"Morgan, are you mad at me for something?"

Morgan palmed his face.

"No. I just really want to keep my promise, but you are incredibly beautiful and... desirable. Plus, I lied! I've never been a scout! Go to bed London!" Morgan growled.

"You think I'm beautiful and desirable?" London smiled softly, looking pleased.

Morgan stood up, while huffing.

Morgan stormed around to her side of the bed. Morgan scooped up a startled, squealing London.

"I'm a man London! I would never hurt you, but... I'm keeping you at a distance! I have a job to do, and I never should have asked you to kiss me! Let's pretend this never happened. It's better this way, no distractions."

Morgan placed London on her bed.

Morgan started to stand but London had her hands still wrapped around his neck.

"Before you go, I need to say something."

Morgan unpeeled her hands, sitting as far down towards the foot of the bed, as possible.

"What?" Morgan asked quietly.

"You're right." London sobbed.

Morgan looked suspicious. "What do you mean, I'm right?"

"I'm damaged Morgan. As much as I like kissing you... I have a lot of baggage. You deserve the family that you envisioned when renovating this house. I'm not sure that I could ever get beyond everything Trent put me through. Thank you for taking me in, for helping me, but you are right; we can't get distracted. Because the second we lose focus, he will get me, Morgan. He will!"

London laid down, she rolled away from Morgan, bringing the covers up to her chin.

Morgan sighed.

"London don't fret. You must trust me. I will keep you safe." Morgan promised.

London said nothing, she was burrowed under the covers, crying softly.

Morgan got up slowly, he turned back towards his room.

Morgan lay back down; he turned his head to where London was only moments ago.

Morgan glanced out the window. The sun was getting ready to rise. Morgan decided to get up and start the coffee.

Maybe he would get on his computer and do some more digging on Trent and his family.

Episode 10, London Meets Grady

The more Morgan investigated the Foresters, the more he realized that they were going to be a problem.

Trenton Forester the first, built his empire while stepping on the little people. He ruined lives, ran out business, inserting his stores into communities. Once established, he could set his prices as he saw fit, and he did.

Morgan found a picture, a three-generation photo, all three Forester men together. The looks in their family run strong; all three men, blonde, very good looking, athletic.

London was right, Trenton looked like an angel. He would come across as the victim in a courtroom. London never reported any of his crimes. *What was his next move?* He wondered.

Morgan felt London behind him. He turned his head slightly, while swiveling his chair.

London stared at the screen, peering at the Foresters. London looked sad, and scared.

"How do I fight that, Morgan?"

"I'm working on that; you have to trust me London."

London looked down at Morgan.

"I do trust you, Morgan. You have no idea how much I trust you."

Morgan smiled.

"I'm glad."

"Trenton is a lawyer. I think... I'm going to have to get a public defender. He knows about the baby; he's going to want to take it from me."

Morgan picked up the phone, he dialed a number.

"Hey, Grady, Morgan here. Any chance you can squeeze me in with a friend? We need some legal advice."

London's heart pounded. Coming out into the open with all of this was happening, but it had to happen. London was so happy to have Morgan on her side.

Morgan hung up.

"He said to head on over, let's get ready to go." Morgan encouraged.

"I'm ready, I'll go make a decaffeinated coffee, while you get dressed."

Morgan left to get ready.

An hour later they stood in front of Grady's office.

Parker, Parker, and Murphy Law Offices

"This Grady... he knows his stuff?" London asked quietly.

"Grady is brilliant! He is more than a match for the Foresters. Top in his class, cut-throat, but so pretty that he holds jurors in the palm of his hand."

"I told you I don't much care for lawyers, Morgan."

"You also said you didn't like cops, if I remember." Morgan arched an eyebrow at London.

London blushed, she gave Morgan a slight shove, he didn't move an inch.

"I don't hate all cops… anymore." London admitted.

"See! You will love Grady in no time."

When they went in, they were immediately ushered into Grady's office.

Grady literally resembles *Pierce Brosnan!* A much younger version but totally that type.

London stood there, she realized her mouth hung open, she quickly shut it.

"I have that effect on people." Grady said with a grin.

"Have a seat, fill me in and let me see if I can help you."

London started out slow, but then the words tumbled out. From beginning to end, she left nothing out.

When she was done, Grady looked grim. Morgan resembled stone and London felt dog tired.

Grady came around his desk. He squatted down in front of London and took one of her hands.

"Let me help you London. I'm not telling you that it is going to be easy, but I've taken on bigger fish than the Foresters."

"I have no money! No way to pay you!"

"You let me worry about that. Truth is I've been watching the Foresters for a while now. They are sleezy and corrupt. I've been itching to tackle them."

Grady sat back down.

"Did you ever report anything he did to you?" Grady asked.

"I tried but when I went to the police, they told me to go home. He has the police in his pocket. I told them that he raped me, they laughed at me."

Morgan practically roared hearing that.

Grady snapped a pencil in half.

"Did you ever have a rape kit done?" Grady questioned.

"Once... just the one time. I was beat up so badly, that when I went to the shelter, they took me to a hospital. But... then... Trenton found me, and I am here."

Grady grinned.

"We got him! We have proof that he beat you and raped you! This is good news London! Where was the rape kit done? I will also need the name of the shelter and where it was. I need names of anyone that saw you at the shelter, and who worked with you."

Grady handed London a notebook and pen.

London started writing.

Morgan seemed to be calming down.

Grady looked towards Morgan.

"I assume she's staying with you, Morgan?"

"Yes, I'm on an extended leave of absence. My place has security, cameras, you need a code to get in. It's secure, but there is room for improvement."

Grady grinned.

"About that... I have a friend. She's amazing at what she does! I'm going to make a call. You will be very impressed with her mad skills."

"I appreciate you, Grady. You have no idea how much this means to me."

Grady took the notebook from London.

"You saved my life Morgan. You won't be paying me one single dime."

London gasped.

"You saved his life?"

"He's exaggerating."

Grady looked at London.

"Sit this guy down and make him tell you my story, London. It really tells you the kind of man you have here. He's a keeper, you remember that."

London blushed.

Morgan huffed.

Episode 11, Loss

London lay in her hospital bed; her heart was breaking; she was sure of it.

The doctor that took care of her before, stood by her bed. Morgan and Doc talked quietly but she could still hear their conversation.

Doc stepped towards London.

"I'm so sorry London, the baby never stood a chance. I was afraid this was going to happen but... we couldn't save him."

"It was a boy?" London sobbed.

"Yes. When I first met you, you were malnourished, dehydrated, and trying to go into labor. I know this is hard to hear, but sometimes these things happen for a reason. I truly am sorry for your loss London."

Doc patted her hand and left the room.

Morgan did not know what to say, he didn't know if he should hug her. Morgan felt beyond useless.

London cried, tears tracking down her cheeks.

"London, tell me what I can do for you. I don't know what to do." Morgan fretted.

London looked up; misery written all over her face.

"I had a baby boy, Morgan. With everything I've been through, my baby never stood a chance, because of Trent!"

Morgan pulled a chair up to her bed, he sat down, picking up her hand.

"I can't begin to understand any of this London, but... I think that the stress of running, going hungry, and thirsty. Your body couldn't deal with your pregnancy. You did nothing wrong! You're right, your ex is to blame! If he loved you and cared for you, none of this would have happened."

London nodded.

"I feel that all of this is his fault, I really do! Soon, he is going to know where I am. Grady is going after him, he will find me, Morgan."

Morgan's face turned to stone.

"Then, he's going to be finding me, as well." Morgan stated grimly.

London's hospital door opened.

Stella stuck her head inside.

"Can I come in, honey?"

London sat up. London's arms outstretched towards Stella. London began to cry in earnest.

Stella stepped inside. She raced over to London throwing her arms around her.

Morgan stood up.

"Is Alden here Stella?"

"He's in the waiting room, on this floor."

"I'll go track him down. I'll be back sweetheart." Morgan stated, as he left the room.

Stella arched her brows at London.

"He called you sweetheart, London!"

London waved her hand around.

"He was just being sweet, it's not like that between us." London stated.

Stella didn't look convinced.

"I've known Morgan a very long time. I have never heard him call any woman, sweetheart."

London looked a bit concerned.

"No... he... it isn't... I can't!"

Stella saw that London was getting upset.

"Wait, honey, calm down! You just lost your baby; you don't need to be worrying about anything right now. I was just... surprised, that's all."

London laid back on her bed.

"I'm so tired Stella. I can't stop crying. I am so sick of being scared, and tired, and now... I feel empty."

"Oh sweetie, I want you to know that I completely understand how you feel."

London eyed Stella.

Stella nodded.

"I miscarried also. Between Ben and my twin boys. I got pregnant far too quickly after Ben. I knew I couldn't possibly handle another small baby but... when I miscarried... I felt so sad. Doc told me that sometimes the body knows what's best for us, but it still hurts!" Stella shook her head.

"Doc told me the same thing, Stella. Trent beat me so badly; he controlled what I ate and drank. Ultimately, he tried to murder me."

Stella grabbed London's hand.

London went on to say, "Trent wanted a baby so much, but because of him, I lost that baby." London stated.

Stella nodded.

"He has an awful lot to answer for London. I think... you need to start talking to someone."

"Doc already set me up with someone; they are going to come to the house. Doc sure is a nice man."

"He is the best!"

Episode 12, "I feel... like... I need to run!

Weeks flew by. Winter began to subside. Spring was just around the corner.

London was feeling pretty good. She was all healed up from the miscarriage. The days of feeling blue and down mostly disappeared.

Morgan went back to work, he had to.

London spent her days cleaning and cooking.

Today, London was outside, she stomped on the shovel, forcing it into the ground turning the soil. London hadn't asked Morgan if she could put in a small garden, she probably should have, but she needed to be out in the fresh air! She needed to move her body, and she needed this garden!

London bent down, pulling more rocks out of the soil. She steadily placed them in a pile. London had to admit that her pile of rocks was getting very large.

London heard a car.

London started to toss the shovel to make a run for the house but when the truck came around the curve in the driveway, she realized it was Morgan.

Morgan stopped the truck, he eyed London, heading her way.

London chose a spot beyond the main yard; at least she wasn't ripping up his beautiful lawn.

Morgan stopped, he eyed her pile of rocks, and the churned-up dirt.

"You know I'm the sheriff, right?"

London shrugged.

"Uh… yes? Why?"

Morgan looked around.

"I'm trying to see where you hid the body." Morgan grinned at London.

London sucked in a breath.

Why did this man have to be… so… everything!

"No body, yet. I'm… working the soil to possibly plant a garden."

"In this rocky area? Uh… I don't think you are going to get a thing to grow here, London."

London stuck her chin out, looking irritated.

"Are you saying you would prefer that I dig elsewhere?"

Morgan had the audacity to twinkle at her!

"I wasn't saying that London. I was saying this is probably the worst stretch of soil on this property."

London jammed the shovel back into the soil viscously.

"This spot is fine! That's the problem, so what if it's hard work. If I'm here, I will get vegetables to grow!"

Morgan stopped smiling.

"What do you mean? *"If you are here?"* Morgan asked.

London stopped digging. If it was possible, she looked even more irritable.

"I can't stay here forever, Morgan. I need to get my life going. I can't keep depending on you and everyone else to take care of me. I need to stand on my own two feet! I've never lived alone Morgan. I lived with my parents, until they were killed. Then, I lived with my spinster aunt; she was my last living relative. I met Trent, right after I met him, my aunt passed away. Trent and I got married immediately."

Morgan started to say something, but London was already charging towards the house. London leaned the shovel in a corner on the porch.

Morgan followed her.

"London! I've told you, repeatedly, that you are not a bother. I like having you here."

London turned around to face Morgan.

London looked like a scared, wild animal, that was cornered.

Morgan saw London's hands curl into fists, she sucked in an agitated breath.

"Morgan... I feel... like I need to... run." London whispered.

Morgan couldn't have stopped what he did next if he tried.

Morgan lunged for London pulling her in for a hug.

London hugged him back.

"What is this London? Talk to me!"

London pulled away. London went inside, she walked towards the roundtable in the foyer. London reached down, handing Morgan a thick envelope.

Morgan took the envelope.

Braken & Braken Law Offices practically leapt off the envelope.

Morgan saw that the envelope was open.

Morgan grabbed London's hand, towing her to the living room. Once there he motioned for her to sit.

"Do you want to tell me what it says, or would you like me to read it?"

"Go ahead and read it, then we can discuss it."

Morgan pulled out the legal documents. He read every word, twice. Morgan put the papers away, leaning towards a dejected London.

"So, because he knows where you are, you want to run?"

London sighed.

"I want to run, but I know I can't. I'm scared, Morgan. That man dug my grave! I lay next to that grave, broken and bleeding. My fear is that if he gets his hands on me again… he will finish the job."

"Never going to happen, London. I wouldn't go back to work until I knew the security system was up-and-running. We have more security than our local bank."

London grinned, slightly.

"I'm worried about going to court. Just being in the same courtroom with him… I shake just thinking about that. Then, I get ticked off because I'm such a wimp!"

"I have a remedy for that."

London looked intrigued.

"What? What remedy?"

Morgan picked up his phone.

"Hey Luke, I have a lady here that needs to learn some self-defense. When can she start?"

London's eyes widened.

Morgan said goodbye, he turned towards London.

"What do you think London, are you ready to learn how to drop a man?"

London's smile turned evil.

"Oh yes. I am so ready. Let's do this!"

London surged to her feet.

"When do we start?" She asked.

"He said come on over now."

London raced for the stairs.

"I'm going to go put on fighting clothes!"
Morgan snickered.

"You have fighting clothes?"

London stopped halfway up the stairs.

"I have comfortable spandex leggings and a sports bra, those should do."

London didn't see Morgan's mouth drop open.

Morgan rubbed the back of his neck. *London in a sports bra and tight leggings? He wondered if he was going to be able to handle the sight of London dressed like that! London may be petite, but she had put on some weight. The weight gain had done her some good. London had filled out in all the right places.*

Morgan groaned; he headed upstairs to change out of his uniform. Morgan was sure that this woman was going to be the death of him.

Just as he headed into his room, London sailed out looking far too good in her *fighting clothes.*

"Hurry up Morgan! I want to punch something!"

Morgan growled.

"So do I." Morgan grumbled.

London looked confused as she sailed past Morgan.

Morgan noticed that London coming towards him, or walking away, was a beautiful sight.

Morgan closed his eyes.

"I'm going to work out until I drop." Morgan said out loud to himself.

Episode 13, "I did it! I got yah!"

London faced her tormentor, Luke.

Luke Charles spent the last few months doing his best to teach London some basic fighting skills. He taught her how to grapple. Putting her in uncomfortable holds, while taunting her. In an odd way it made London face a few of her fears. Even now, Luke once again had her pinned. She could feel his hot breath on the back of her neck, and it ticked her off!

"You are not thinking London! You are feeling! What do you do when someone has you from behind? I'm not made of glass girl, and neither is your attacker!"

London elbowed Luke in the ribs. When he loosened his grip a bit, she brought her head back, enjoying his grunt of pain when her head hit his nose.

Luke let go, gripping the bridge of his nose.

London faced him now, standing, with her fists up, ready to attack again.

Luke waived her off.

"Down girl! You win!"

London squealed with happiness.

"I did it! I got yah!" She screamed.

"Pretty sure my nose is broke." Luke whined.

London looked concerned. She started to take a step towards him, but she saw that special glint in his eyes.

London growled putting her fists back up.

Luke nodded.

"Well, I think you finally figured it out." Luke drawled.

"Figured what out?" London growled, still at the ready.

"If your attacker seems to be all done in? Don't believe it. From what you've told me about your ex, he will use any advantage at his disposal."

London nodded.

Luke tilted his head back to slow down the bleeding.

"Seriously girl! I'm done for real this time." Luke moaned.

London started to turn away; her face turned to stone. London turned back towards Luke with a determined look on her face.

London lunged forward, with one roundhouse punch she hit Luke in the jaw, hard! Luke landed on his butt, letting out a whoop of laughter.

London pointed her finger at him.

"Now... you are done!" London replied, with a grin.

London and Luke glanced towards their left when they heard laughter.

Morgan snuck in; he must have seen the entire thing. Morgan had his phone aimed in their direction.

Morgan sighed with happiness.

"I will be able to enjoy this moment, for the rest of my born days, Luke." Morgan chortled.

Luke sneered at Morgan.

"Don't you go posting that online dude! I'll be out of business if people see this here girl, setting me on my backside!"

Morgan pocketed his phone.

"This video is for my enjoyment only. I might send it to London though, let her watch it over-and-over, for confidence building reasons, of course."

Luke sighed and shook his head.

"Get out, both of you! I need to straighten my nose, again!"

London looked horrified.

"Did I really break your nose?" She cried.

Luke nodded at her.

"And I am so proud of you girl! My work here is done!"

London looked shocked.

"No! I'm not done! I'm working on strength and speed. I still need you, Luke!" London demanded.

"That's what I like to hear; a woman saying that she NEEDS me."

Luke waggled his eyebrows at Morgan.

"She loves me." Luke told Morgan.

Morgan scowled at Luke.

Luke went on to say, "Luke and London... it has a beautiful ring to it, you think?" Luke teased.

Morgan crossed his arms, looking annoyed. Morgan glanced in London's direction to see what her reaction to this entire situation was.

London had a slight smile on her face.

Morgan did not like that! Not one bit!

London sashayed towards a now wide-eyed Luke.

Luke started to back away, he gulped, looking a bit shook up.

London stopped in front of Luke. *"She looks far too sexy!"* Morgan thought.

London brought her finger up to Luke's mouth. Luke was terrified that she was going to caress his lips... or something!

London tapped Luke on the nose, hard!

Luke yelped, doubling over, holding his very sore nose.

"You don't attract me at all Luke Charles! Stop teasing me! I'll be back in two days for my next lesson!"

London started to walk away, but she stopped, she turned around and said, "You might want to put some ice on that."

London turned, striding over to her bag, she picked it up, slinging it over her shoulder.

"You coming Morgan? I'm starving!" London exclaimed.

Morgan shut his mouth; he realized it was hanging open.

Morgan glanced back towards his buddy Luke.

Morgan followed London; he spoke over his shoulder.

"You heard her Luke Charles; you might want to put some ice on that." Morgan's voice was meant to irritate Luke, and it did.

Morgan snickered as he left the building.

Episode 14, Big Event! King or Queen for a Year

London was in absolute shock! She had to admit that she had never seen anything like this event before.

The Westman's turned at least five acres into an obstacle course. There were pits of mud, a man-made climbing wall, tug-of-rope contests. London looked to her right, people were throwing axes and knives! London turned again, looking to her left. London saw a wall of nets, the Westman boys were all climbing the thing as fast as they possibly could. London was impressed when Elijah started to fall backwards. AJ grabbed him, saving him from a very nasty fall. Caleb and David stopped climbing, checking to make sure that their baby bro was okay.

Francine ran around with a first-aid kit, bandaging wounds.

Stella and Alden were fast asleep in lawn chairs, leaning on each other.

Grandma Nettie and Pop each held one of the twins. They cooed and jiggled the babies while Stella and Alden caught a few z's.

London felt her eyes well up. If her child had lived... no she couldn't think about that. London blinked her tears away.

London searched the crowd looking for Morgan.

London watched as half the town lined up for the running portion of the games. London spotted Morgan with a number attached to the front and back of his shirt. Number 1, of course. Morgan really was a good man, but he could never be hers, that she was sure of.

About thirty guys and gals lined up to run the five-acre race. The Westman boys were done with the wall of nets, they too were lined up.

London heard someone yelling, then a cap gun went off. The runners surged forward. London watched as Morgan put on a burst of speed, but then he slowed down a bit, finding his pace. The young Westman's quickly fell to their knees, they ran too fast, too quickly. London watched as AJ and Morgan stayed neck-and-neck.

London realized that AJ and Morgan must have been training for this event.

One-by-one the runners gave up. Some sat down, right where they stopped. Some turned back, walking up the hill, smiling good-naturedly at their hecklers.

London stood up, she wandered to the other side of the property. London stood at the roped off area, waiting for the runners to appear from the tree line. London got excited when she saw that only Morgan and AJ were left and the race was going to be extremely close.

Morgan had the biggest grin on his face as he ran next to AJ, AJ's grin was just as wide.

The two guys had to race up the last hill. Then, they had to Leap onto the wall of nets. Climb as fast as possible, flip over the other side, dropping down onto a giant blow-up... thing! London thought it looked like a giant mattress, like firefighters used to save jumpers.

After they land on the mattress thingy, they must somehow fight their way off that thing and race to the finish line. Whoever ran through that ribbon first, was crowned the King or Queen for a year. London knew that the points were close, too close!

Morgan and AJ crested the hill. They both put on speed, leaping onto the wall of nets. Morgan was good... but AJ was younger, and fast! AJ went up the wall of ropes like a monkey. When he got to the top he yelled, "I'll wait here for you Morgan, just to give you a fighting chance. Plus!, I don't want you to feel bad, old man!"

"Who are you calling old, AJ? I suggest you move faster, because here I come!"

Morgan surged forward, grabbing AJ's ankle in the process. AJ laughed while trying to wriggle free.

"See! You need to cheat to win, Morgan!"

By now Morgan was sitting at the top of the wall, facing AJ.

"I'm not cheating. When I cross that finish line first, I hope you don't cry too hard."

Morgan dropped down onto the huge safety mattress. Morgan figured he had this race in the bag. What he hadn't counted on was AJ free falling on top of him.

All the air left Morgan's lungs as a giant, almost man, landed on him.

"Dang kid! What are your parents feeding you?" Morgan complained.

"Cow! Cow, and oh yeah! More cow!"

AJ pushed himself off a flattened Morgan, he rolled with expert skill off the giant safety mattress.

Morgan scrambled to catch up, but AJ was flying across the yard towards the finish line. Morgan was right behind him, he picked up speed. They were now neck-and-neck.

Just as AJ was about to cross the finish line he leaped! He looked like Superman flying across that ribbon.

Ben, Caleb, David, and Elijah, whooped with approval, as their big brother beat their favorite sheriff across the finish line.

Morgan groaned, he staggered around a bit, gulping in air.

"I'm getting too old for these games." Morgan admitted.

AJ pinched Morgan's cheek, wiggling it back and forth.

"Is the poor old sheriff getting too old to play with the big boys? Aww! Poor, big baby!" AJ crooned.

Morgan grabbed AJ around the waist, lifting him up off the ground. AJ laughed hysterically.

"Ahhh! Stop Morgan! I'm going to blow my lunch all over your back!" AJ complained.

Morgan quickly put AJ down.

AJ placed his very large foot on top of Morgan's shoe and shoved!

Morgan went down.

"Just kidding! I have hardly eaten a thing! I'm starving! I was waiting to eat once the running portion was done."

AJ held out his hand to help Morgan up.

Morgan eyed AJ's hand.

"Come on! Have a little trust man!"

Morgan took AJ's hand, soon he was standing back on his feet.

"Congratulations AJ, very good race!" Morgan exclaimed.

A gaggle of pretty girls ran over and crowned AJ the winner. Morgan couldn't believe the amount of giggling going on.

Morgan wandered away from AJ's fan club, but he did notice that one young lady did not look too happy.

Sarah Trent stood looking at the group of girls surrounding AJ.

"Hey Sarah, how are you today?" Morgan asked.

Sarah looked up, she shrugged.

"Isn't your sister Mary going out with AJ?" Morgan questioned.

"Sort of... I guess. Well, no... our parents won't allow it. Plus, my sister is so stupid! Alden James really likes her, but all she does is homework! She has a fit if she gets one question wrong on a test! If Alden James liked me..."

Morgan realized in that moment that Sarah had it bad for AJ.

Morgan sat down next to her.

"Life is kind of funny sometimes Sarah."

"What do you mean?" Sarah's face turned a deep shade of pink.

"Time is a funny thing. When we are young, we can't wait to grow up. When we grow up, we wish we were young again. Enjoy your life now, embrace it! Down the road if you and... Alden James... are meant to be, it will happen."

Sarah glanced up at Morgan.

"You think Alden James could ever like me, for me?"

Morgan nodded.

"He'd be a fool not to. You, young lady, are a beauty."

Sarah smiled shyly, her braces peeking out.

"Thanks Mr. Morgan." Sarah stood up, racing away to find something to do.

"Wow! So, you also have matchmaking skills?" London asked.

Morgan grinned at London as she took a chair next to him.

London had one of the twins, he had no idea which one. London snuggled the baby, breathing in all the baby smells.

"Fourteen is a rough age, for both girls and boys. I remember those days." Morgan shivered on purpose, dramatically.

"The horror of it all!" Morgan exclaimed.

London grimaced.

"Yes, I do remember the wonder years of puberty. The greasy hair, the pimples, the armpit smell that never goes away!"

"You smelled like armpit? Egads woman! Move down a chair!"

London rolled her eyes. London shook her head at Morgan.

"I did not just run a five-acre race, you did. You are right, I should move down a couple of chairs, you stink Sheriff!"

Morgan ripped off his smelly shirt, wiping his armpits with it.

"Is that better?" Morgan glanced at London.

London was eyeing him up and down, she tried to look everywhere but at him.

"Is my bare chest upsetting you?" Morgan teased.

"No! Shut it, Morgan! I'm hungry! I'm going to the buffet table." London started to flounce away with the baby.

"Any chance you feel like making me a plate, London? I had this ginormous farm boy land on me. I'll never be the same again!"

London giggled.

"Ok, sure! Rest up old man."

Morgan frowned, but London was already on the move.

While London was getting their food, Morgan felt a change in the air. It never made any sense to him but when there was danger, Morgan seemed to feel it. Whenever it happened, he never ignored it.

Morgan casually scanned the grounds, something was off.

Everywhere he looked he saw people laughing, having fun.

Morgan's eyes landed on a car that seemed out of place. He wasn't sure how long the car had been there, but it didn't belong near the Westman farm.

The car was expensive, parked at the end of the Westman driveway. It was black, sleek, with tinted windows.

Morgan stood up, he started towards the driveway.

The car revved its engine.

Morgan moved faster.

Morgan heard shouting but he kept running, keeping his eyes fixed on that car.

The car revved again; the tires spewed gravel.

Just as Morgan reached the vehicle it peeled out, spitting dirt and stones everywhere.

Morgan managed to thump his fist on the passenger side, but the driver kept going.

Morgan stood at the end of the Westman's driveway, watching the car disappear. It had no plate.

Morgan glanced towards the yard. Everyone stopped what they were doing to see what was going on. You could have heard a pin drop.

London had one hand on her chest, sucking in air. Her other hand opened, dropping their food to the ground.

Alden and Stella heard the noise and woke up.

Alden raced up to Morgan.

"What just happened here, Morgan?"

"I can't prove it, but I believe London's ex just stopped by for a visit."

Alden peered down the road.

"What are we going to do about this Morgan?"

Morgan tilted his head, looking very determined.

"We win the war Alden. This guy likes to beat up on women, he likes to win skirmishes. Me? I plan on winning the war, Alden. This guy is going down for his crimes, he will never touch her again!"

"You have all of us too Morgan. I'm not getting much sleep these days, but you can still call on me, day, or night, if need be."

Morgan nodded.

"I appreciate that. I'm going to head on over to London; she's looking a bit pale."

Alden walked with Morgan.

"You... like her... a lot don't you, Morgan."

Morgan eyed Alden.

"I'm protecting her. I can't have those feelings, Alden."

Alden nodded.

"You know Morgan you are quite the looker, according to every woman in Newaygo County. I hear them all talking, you know. They say, *"Morgan has dream appeal, and his eyes are to die for!"* Alden batted his eyelashes at Morgan provocatively, while making his voice sound feminine.

I've also heard women talking, saying, *"What a studmuffin!"* Pretty sure one of them said, *"Dreamboat!"* Old Mrs. Loudry said, and I quote. *"That man puts the F in Fine and the G in Gorgeous!!!"* Alden thumped Morgan on the bare back vigorously.

"Honestly man, Mrs. Loudry went through the entire alphabet where you are concerned. She said, *"A for Adorable, B for Beef Cake, C for...."*

Morgan stopped walking dropping his head to his chest.

"Stop it, Alden! You have got to be kidding me?" Morgan huffed.

"Take a look around man! You are standing here bare chested giving every woman here, heart palpitations."

Morgan looked around, he realized that every woman on the property, seemed to be... ogling him.

Morgan blushed, he stepped behind Alden, he peeked around him.

Alden shouted with laughter; his head thrown back.

"Come on man, I'll loan you a shirt."

Morgan stayed close to Alden till he got his shirt. Then, he wandered over to a very subdued London.

"How are you doing London? You, okay?" Morgan asked.

When London looked up, he had to admit that he was pleased to see fire in her eyes.

"No more running Morgan. I'm done running. But we must stop him, we must make him face the consequences for everything that he did to me!"

Morgan held out his hand.

London rolled her eyes, but she took his hand.

"I know darn well you only want to hold my hand Morgan, to keep all of these women away!" London exclaimed, laughing out loud.

Morgan smiled, shrugging.

"Ah! Yah caught me!" Morgan admitted.

Morgan glanced around the property; he realized that Alden was right. It seemed that there was, indeed, a lot of eyes watching him.

"Please don't let go of my hand, London! Not for one single second, you promise?" Morgan pleaded.

London let go of his hand.

"I have to go to the bathroom; man-up, Sheriff Dun!"

Episode 15, What Just Happened Here?

"What do you mean we can't get a restraining order?" Morgan shouted.

Grady sighed.

"The judge won't approve it. You have no proof it was him. There must be two proven incidents, for the judge to agree to a restraining order. I'm still waiting on the rape kit, and some of the witnesses that were aware of London's problems with Trent, are backing out. I believe they are being coerced or threatened, but they won't talk. Our court date is two months away and this case is starting to fall apart."

London paced back and forth; she stopped to face Grady.

"What about Miss. Hill? She oversaw the shelter that I was at. I don't think Trent could scare her. Miss. Hill is a force of nature!"

Grady nodded.

"I have Miss. Hill tucked away, safely. She is willing to testify, no matter what, but she was... pressured to remain quiet."

London sat down heavily.

"Two months? Do you know what Trent can achieve in two months?" London murmured.

"This isn't all bad London." Grady stated. "I want you out in public more often. Stop hiding! He needs to see you around town. If he sees you, he will try to make a move on you."

Morgan surged to his feet.

"Are you out of your mind? This man raped her, dug her grave, his intent was murder!"

"But maybe he doesn't know that you lost the baby London. I don't think he is going to hurt you. The only way to draw him out is for London to be the bait. I know it's a lot to ask but I think seeing her will make him bold."

London nodded.

"I agree with Grady."

Morgan looked exasperated.

"Of course, you do London! You are both certifiable! I fight to keep my people safe! I do not endorse throwing her to that WOLF, like a big DOGGY TREAT!"

"I'm not trying to open old wounds here London, but how do you think you would feel, wearing one of those kid harnesses? Make it look like you are walking around town with a baby."

Morgan ground his molars, glaring at Grady.

London sucked in a breath.

"If it means catching Trent... I'll do it!"

Morgan threw up his hands in disgust, he sat down heavily.

"If we are doing this, London. You will be wired at-all-times, do you understand?" Morgan demanded.

London rolled her eyes at Morgan.

"Yes! I understand! I get it! Trust me Morgan, I do not want Trent to ever get his hands on me again! I will follow your rules to the letter."

Morgan looked somewhat satisfied, but he still crossed his arms, continuing to scowl.

London went to find the restroom.

Morgan stayed behind to chew Grady out.

Grady was ready for him.

"I know Morgan, this is not what I want either. Trent is slick, he must be lured out. It's better to have her surrounded by our finest police officers than for Trent to get a hold of her when she's alone and vulnerable."

Morgan didn't look happy, but he nodded.

Grady sighed.

"I can tell what you feel for her man. I promise you! I am doing everything on my end to get this guy. It's starting to look like he will get away with everything unless we fight as dirty as he is willing to fight."

"I'm just trying to help her Grady, there is no US." Morgan denied.

Grady leaned back, smiling slightly.

"Is that so?"

Morgan nodded, looking annoyed.

"Well... then maybe you wouldn't mind if I ask her out to dinner? That wouldn't bother you, at all?"

Morgan looked away from Grady, he didn't want Grady to see the truth in his eyes.

"She's been through a lot, Grady. She would never go out with the likes of you. I don't think she would be interested." Morgan stated.

"I can be very persuasive." Grady purred.

Morgan glared at Grady.

London strolled back in.

"Morgan and I were just discussing something London. I told Morgan I was going to ask you out to dinner, but Morgan said, *"You would never go out with me, that you would never be interested."* He basically forbade you."

London glared at Morgan.

"How dare you try to answer for me, Morgan Dun! Besides, what is wrong with Grady? He seems like a perfectly respectable man!"

Morgan surged to his feet.

"I never said that! He's trying to trap you into going on a date with him. Be my guest! If you want to go on a date with a LAWYER that's fine with me! I distinctly heard you say, at one point, that you didn't like COPS or LAWYERS."

London sputtered.

"I happen to like you and you are a cop! I happen to like Grady too! For a lawyer he's pretty darn awesome, wouldn't you say?"

"Yes! He's, my friend! Well! I thought he was my friend!" Morgan glared at Grady.

Grady roared with laughter.

"I'm just messing with you guys! I would NEVER date London."

London looked offended.

"What? I'm not your type? Do I not appeal to you? And to think I stuck up for you Grady!

Well, too bad for you Grady, because you are picking me up at six! Don't be late!" London huffed, while storming out of his office.

Morgan and Grady both stood there in stunned disbelief.

"What just happened here, Morgan?" Grady gasped.

Morgan shook his head, his eyes landed on Grady.

"I guess... this means you are going on a date! With London!" Morgan gritted through his teeth.

"Dude! I was just messing with you! How do I get out of this? I have a headache, right?" Grady questioned.

Grady grabbed his hair.

"I have to wash my hair, that's an excuse that women always use!" Grady exclaimed.

Grady paced the office.

"Sudden family emergency? Maybe, my Great Aunt Edna died!" Grady shook his head no.

"That one wouldn't be too believable. I don't even have a Great Aunt Edna! Why Morgan? Why, don't I have a Great Aunt Edna?!" Grady exclaimed, sounding panicky.

Morgan grabbed Grady by the front of his shirt reeling him in real close.

"You touch her… you die. If you are late…
you die. Basically, I feel the need to… hurt you…
but she's EXPECTING you!"

"I… no… I didn't mean for this to happen!
Help me, Morgan!"

"You better be home by ten o'clock and
don't tell her I said that!"

"I swear man! I don't want your woman!"

"She's NOT MY WOMAN!" Morgan shouted.

Grady uncurled Morgan's fingers from his
shirt.

"You keep telling yourself that Morgan.
We've been friends for years and you want to
bury me! You sir… are in love with her!"

Morgan growled at Grady.

"You see Grady, I can't love her, I need to
keep her safe."

Morgan turned on Grady aggressively.

"Have a great time tonight! You better
make sure she has fun, Grady! That woman
needs a bit of fun!"

Grady looked floored.

"You want me to make sure she has… fun?"

"Not too much fun!" Morgan growled at
Grady.

"I swear! She will have a great time, but
only… a little bit of fun."

Grady looked worried.

"The thing is Morgan... women fall in love with me all the time! I don't mean for them to do it! Uggg! It's a curse! What if she falls in love with me, Morgan! That is a very real possibility, dude!"

Morgan rolled his eyes.

"Be at my house by six." Morgan stated, pointing his finger at Grady.

Grady sat down behind his desk, he put his fist to his chin, looking pouty.

"But I don't want to go on a date with London." Grady whined.

"Well, you should have thought of that before you started this crazy train, Grady! Maybe you should consider, GROWING UP!"

Morgan slammed the door on his way out.

Grady crossed his arms.

"Maybe, I don't want to grow up you big... stupid... dummy." Grady whispered.

Morgan whipped open the door.

"What was that?"

"Six! I'll be there by six o'clock sharp!"

Morgan left... again.

Episode 16, Date Night With... Grady.

London fretted. She changed her dress three times. London finally settled on the red dress. London knew, with her coloring, that red looked fantastic on her.

Morgan knocked at her bedroom door. He opened the door when she told him to enter.

Morgan stopped; London looked fantastic.

"London, you look... incredible." Morgan whispered.

London had to admit she was a nervous wreck. *How did she get herself into this farce of a date? With Grady, no less.*

London held the front of her dress up.

"I can't get the zipper done up Morgan. I hate to ask but.... "

Morgan stepped forward. He started to zip her dress up, but he saw a long scar on her back. Morgan eased the dress aside, realizing that she had a couple more.

London gasped, she tried to move away, but Morgan took ahold of the backs of her arms.

"London? How did you get these scars?"

London's head dropped.

Morgan knew before she spoke, he just knew.

"Trent... cut me."

Morgan must have squeezed her arms a bit because she gasped.

Morgan let go immediately.

"London." Morgan said softly. "Did he do that to you anywhere else?"

London sighed, she felt defeated.

London let her dress drop to the floor. She kept her face averted, as Morgan looked her over.

Morgan walked to the front of her. London had several scars on her chest and abdomen.

Morgan bent down, he pulled the dress up over her hips, he slid her arms back into her sleeves. Morgan went around behind her, zipping her dress up gently.

"Doesn't matter what he did to you London, you are beautiful. I'm sorry he did that to you. Scars fade, they are just scars." Morgan shrugged. "I have a few myself darlin."

London looked up into Morgan's eyes.

"He wouldn't take me to the doctor. That's why some of them are so bad. I needed stitches. I'm always going to be that person that must wear a shirt over their bathing suit. I don't want to scare children."

London sniffled.

Morgan hugged her.

"When this is all over, if you really want to have those scars fixed, I'll set you up with the right doctor. You shouldn't have to carry around what that man did to you for the rest of your life."

London nodded.

"I might take you up on that, but I would have to get a job first, so I can pay for it. That kind of surgery isn't cheap."

Morgan stood back; he eyed London.

"I must say, you dropping that dress was so hot!" Morgan exclaimed. Morgan wanted to lighten the mood, by teasing her.

London gaped at Morgan.

"What? Stop it!" London giggled.

"Seriously! First you climb into my bed and then you do a strip tease! Whoeee! I'm going to take a cold shower while you are gone."

London giggled again.

"I'm ugly!"

Morgan arched his eyebrows.

"Just so you know London, you could never be ugly. You are breathtaking! Plus, I saw your bra and panties! You hussy!"

London hit Morgan with her purse as they went down the stairs.

"Stop it! I'm going to fall down the stairs because you keep making me laugh."

"Fine! You are so ugly... your mama tried to make the doctor stuff you back in after you were born." Morgan teased.

London screamed with laughter, grabbing the banister.

"You are so ugly... your dog put you up for adoption!" Morgan exclaimed.

London sat on the stairs.

"Dangit Morgan! I can't even walk!" She squealed.

"You are so ugly, when you walk into the bank... they turn the cameras off!"

London threw back her head and roared.

"Stop! When I stop laughing, I'm going to hurt you, Morgan!"

"One more London." Morgan stated.

London grinned, eyes twinkling.

Morgan bent down and put his face level with London's face.

"You are so... beautiful London... you take my breath away." Morgan whispered.

London went still.

Morgan leaned in; his lips brushed hers gently.

The doorbell rang.

Morgan froze; he pulled away. Morgan took London's hand, steering her towards the door.

Grady stood on the porch with flowers and a big box of candy.

London smiled taking the flowers and candy.

"Thank you, Grady."

"Let me take that stuff for you London."
Morgan set them on the round table.

London suddenly looked uncertain.

"You have fun London; I'll wait up for you."
Morgan stated softly.

London nodded, heading out the door with
Grady.

"You look incredible, London! Red suits
you!" Grady exclaimed.

Morgan slammed the door.

Grady and London both jumped.

Grady grabbed his heart, looking very
nervous.

London grinned.

Episode 17, "I'm Going to Break Him in
Half!"

Morgan glanced at his cell phone, again.

Morgan texted London, for the third time.

*"Still good, Morgan. I had steak! Stop
worrying!"*

Morgan decided to text Grady.

*"Take a picture of her so I know she's having
fun!"*

"Dude! You are such a nerd!"

"Do it!"

"Fine! You, stalker!"

Grady sent a pic of London, she held up a wine glass, with a big smile on her face.

"We are turning off our phones now! Because you seriously need professional help!"

Morgan typed frantically. Morgan absolutely did not want them to turn off their phones.

Morgan dropped a cuss word when he saw their green dots disappear, showing that their phones were, indeed, off.

"I'm going to break him in half!" Morgan shouted to the ceilings.

Morgan dropped into his recliner. He picked up his remote, scrolling... scrolling... and scrolling.

Morgan sighed, turning the tv back off.

Morgan opened his text message again; he tapped on the pic that Grady sent him.

London's face appeared on his screen. *She's so beautiful. I think she must be the bravest person I've ever met.* Morgan thought.

Something in the background caught his attention. Something about the photo was bugging him, but he couldn't quite put his finger on it. Morgan scanned the photo, looking for what, he wasn't sure, but his radar was going off. Morgan froze. In the background, Morgan could see only half a man's face. He was obviously off to the side, in the background, half in the photograph, half out. The man's face was blurry. Morgan wasn't sure but the guy in the photo reminded him of Trent.

Morgan surged to his feet. Morgan ran to his office, grabbing the three-generation photo of Trent and his family. Trent's face stared back at him; he held his phone next to it. He couldn't be sure, but his gut was screaming *yes*! They guy in the photo could be anyone, but Morgan wasn't taking any chances.

Morgan dialed Grady's number, but it went straight to voice mail. Morgan was sure that he would get the same, when dialing London. When her voice mail came on, Morgan roared, while heading for the door.

Morgan hit the speed-dial for the station, someone at the station picked up.

"George! This is Sheriff Morgan Dun, get someone over to the Steak House on main street, fast! London is there and possibly her ex-husband!"

Morgan lived North of White Cloud, he knew that someone from the station would get there before him but still he hit ninety miles an hour and floored it even more.

When Morgan got to the one and only stop light in town, he knew in his gut that it was bad news.

Morgan pulled into the parking lot of the Steak House. At least three police cars were already there, lights flashing. Morgan watched in horror as an ambulance loaded someone into the back.

Morgan sprinted to the ambulance; he peered inside seeing his buddy Grady on a stretcher.

"Is he conscious? Can he talk?" Morgan asked.

Grady mumbled something.

Morgan's second in command stepped up.

"We've got roadblocks going up in every direction, boss. Grady's car is gone, it has *Star Tracker*, so we should be able to track it. We are trying to get someone from the company on the phone right now."

Morgan nodded, still looking at Grady.

A paramedic stepped up.

"He's got a concussion for sure Sheriff Dun. He asked for something to write on before he passed out. I couldn't make sense of it, maybe you can."

Morgan took the slip of paper; he watched the paramedics shut the doors.

"Henry! Keep me posted, call the station, ok?" Morgan asked the medic.

"Will do Sheriff."

Morgan jumped in his squad car, he flicked on his interior lights. On the single piece of paper was written, C Pl_a.

Morgan scratched his head. What Grady's note was supposed to mean, he had no idea.

Morgan went to the station. He passed the note around, hoping that someone might be able to figure out what it meant.

"Do we have anything at all to go on guys? What's going on with the roadblocks?" Morgan questioned.

George stepped up.

"There are so many back roads out of town, we are sure that he got out."

Morgan turned towards the nearest desk and promptly flipped it.

The station went dead quiet.

Morgan sucked in a breath.

"I want all units from here to the county line, up and down every side road! I want an APB, state-wide! Put out a BOLO for Trenton William Forester, the third! Forester is six-one, he weighs two-hundred-ten pounds, blonde hair, brown eyes. He is to be considered armed and dangerous! Charges? The kidnapping of London

Forester, she was last seen in a red dress and heels, five-foot-seven, blonde hair, blue-eyes, approximate weight, one-hundred-twenty pounds!"

Morgan turned towards George.

"Tell me you got all that!" Morgan shouted.

George nodded vigorously.

"Yes, sir boss! I'm on it!"

"Where are we with Grady's *Star Tracker* for his car?!" Morgan roared, again.

Episode 18, London's Point of View

London and Grady finished dinner.

"Did you have a good time, London." Grady asked.

"Honestly, I must admit that I had a great time. Probably, because you've been a perfect gentleman. Plus, you didn't make a single move on me."

Morgan turned to open her car door.

"Morgan threatened to hurt me... or was it kill me... bury me... maim me? I want to live! I look on you as my client and... friend."

London smiled at Grady.

"I look at you as my lawyer and... friend too."

London snickered at Grady.

"I want you to live too." London teased.

"I'm glad that's settled! We should do this again! This friend thingy! I can honestly say, I've never had a woman as just a... friend. It is so nice!" Grady exclaimed.

London stopped smiling, horror crossed her face, she couldn't get any words out.

Grady dropped to the pavement. Trent stood above him with his handgun. Trent flipped the gun over and pointed it at Grady's head.

"Please!" London cried. "Please don't hurt him! I'll do whatever you want, just don't hurt him!"

Trent's gaze made London shiver.

"Get in his car, now! You and I have a seaplane to catch."

London climbed in.

Trent slammed the door shut.

When Trent got in, he turned towards London. London faced forward, frozen in fear. She couldn't even look at him.

Trent reached out, sliding a stray curl behind London's ear.

"Buckle up sweetheart... I wouldn't want you to get... hurt." Trent whispered.

London clipped on her belt.

Trent grabbed her chin, turning her face towards him. Trent ground his lips against

London's lips. London felt bile rise into her throat.

Trent reversed the car, racing down Main Street.

The only thing that crossed London's mind was, *"Where is a cop when you need one? The man is doing ninety in a twenty-five!"*

London could feel hysteria boiling up inside her, a giggle slipped out.

Trent eyed her.

"Glad you're having fun over there."

London glared at Trent.

"This is not fun, Trent! You need to stop this insanity! We are divorced! This is kidnapping! You will never get away with this!"

Trent sped by White Cloud High School. Trent took the first curve so fast, she thought they were going to end up in the trailer-park!

"Slow down Trent!"

Trent eyed London, he hit the gas harder.

Was he trying to kill them? Somehow, she just couldn't see Trent taking them both out in that manner. No, he'd want to torture her first, he loved to torture her. This was Trent just trying to scare her, as usual.

"I must say, you seem to have come out of that shell of yours! I don't like it! I'm going to have to do something about that little problem."

London lost it.

London unbuckled her seat belt. She launched herself at Trent, nails scratching, fists pounding.

Trent started cussing, trying to fight her off, while trying to stop the car. Trent got the car to stop. London wrenched her door open, falling to the ground. London heard Trent coming after her, she ran right out of her heels, putting on a burst of speed.

She might have gotten away if she hadn't tripped.

Trent picked her up by her hair, and back handing her across the face. Trent half-carried her to the car, shoving her into the trunk.

London tried to fight her way back out, but when Trent pulled back his fist, she went completely still.

"That's better!" Trent huffed.

Trent put duct tape over her mouth, he taped her wrists and ankles.

"I wouldn't have to do this if you would just cooperate!"

Trent slammed the trunk, the car started moving again.

London knew which direction they were going; they were between White Cloud and Jugville.

London's face burned from Trent's abuse.

London paid close attention to how Trent was driving. He slowed down, probably because he figured he didn't want to get pulled over.

Trent stayed on the same road; she could feel the car taking several curves. Trent took a left, driving down a straight road for quite a bit. Trent seemed to be going off-road, London got bounced around, getting even more bruises.

While Trent drove, London thought about all the training Luke taught her.

Luke taught her one day how to get out of duct tape. *There she lay on her foam mat, in the gym, all taped up! Luke showed her step-by-step how to free herself.*

Thankfully, right now, her hands were taped in front of her, not behind her back. That made things easier. She reached up, ripping the tape off her mouth.

Luke told her to bring her arms up above her head, pull her arms down fast and out at the same time. London rolled onto her back, London put her arms above her head, as high as possible. She was thrilled when the duct tape split apart, leaving her hands free. London quickly untapped her ankles.

When Luke opened the trunk, she was going to fight harder than she had ever fought.

Episode 19, Meanwhile, Morgan.

George was on the phone with *Star Tracker*.

"What? What do you mean the car is in Jugville?" George questioned.

The entire station went quiet. Morgan charged over to stand by George.

"Sir, the car has stopped, it is out in the middle of nowhere."

George hit the speaker button so everyone could hear the conversation.

"Ok, so Grady's car is where?"

"I am not finding an actual address, but it seems to be... near...Coonskin Creek and Robinson Lake? Does that make any sense to you all?"

George's eyes widened.

"I know what he's doing! Thanks, lady, for all your help! Bye!"

George hung up.

"Give me that piece of paper again, Morgan!" George exclaimed.

Morgan whipped out the paper that Grady wrote on.

C Pla was scribbled across the paper.

"I know what this means! It means Seaplane!"

Morgan grabbed the paper, he peered at it.

"He's got a sea plane, guys! He's probably got it parked right there at the mouth of Coonskin Creek; all he has to do is take off from Robinson's Lake! He is going to put her on a plane and fly her out of there! Move! Move! George you are with me!"

Morgan turned towards one of the other officers.

"Check with the airport, see if they know anything. Does he even need a flight plan for one of those? How far can he get before fueling? Check into that just in case he makes it into the sky. See if you can find out what kind of plane he has. If it's got twin engines, he can go far."

"I'm on it, boss!"

Morgan and George raced down Main Steet passing the school.

"George, what road do we take to get to where Coonskin Creek and Robinson Lake come together?"

"Main Street is technically East Wilcox Avenue, that turns into E. Echo Drive."

Morgan scowled.

"Jugville area can get a bit confusing for such a small village." Morgan said.

"He had to have taken South Ransom Road. Then, he would have to go two-tracking, till he reaches Coonskin Creek."

George looked up. "Turn here, boss!"

Morgan turned left on to South Ransom Road; he stomped on the gas pedal.

George was used to defensive driving, but Morgan seemed to be *Nascar* driving! George grabbed the handle up above, he found himself trying to stomp on the floor, on the passenger side of the car.

"Dang! I wish I had my own brake pedal right now!" George thought.

"Where's Zeb?" Morgan asked George.

"Zeb is behind us... EVERYONE is BEHIND us Morgan!" George practically screamed.

"I need him to speed up and get our patrol boat in the water! He needs to get in front of that plane if he can!" Morgan exclaimed.

The patrol boat can hold up to three officers; it sits high in the water. The patrol boat glides effortlessly across ponds, lakes, and can even be used in rivers. The boat is small but fast.

"I'm just not so sure that Forester would even stop, boss."

Morgan growled.

George quickly regretted that statement.

Morgan put the pedal to the floor.

George prayed.

Episode 20, Come Out! Come Out! Wherever You Are!

London felt the car stop. She braced herself, waiting for Trent to open the trunk. When he didn't and some time went by, she decided that breaking out of the trunk, on her own, might be the best idea.

London pushed until the backseat gave way. London crawled through the opening, scanning the front seat. Trent wasn't anywhere in sight.

London couldn't believe how bright the moon was tonight.

That can be good for me to get away, but also bad, because Trent will be able to see me, just as good as I can see him! She thought.

London peeked up, to look around. Outside of the car, she could see a... PLANE?! She now realized that Trent's getaway plan was to fly off and away.

London moved a bit, she felt something by her foot. London grabbed it, it was a duffle bag. London peered at the plane again, she could see Trent moving around. London unzipped the bag. Inside were... clothes? It looked like Trent packed some clothes for... they were her size!

London grinned.

"Well, thank you, Trent; don't mind if I do." London whispered.

London pulled out black leggings, socks, and shoes, she pulled out a shirt that was black with a large, white logo. London turned the shirt inside out; the logo wouldn't show if she wore it that way. Her hair would be a dead giveaway, it would be well seen in the moonlight. The shirt was long, so London ripped the bottom, towards the hemline, all the way around. London got undressed, awkwardly, wiggling around in the back seat. Her hair was already up, so she wrapped her makeshift scarf around her head. When London was done, she knew when she opened the door, the interior lights would come on. There was no way that Trent would miss that.

London eyed where Trent was still standing, she raised her arm towards the cover for the interior light in the back, she pulled it off, yanking out the bulb. London eyed the other two, she did the same.

London kept her eyes on Trent, while opening the car door slowly and quietly. London was so happy that Trent seemed completely focused on whatever task he was doing.

When London got the door open, she eased backwards. She was face down, with her eyes trained on Trent.

Trent had plans for her, she knew that at some point his plan was to get rid of her, but she also knew how evil he was. He'd make her suffer until he was done with her.

London's right foot got caught between the floorboard and the door. The dress she discarded was wrapped around her shoe. *Dang this is so awkward!* She fumed.

London finally hit the ground; she stood up slowly looking for Trent, but she couldn't see him! London stretched up a bit more, her gaze zipping around as she frantically looked for him.

"Going somewhere?" Trent whispered.

He was directly behind her!

London spun around, Trent's right hand came up, clutching her throat. Trent squeezed, cutting off her air supply. Trent pushed until she was trapped between him and the car.

London fought, she knew if she didn't do something quickly, she would be unconscious soon.

London punched straight at Trent's face, she felt very satisfied when she heard cartilage crunch. Trent roared but hung on tighter. London was starting to see spots, she straightened her fingers, jabbing him in the throat causing Trent to release her.

Trent made a grab for her as she rolled under the car.

"I must say, London, you have picked up some moves!"

"You have no idea, Trent!" London shouted.

"Come on honey! Come on out of there so we can have a chat!"

Trent made a grab for her, but she scooted backwards.

"Tell me Trent, what exactly is your plan here? I must say, I am very curious." London mocked.

"My plan? Oh... I'm so glad you asked. You give me the child I've always wanted and if you are a good little wife... I let you live."

"Anyone ever tell you that you are insane, Trent! I want nothing to do with you!"

Trent peered under the car; his eyes glinted dangerously.

"I just want you back with a baby on the way. But if that doesn't agree with you... well, you are quite disposable. You get what I'm saying? You will do as I say, London. If you don't, then one-by-one, all the people in this town that you seem to care about, will come up missing.

You know I'll do it, London. You can't keep all of them safe, all the time." Trent promised.

Trent's grin turned evil.

"That woman you seem so fond of and her twin baby girls. Hmm, brakes fail, accidents do happen, so sad." Trent stated.

London started to shake, first with fear, then with rage.

London told Trent to back away from the car, so she could get out. She had no intention of letting him hurt anyone in this town.

Trent backed away while smiling, he figured he had her cornered. He thought that he had won.

London stood up, dusting herself off.

"So, you want me to provide you with a child. Why is it that you haven't asked me about my son?" London asked.

"Don't you mean, our son?"

"No! My son! You were nothing but a sperm doner!"

"I asked around. I saw you at the picnic holding a dark-haired baby. I knew that couldn't be our child. I was told... *Poor London lost her baby."*

Tears filled London's eyes.

"You are insane, and heartless! You don't care about anyone but yourself! Maybe growing up without a mom did something to you Trent! You need help!" London cried.

Trent roared with laughter.

"You think that because I didn't have a mommy that I am in some way broken?"

Trent took a step towards London; she took a fighting stance, putting up her fists.

"You are going to fight me, London?" Trent sneered at her.

"To the death if I must! Yours or mine, doesn't matter! I will never be beaten, raped, or almost murdered by you, ever again! Today, this all ends, one way or another."

Trent crossed his arms, widening his stance.

"I'd like to tell you a story, London. I didn't have a mommy... because she had an... unfortunate accident."

London felt the hairs on her arms and neck stand on end, even her scalp tingled.

"You... killed your own mother?"

Trent shrugged.

"Truth is London, she was my first victim... not my last."

London gasped.

Trent shook his head at London.

"I've killed so many that I've lost count. I thought that killing my own mom would... make me feel something, but nope. One night I saw her standing at the top of the stairs, it was dark. I gave her a push and down she went, tumbling down the stairs. She was dead before she hit the foyer."

Trent seemed to think that was hilarious, he doubled over laughing.

"Everyone came running. I of course sobbed my little eyes out. They all felt so bad for me... after all, I was just traumatized! I saw my mom die, right before my eyes!"

"You are so twisted Trent!"

"You don't know how twisted, London! Let's just say that I'm probably the best, unnoticed serial killer, walking around."

"Why are you telling me all of this? Aren't you afraid that I'll tell the whole world?"

"Go ahead, tell. Just remember what I said, the people you love? I will end them all! I have one more story to tell you, this one is to DIE for! I met this girl, the last few months before graduation. Yep, you guessed it! It was you! I looked at you and I thought that you would make the perfect incubator for my heir. Docile, shy, obedient, you my dear, would give me the child that I wanted, then... "

Trent made a slicing motion across his own throat.

"Well, after you gave me an heir, I wouldn't need you anymore."

Trent held up his index finger.

"But... you had a relative London."

London took a step back, bumping into the car.

"What are you saying Trent!" London sobbed.

"Oh, don't look so sad, London; your aunt was old, she was ready to go. I have to say, smothering her was quite satisfying. I'd let her get just enough air to give her hope... then press harder."

London's breath sped up; anger flowed unchecked throughout her system. London felt strong! She'd never felt this strong before.

All of London's training kicked in.

London lunged at Trent. Trent wasn't expecting it, she managed to connect with his face. Trent went down with a roar, he tried to get up, but London was all over him. She took every ounce of her rage and fear, and she put it into every punch and kick.

Trent did stand at one point; Trent blocked a couple of her punches.

Trent was actively fighting back now that the shock of London attacking him wore off.

"My! My! You have been training, haven't you." Trent mocked.

Trent had a black eye, a swollen lip and blood running down his face from his previous nose injury.

London didn't have a scratch on her, but her knuckles were messed up.

Trent dodged another punch, turning London around, he pulled her up tightly against his chest. Trent bent down, whispering in London's ear.

"When I'm done with you... you are going to beg me to kill you."

London remembered breaking Luke's nose.

London snickered, then she giggled out loud.

London brought back her head fast and hard. *Trent's nose would never be the same again! London had hit it at least two times tonight.*

London spun out of his arms, she stepped in close, kneeing him in his man parts.

Trent held his nose with one hand, and his man parts with the other.

Trent looked like he was going to be sick.

"Not looking so pretty now, are you Trent?" London mocked.

London put her face down close to Trent's face.

"I notice you are limping pretty bad there Trent. Exactly how messed up is your foot, from the wheel of my car?" London cackled with glee.

Trent glared at her from the ground.

"Don't worry London, I have every intention of making you pay for that one!" Trent shouted.

London figured right about now was a good time to beat feet and make tracks. London would let the police handle this psycho.

London sped off into the trees, she had no idea where she was, or what direction she should take, so she just poured on the speed, crashing into the brush like a crazed rhino.

London found some thick brush, she dived into it, figuring she would hide for a while and catch her breath. She had a stitch in her side, when she tried to suck in air, it hurt so bad!

I need to work on cardio, and maybe some distance running. Egads! I'm feeling the burn! She thought.

"Come out! Come out, wherever you are." Trent sang.

London knew she couldn't stay put forever; he would eventually figure out that she was hiding.

"You know London, the moon is so lovely tonight. Why don't you come on out so we can spend some... quality time together." Trent's voice sounded mean and hateful.

London had a pretty good idea what Trent meant by that statement. London shivered. *Obviously, I didn't kick him hard enough down under!* She thought.

Trent sounded closer, too close! He stopped right where she was hiding.

"London, it doesn't have to be like this. Why don't you come out of there before I get angry! You know what I'm like when you make me mad."

London couldn't sit still one more second. It was fight or flight and right now... flight was taking over. Every bit of her training went right out the window!

London came out of hiding; she got maybe two steps, and he was on her. Trent threw her to the ground, coming down on top of her. London saw stars! When he tossed her to the ground her head hit something. London could feel blood pooling out from the back of her head.

Trent backhanded her a couple of times, she saw more stars. Trent was ripping at her clothes. She knew where this was going, she'd been here before.

London felt weakness take over her body, she froze in terror. She couldn't stop him, she never could.

By now London was naked, and Trent was removing his clothes.

London heard a siren.

Trent stopped.

London looked up at Trent through swollen eyes.

She sucked in a breath when he turned... and raced away.

London rolled to her side, she curled herself into a fetal position.

He had almost done it, again.

Thank goodness the police showed up.

How they found them, London could not fathom.

London couldn't yell for help; she couldn't find the energy to even move.

London could hear Morgan yelling for her, other voices as well, but they all sounded so far away; she was unable to respond.

George eventually found her.

Everything seemed so quiet. She could see his lips moving but she couldn't hear him. Then, Morgan was there, covering her up. So many people were running around, yet the quiet was deafening.

London was placed on a stretcher. She didn't remember the ambulance ride, she didn't remember Morgan crying and holding her hand, she didn't remember any of it.

Episode 21, "I'm in a hospital, again!

London opened her eyes; she heard a monitor beeping furiously. A nurse raced in, at the same time Morgan sat up.

London eyed Morgan and the nurse.

"I'm in a hospital, again! Dag-nab-it-all!" London growled.

Morgan laughed while tears shimmered in his eyes.

"Of course, you wake up and say that. Most people wake up and say, *"Where am I"* But not you London!" Morgan huffed.

London tried to roll her eyeballs, but it hurt too much.

"Well, it is pretty obvious where I am; what with the lights, the beeping machines, and the uncomfortable bed!"

"I am so sorry that the people that have been trying to save you, provide you with such shotty service." Morgan teased.

Morgan turned serious.

"You scared the life out of me London. I think I aged ten years when we found you." Morgan eyed a very calm London.

"So… what happened, exactly?" London asked.

Morgan stood up straight, very fast.

"You don't remember?"

London shook her head no.

Morgan gaped at London; he looked completely; gob smacked.

"Uh… hold on, let's get the doctor in here." Morgan nodded at the nurse; she took off at a run.

Morgan stood awkwardly by London's bed.

Dr. Wills flew through the doors.

"Well! Hello again, London! How are you feeling?"

London looked suspiciously at… everyone.

"Fine, why am I here?"

Dr. Wills arched both eyebrows.

"What's the last thing you remember?"

"I was at the Steak House with Grady. We had a nice dinner, it was delicious."

Morgan's mouth dropped open.

Dr. Wills took out his stethoscope, twirling it in his fingers.

The nurse's eyes were wide open; she too, had a very shocked look on her face.

"Look! Just lay it on me doc! Don't sugar coat it! Why am I here?" London questioned.

Morgan sat down, taking London's hand.

"After you and Grady got done eating, when you got to the car, Trent hit Grady over the head and kidnapped you. Does any of that sound familiar?"

London glared at Morgan.

"Are you making this up? Are you for real?"

Morgan hesitated.

"After he took you, we figured out where you were because Grady's car had tracking service. Why he took Grady's car, we could not figure out. We never found any vehicle registered to Trent. It's like he dropped from the heavens. When we got there, we found you... naked and beaten. Trent had a seaplane, he got away."

London yanked her hand away from Morgan.

"Did he... rape me... again?" London asked.

Dr. Wills spoke up.

"From our examination, no he did not. You had a bad bump on the head, as well as a three inch cut. We think when he tossed you, you must have hit your head on a rock or a branch. You have a couple of black eyes, a split lip, a concussion along with stitches to the back of your head, and a couple of cracked ribs."

London nodded, still quite calm.

"So, all-in-all, it could have been worse." London stated.

Morgan growled with frustration.

Dr. Wills eyed Morgan severely.

"I don't understand what is happening here, Doc!" Morgan exclaimed.

Doc sat down.

"London, let me ask you a few questions."

"Ok."

"What's your name?"

"London Marie Forester."

"How old are you?"

"Twenty-three."

On and on the questions went. London knew everything from her childhood. She remembered her aunt, and college, and being married to Trent. London remembered everything he had done to her, but she didn't remember leaving the restaurant with Grady. Everything after that was a blank slate.

"What does this mean Doc?" Morgan asked.

"I'm no expert but I believe London has post-traumatic amnesia."

"What is that?"

"It is a state of confusion or loss of memory immediately following a traumatic event. For example, many people do not remember what may have taken place during a car accident. It's the body's way, the brain's way of protecting the individual from traumatic events. I'm going to have psych come up and evaluate her further."

"Will she ever remember what took place?"

Doc shrugged.

"Like I said, I'm going to have psych come and talk with her. This is not my area of expertise." Doc stated.

London glared at them all.

"I feel fine! A bit sore but other than that I would love to leave!"

Morgan looked concerned.

"No! You have cracked ribs! You have a concussion, and you seem a bit forgetful!" Morgan huffed in outrage.

London glared at Morgan. With her two black eyes it had the opposite effect. Morgan sat down heavily, gripping his hair.

"Actually London, you can probably go home tomorrow. Your ribs are taped up. I want to keep you one more night for observation. You can heal at home just as well as you can here."

Morgan was shocked.

London grinned.

"Well! Alright then! I knew I liked you, Doc! By the way, I'm starving and thirsty!" London exclaimed.

The nurse grinned.

"I'm on it, London! My name is Betty, I'm your nurse for the night. I'll bring you a menu and a drink right away!"

"I guess this place isn't so bad, but I don't want to make a habit of this." London grinned.

London got kind of quiet.

"Morgan, you said... Trent got away? Does that mean the police are trying to find him?"

Morgan frowned.

"Trent claims he was never here. He has ten people willing to testify that he was in his hometown. The car had zero prints, he must have worn gloves or wiped it down. Grady didn't see who hit him, so there's no proof there. You don't remember, so we are at a standstill with that. I asked Grady why he wrote down C Pla, which stood for seaplane; he said he has no memory of doing that. You both have head injuries! I am beyond frustrated! I cannot believe that Trent is going to get away with this!"

London sighed.

"It's not that surprising, Morgan. Trent is evil. His family is beyond rich, they can buy people off with a snap of their fingers."

Morgan sat back down.

"If you remember anything, London, I need you to tell me right away! I hope you can remember!"

Morgan hesitated before speaking again.

"Then again... part of me hopes you never remember." Morgan whispered.

Episode 22, Liar... Liar... Now... What?

I really did have amnesia, but then it all came rushing back that same night. I had to lie though. Trent said that he would go after everyone I love, one-by-one! Trent is a serial killer! His first victim? His own mother! Who knows how many people he's killed? He even killed my aunt! She was the sweetest woman.

I had to lie!

Grady got ahold of Trent's lawyer, he had to admit to him that I didn't remember the events of that night. That's good! Trent believes he got away with it, but that doesn't mean he won't stop coming after me... that doesn't mean he won't come after Morgan or Stella, all the people I've come to love! I do love Morgan! So much! But I must separate myself from him!

The problem is... Morgan won't stop hovering!

Two weeks later and the man was attached at the hip.

Morgan sat down next to London, on the front porch swing.

"Dinner is almost done; I hope you like fish."

London smiled.

"I love fish, what kind?"

"Walleye. Alden and the boys stopped by and dropped it off. I love it when that man catches a lot of fish, I always reap the benefits."

London nodded.

"You seem quiet London, anything on your mind?" Morgan asked.

"I'm all healed up Morgan; I want to get a job."

Morgan surged to his feet.

"No! You can't do that, London! I can't protect you!"

"I am not your responsibility anymore. I am getting on with my life. It is wonderful that you have worked so hard to care for me, to watch over me, but it's time for me to go."

Morgan paced back and forth.

"No! London, he will come for you! At least if he comes here, I have security cameras."

"I can have security cameras wherever I go, Morgan! Please! This is probably the hardest decision I've ever had to make! I have to stand on my own two feet! I have to take care of myself! I never have!" London screamed.

Morgan sat down next to London; he took her hand.

"I love you, London. I love you like I have never loved anyone before! I love you and I want to marry you. I don't ever want to be without you."

London almost caved in. Here sat the man she loved, declaring his love for her, opening his heart, begging her to stay.

London pulled her hand away.

"I can never be to you, what you want, Morgan. I'm broken, I don't want to be touched, not by you, not by any man!" London hesitated.

London knew she had to end all his hopes.

"I don't love you, Morgan. I like you. I appreciate you, but I... don't feel that way about you, I'm sorry."

Morgan turned white, he stood up with his back to her, he clenched his fists.

"I see. Well then, that certainly changes things, doesn't it." Morgan whispered.

London was so happy that Morgan had his back to her, she wasn't sure how long she could keep this up. When Morgan stormed into the house, slamming the front door, London jumped.

It's better this way. I'm dying inside, but this will keep him safe! If Trent comes for me, he will only get me! Not the man I love, and not the people I love! So be it!

London went upstairs to pack.

Neither one of them could stomach eating; Morgan tossed the food out.

Episode 23, Confession

Life was so strange. Who knew that you could miss someone so fiercely that your whole body ached.

London got a job at the local library. London had a small apartment above one of the local shops in town. She was able to walk to work every day.

London knew that Morgan truly loved her. Even as mad as he was at her and as heartbroken as he was, he still made sure that her apartment was saturated with cameras and all the latest safety measures. Even her doorbell took pictures, as well as videos.

London had every other Saturday off, and every Sunday. The library wasn't even open on Sundays.

London's apartment was small, but it was just her. She had to trek up a very long flight of

stairs, but she figured it was helping her get stronger.

London was still working with Luke.

London walked in, just as Morgan was walking out.

London froze.

Morgan froze.

Luke looked disturbed.

"Hello... Morgan." London whispered.

Morgan just nodded, storming out.

London's eyes filled with tears; she sat down heavily.

Luke raced over, putting his arm around London. Luke turned the sign to CLOSED. London gaped at him.

"What are you doing? You aren't closed!"

"I am right now! You and I are going to have a strong cup of coffee and have a chat!"

Luke led London to a sitting area. When Luke came back, he handed London a strong cup of coffee.

Luke took a swallow of his coffee, then his eyes slid to London.

"Why are you making that man suffer? Anyone with eyes can see that he loves you!"

London looked outraged.

"Don't try to lie to me, London! I'm on the outside looking in. I can see what's right in front of me! Morgan, the poor sap, he believed every lie you fed him! Why are you doing this, London? That, I can't figure out, at all! But there is something you should know about me. I have a confession to make."

London gulped, wiping her tears.

"What confession?" London sobbed.

"See, the thing is... I'm your trainer... anything you say to me, and I do mean... anything... stays between us. I'm like a built-in therapist! If I were ever to reveal anything one of my clients tells me... they have the right to take three shots at me, I can't fight back, at all! So, you see, you can tell me anything and I can't spill the beans because this man right here? I don't like getting beat on! I prefer to beat others. Maybe I have anger issues." Luke wondered out loud.

"But he's your friend." London sighed.

"You are my friend too."

London looked up in surprise.

"So... anything I tell you... you will not tell him?"

"Scouts honor! You have my word! If ever I tell, you can beat my hind-end!"

London giggled.

"So, if you tell… I get to hit you three times, anywhere on your body… and you can't fight me off? Is that about, right?

Luke gulped, looking a bit green around the gills.

"That's right, anywhere on my body." Luke squeaked.

Luke took London's hand.

"Sometimes telling someone takes that burden away that's weighing you down. Share with me girl! Tell Uncle Luke what's really going on."

London took another drink of her coffee.

"I don't have amnesia." London whispered.

Luke roared; his eyes went wide. Luke began to pace back and forth. Luke gripped his brown hair, making it spike up in all directions. Luke looked around frantically.

"Oh, my goodness! I should not know this! I can't know this! What was I thinking? He's going to kill me if he finds out I know this and I didn't tell him!"

London tried to hide her smile.

"Girl! Don't you be smiling like that! Don't tell me anymore, not one more word!"

Luke sat back down, squirming, looking curious as well as defeated.

"Okay! Why did you hide the fact that you had amnesia? Wait… you lied about having amnesia?! Why did you do that?"

"Because I have to keep everyone I care about safe from Trent!" London sobbed.

Luke tilted his head to the side, looking very Pit Bull confused.

"Huh? Wait a minute! So, you are protecting all of us from Trent?"

"Yes."

Luke looked even more confused.

"Why pretend to have amnesia?"

"At first, I really didn't remember, I wasn't lying. I did have amnesia, but by that same evening, I remembered everything."

"Okay… continue."

London filled Luke in on everything that happened. She left nothing out. When she was done, Luke fell backwards, sagging into the couch.

"That won't work, London! Trent is a killer, he likes it! He's sick and twisted, and no way can you go up against him by yourself! You must let me help you!"

"Look at how he gets away with everything, Luke!"

"True, but... we can set a trap! I'm good at setting up booby traps!" Luke rubbed his hands together gleefully.

"There's more, Luke." London whispered.

Luke leaned forward.

"What?"

"I really am busted, as much as I... care... about certain people... I'm just not sure I could ever be what he wants me to be. Trent damaged me, Luke."

"London, given enough... time... and patience... I do believe that you and Morgan can work this out if you get my drift."

London snorted.

"As hot as that man is, you just might be right, Uncle Luke." London giggled.

Luke roared; London joined in.

"Ok, so, are you still seeing your therapist?"

"Yes, every week."

"Have you brought this issue up with her?"

London looked miserable.

"This is such a small town, Luke. I trust her, completely, but... how is talk therapy going to help me figure this out?"

Luke nodded.

"Do you feel better after talking to me?" Luke questioned.

London thought about that for a minute.

"You know what, I do feel better!" London exclaimed.

"I think that talking about the details, over and over, what he did, all of it? In a weird way, might desensitize the issue for you. Like if you keep writing it down, in a journal, over and over, it doesn't hurt so much."

London looked stunned.

"How did you get so smart, Luke?"

"I have four sisters! Four younger sisters! I'm the only guy." Luke groaned.

"I had no idea you had four sisters! I bet you buy stock in chocolate!" London giggled.

"I buy that stuff every time I stop at my mom's." Luke insisted. "I walk in and throw it at them!"

Luke narrowed his eyes at London, pointing his finger at her.

"I can tell you for a fact that the multi-pack of tampons is your best buy for your buck! I can tell you which menstrual cramping medicine each of my sister's prefer! I know exactly which week to stay away from my mom's house, because they are like synchronized swimmers! Women live together long enough, and they all cycle together, and I am not talking about bikes!"

"Stop! You are killing me over here! Now, I have ta pee!" London laughed.

"It's a warzone, I tell yah! Now do you see why I'm still single?" Luke crossed his arms, looking mule-like.

When they were both done laughing and after London peed, Luke brought up the subject again, about trapping Trent.

"We have to get him, London. Let me think about this some more. We will talk again, soon. You ready to learns some skills today, lady?"

"Luke, when he attacked me, to rape me again, I froze. All my training went out the window! I was back to being that terrified woman, with no way out!"

Luke nodded.

"Your knee-jerk reaction is to submit. I'm going to teach you how to get beyond that, to keep fighting! Are you ready?"

London stood up.

"I am so ready Luke, help me."

"Always girl! Uncle Luke's got this."

Episode 24, Are You Serious?!

London glared at Luke.

It had had only been one week! One week since she unburdened herself to *Uncle Luke*! Now she wanted to bury him!

"I'm sorry! It all just came out! He's on his way here! No don't hide! Sheesh woman!"

"What happened to you being like a THERAPIST?"

Luke pointed at his own chest, with both thumbs, eyes wide.

"But I have no degree! You can't hold me to that!"

"What about, SCOUTS HONOR?"

Luke shook his head, looking uncomfortable. Luke seemed to be looking everywhere BUT at her.

London glared at him.

"You were never a scout, were you?" London gritted the words between her teeth.

"Yes, that would be a big NOOO." Luke emphasized the O and shrugged.

London slapped Luke on the shoulder, hard.

"Luke, are you serious right now?" London screamed, while doing the angry dance.

"He's on his way over here? What am I supposed to say to that man? He is so mad!" London exclaimed.

Luke grinned big.

"You got this! Plus, we need his help to set our trap! I think you should go with the flow." Luke tried to look wise, he even crossed his arms and... winked at her!

London was about to open a big ol can of whoop butt on him, but the door burst open. In stormed a very large, angry looking sheriff.

Morgan advanced on London, stalking her really.

London's eyes went wide.

"Morgan... uh... how are you? Me... I'm doing ok." London gulped.

For every step that Morgan took forward, London took one step back.

London finally dove behind Luke, she gripped his shirt tightly keeping Luke between her and a very steamed, Morgan.

London peeked over Luke's shoulder, moving, and weaving with him.

"Dude! You're in my face! Back up!" Luke told Morgan.

Luke tried to move to the right and then to the left; he even tried to turn around, but London held on tight.

Morgan grunted, trying to move Luke out of his way.

"I think... we all... just need to take a breath... and calm down." Luke said in a sing song manner.

Morgan slugged Luke in the stomach hard enough that Luke doubled over.

"Dude! Why did you slug me? I'm the one that told you the truth!" Luke wheezed.

Morgan eyed Luke.

"But you waited a whole week to tell me, Luke." Morgan's voice was low, and deadly.

London squeaked, losing her grip on Luke as he dropped to the floor.

London turned on Morgan.

"How dare you hit, Uncle Luke!"

Morgan arched an eyebrow, tilted his head slightly, placing his hands on his hips.

"Uncle... Luke?" Morgan questioned.

London planted her hands on her hips, imitating Morgan. She stuck her chin out as far as she could, looking onery.

"What do you know? Maybe he is my uncle, five times removed! You think you know everything, but you don't know squat!"

Morgan shook his head, his eyes closed slightly, then he roared while grabbing ahold of London.

Morgan's lips landed on London's, he wasn't gentle, he ravaged her.

London was so angry that she kissed him back, just as fiercely.

All her fear, and her rage, she put all of that into their kiss.

Luke stayed on the floor, at their feet.

"Huh, well, there yah go! All's well that ends well! Good ol me! Saving the day! But do I get a thank you? No! I get slugged in the stomach. That's a fine howdy do! Uggg my gut hurts! I think you cracked a rib, Morgan!" Luke whined.

Morgan and London didn't hear a word he said.

When they pulled away, they were both breathing hard.

Morgan smiled down at London.

London stepped back a couple of steps; London was visibly shaking.

"As wonderful as that kiss was, Morgan... I'm feeling a bit overwhelmed over here." London admitted.

Morgan picked London up, twirling her in a circle, one, two, three times.

"I missed you woman!" Morgan exclaimed.

London squealed.

"Morgan! Put me down! Stop! I'm going to pee!" She warned.

Morgan stopped, still grinning.

"I think she has bladder control problems, Morgan. You all might want to investigate that." Luke was still wheezing a bit.

Morgan stuck out his hand, to offer Luke a hand up.

"Come on, Uncle Luke, let me help you up." Morgan chuckled.

Luke looked suspicious, he grumbled a bit, muttering under his breath.

Luke took his hand; Morgan hauled him to his feet.

"Ok, now that you two… kissed and made up." Luke snickered at his own joke. Luke slapped his leg, snorting loudly.

Morgan twinkled at London; she blushed.

Morgan started towards London to kiss her again, but London was so freaked out that she eyed the door, wondering if she could race away.

London had to admit that she loved kissing this man, but could she ever go any farther? She just wasn't too sure about that. Plus, London was still trying to keep some distance between herself and Morgan, she needed to keep him safe.

"No! No!... No, more kissing, Morgan! We have stuff to do! We have to get everyone down here, so we can set up, OPERATION STOP THE MANIAC!" Luke shouted.

Morgan couldn't take his eyes off London.

Luke snapped his fingers in front of Morgan's face.

"Focus Morgan! We don't get this right... and she's dead." Luke stated.

Morgan stopped smiling; London frowned.

"Boy Luke you sure know how to kill a moment." Morgan complained.

Luke put a hand on each of their shoulders.

"That's what I'm here for! I live to serve!"

London crossed her arms, she looked quite severe.

"Oh, by the way... Uncle Luke... I get to punch you three times, anywhere on your body... and you have to take it." London purred.

Morgan and Luke's eyes went wide.

"What is she talking about, Luke?"

Luke shook his head, he didn't seem worried, at all.

"I only said that so you would confide in me, London. So, I could fix this whole sorry mess! Remember? I lied about being a therapist, and a scout. I also lied about the three hits! I'm so devious like that. Gotcha!" Luke crowed, he looked quite smug.

Luke glanced at Morgan. When he turned back, London's fist met firmly with his face!

Luke fell flat on his back.

"London! Nice hit! Remind, me never to tick you off!" Morgan exclaimed.

Episode 25, *How Scary Can Something Be... If You Poke It In The Eye?*

London worked hard with Luke, she never wanted to freeze up again!

When Luke pinned her, London felt panic start to rise within her.

"Don't panic London! Think! What do you do if Trent is on top of you? He's bringing his fist back to hit you!"

Luke sat on top of London, he pulled back his fist, snarling at her.

London yelled out, "Poke him in the eyes! Hand thrust to the nose! Punch or jab to the throat!"

"Yes!" Luke exclaimed.

"I think I can come up with at least two more, Luke." London growled.

"What? Tell me." Luke grinned.

"Box his ears! Rip out his hair!" London screamed fiercely.

Luke sat up, he looked very impressed, and a wee bit nervous.

"Yes! That may be what saves your life, London. Remember! *How scary can something be... if you poke it in the eye?* While they are busy grabbing their face, eyes watering, you run away!"

"That's going to be my new mantra!" London squealed.

London spread her arms wide, hollering loudly.

"How scary can something be... if you poke it in the eye?"

London's eyes went wide. "I should make t-shirts!"

Morgan huffed from where he was seated.

Luke and London looked towards him.

"Something on your mind, Morgan?" Luke asked.

"I can hardly sit here and watch you pretend to hurt her. I feel sick at the thought that she might have to face Trent, again! There must be another way!"

London patted Morgan on the shoulder.

"I'm going to have a tracking device on me, just in case! We choose the place; we control the outcome! Morgan, we can do this, we must! I need to get him to confess to his crimes, like he did before! That is the only way he's going down. I will invite Trent to meet me. I tell Trent that I want to make a deal with him. I tell him that I will go back to him, on two conditions... he must tell me why he is the way he is, and he agrees to leave you all alone. The man loves to talk... that will be his undoing." London insisted.

"I can't stand the thought of that man being anywhere near you. Look what he did to you last time! London, he almost raped you... again!"

London nodded.

"Next time! I'm not going to freeze! I refuse to freeze, ever again!"

"We are all set up. Go home, get some rest, you two. One week from now, we catch a snake." Luke stated.

Morgan looked concerned.

"Maybe, you should stay at my place London, it would make me feel better having you near me." Morgan said.

London shook her head no.

"I have a feeling that he's got people watching me. That's why I think it's a bad idea that you keep hovering around me, Morgan."

Morgan scowled.

"You and I are going to have to have a very public... disagreement... aren't we, London?"

London smiled.

"Oh yes, a very public... disagreement."

London laid her hand on Morgan's chest.

"After we... disagree... you have to stay away, so it's believable, Morgan."

Morgan looked grim but he nodded in agreement.

Episode 26, "You are not the boss of me, Sheriff!"

They chose the perfect spot for their disagreement.

White Cloud had a *"Music in the Park"* day. Everyone was at the park!

London sat next to Stella. Stella's entire family was present, even Pop and Grandma Nettie showed up.

Morgan roared up in his police cruiser, his lights flashing. He didn't have his sirens on, but the lights certainly caught everyone's attention.

Morgan slammed his car door, he peered around, until his eyes landed on London.

London let out a gasp. London did her best to look nervous. She clutched at her chest, playing with the buttons on her shirt. Honestly, it wasn't difficult to look nervous, she was nervous!

Stella and Alden glanced at London then towards Morgan.

Alden scowled. "What's got his panties in a bunch?"

"Are you ok, London? Is there a problem here that we need to know about?" Stella questioned.

Pop stood up.

"Morgan is charging this way, and whooeee, he looks like a man that needs a chill pill! This ought to be good!" Pop rubbed his hands together, gleefully.

"Sit down you old coot! You seem to thrive on chaos! What am I saying? You are the chaos!" Nettie screamed.

Nettie tried to yank Pop back down into his chair, but he sidestepped her, hitting record on his cell phone.

In fact, a whole lot of cell phones went up into the air.

AJ smiled slightly. "With all these cell phone up in the air like that, it's really starting to look like a concert here!"

The band even stopped playing, they watched as Sheriff Morgan advanced aggressively towards London.

The park went dead quiet.

The birds and squirrels even seemed to pause.

Morgan stopped in front of London.

Alden surged to his feet.

"Hey Morgan, you are looking... kind of grim. What seems to be the trouble here?" Alden questioned.

Morgan glared at Alden.

"This has nothing to do with you, Alden. Why don't you just sit back down, so I can discuss something with London."

"I don't think I like your tone, man! Take it down a notch, why don't you? There are families here!" Alden shouted.

Morgan got about an inch from Alden's face; they now stood chin-to-chin. Pure aggression dripped from them both.

"Like I said Alden, mind your own business!"

Morgan pushed his index finger into Alden's chest.

Alden shoved Morgan back.

London stood up quickly, stepping between the two men.

"I'll talk to him Alden, but I'll just be over there... if I need you." London stated.

Alden nodded, still frowning at his best friend.

London walked over towards a big tree. Looking around she realized that she picked the perfect spot. They stood dead center in the middle of all the town's people.

Morgan stood in front of her, arms crossed, looking ticked off.

"Do you want to tell me why you plan on moving away from here? What are you thinking? I can't protect you if you leave!" Morgan shouted.

Stella gasped, her eyes rounding. Stella started to head their way, but Alden wrapped his arms around her waist, yanking her down onto his lap.

"How many times do I have to tell you, Sheriff! I am not your responsibility! What I decide to do, that is up to me!"

"You have been my responsibility since the day you drove into my county, handcuffed to your steering wheel!"

The crowd gasped.

"How dare you! How dare you bring up the worst moment of my life! Plus, now the whole town of White Cloud is wondering why I was handcuffed to my own steering wheel! Shouldn't there be some sort of confidentiality clause?"

London pointed her finger in Morgan's face.

"You know what your problem is, Sheriff? You think you own everyone in this town! I think you have a God Complex! I think that badge of yours is going to your head! You know why you are still single? Who could stand you? You are bossy! You think you are always right! You don't listen! I'm leaving because you are smothering me to death! Besides, I'm used to being on the road; that's where I feel safe! Not with you! With you... I feel caged! I never want to see you, or talk to you, ever again!"

"Well! Before you go, let me just say this! Don't come crying to me when your ex-husband tracks you down! All I've ever tried to do is help you and this is the thanks I get? All I can say is... GOOD LUCK!"

Morgan stormed away.

London looked around, her face flaming.

London didn't have to pretend to be embarrassed, she didn't even have to pretend to cry. She was so emotional that it all came naturally.

Stella raced over to London; she hugged her tight.

Alden stood up going after Morgan, he was beyond angry.

Morgan turned around, ready to pounce if Alden chose to attack.

"What is going on with you, Morgan? This isn't like you! Explain yourself!" Alden shouted.

Morgan's expression was fierce.

"She's leaving, Alden!" Morgan shouted. "She's leaving and there is nothing I can do to stop her... and I love her!"

Everyone in the park started talking at once. Some people shushed others; they didn't want to miss anything.

Alden gaped at Morgan.

"Does she know that?"

"I told her! She said that she didn't love me... that she never could! She said she could never be to me, what I wanted."

Alden sighed.

"I get how you are feeling but you went about this all wrong, man."

Morgan's eyes glinted.

"I'm outta here, Alden. I can't be around her, waiting for her to pack up and leave. You might not see too much of me for a while. I don't want to be running into her."

Morgan turned towards the still quiet crowd; Morgan fiddled with his hat.

"I'm sorry I interrupted your concert folks. Truth is... I love that woman, but she doesn't want me."

Everyone gasped, again; turning to look at London.

Some of the women, at the concert, looked at London like she was a nutter.

London had tears streaming down her face.

"I never said that I didn't care about you, Morgan! I... I just don't want to be with you. I can't be with you, not ever. I'm sorry!"

London ran out of the park, she headed for her apartment.

Morgan tipped his hat to the crowd; he got in his car and left.

Pop stopped his recording.

While everyone talked at once, Pop had a very thoughtful look on his face.

Episode 27, We Need to Talk

Everything was in place. London glanced at the watch they put on her wrist. The watch would track her movements, just in case Trent got his hands on her, somehow.

London nodded at Luke, while she dialed Trent's phone number.

"Well, hello London, this must be my lucky day. Why, would you be calling me?"

"I can't keep living like this Trent! Wondering when you will show up again. I don't want you to hurt my friends. Maybe... maybe... we can talk."

The line was silent for a bit.

"Sure. Why not? What did you have in mind?"

"I... I'm scared of you, Trent. You must see that I have a right to fear you! I don't know how to do this! I don't... want to be... alone with you." London whispered.

"Listen to the fear in your voice, silly woman! I just want you to come home to me. I want us to be a family again. Is that too much to ask?"

London realized that Trent was being careful with his words. He must suspect something. London was supposed to lure Trent back here, but she made a snap decision.

"You... tell me Trent... tell me where to meet you... in public! That's the only way I can be near you."

Luke stood up, looking panicky.

Luke was shaking his head no, but London didn't pay him any attention.

Trent laughed softly.

London felt chills race up her spine.

"I like that, London. So... I'm the boss, aye? You will meet me anywhere I want?"

"Within reason, Trent. I'm living on a very small income. I'm working at the local library. I have my own apartment, so I have bills."

"I'll pay your travel expenses."

London gulped.

"Ok… tell me where we are meeting." London whispered.

"Take the phone off speaker, London." Trent whispered.

When the phone beeped, letting her know she had a message, she switched over to it.

On the screen was a picture of Stella and Alden, they were sitting in their yard with their baby girls on a blanket. Another picture popped up, it was a shot of Luke, then Morgan. The last pic gave her chills. A picture of Francine sitting on a bench at the library flashed on the screen. Francine was unaware that her picture was being taken.

London gasped; she immediately switched the phone to private.

Luke charged towards London, looking frantic. Luke still held his own cell phone up, it was on speaker. London could hear Morgan going nuts on the other end.

London hung up the phone and turned towards Luke, she looked calm.

"I'm going to end this Luke; everything is going to be ok." London said softly.

Luke raced up, grabbing London by her upper arms.

"Please, London, tell me what he said! What did he send you?"

London brought her knee up, dropping Luke like a rock.

Luke gasped, holding his man parts. Luke dropped his cell phone, Morgan's voice cut off abruptly.

London kicked Luke's phone out of his reach.

Luke started to sweat, rolling to his side.

"I really should not have shown you that move... uggg! I don't think children are in my future!" Luke moaned.

"I'm sorry, Luke. This ends today, one-way-or-another. Trent will never hurt anyone I love, ever!"

London ran out the door.

Their plan was officially out the window but one way or another, all of this would end today.

Morgan was on the phone with Luke during the exchange but then Luke's cell phone went dead. Morgan kept calling Luke back but got no answer.

Morgan paced his office, roaring at the top of his lungs.

When Morgan glanced out the large glass windows of his office, all his officers were frozen. Some were hunched down in their chairs.

Morgan did what he was supposed to, he stayed away from London. He hadn't gone near her, but now he wanted to race to her side and shake some sense into her!

Morgan's cell rang, it was Luke; he answered quickly.

"Morgan, you there?"

"Oh, I'm here! You put London on the phone, right now!" Morgan hollered.

"London is already on her way to Grand Rapids! I'm in my car, following her! The woman kicked me in my man parts; she got a head start on me. I'm tracking her watch!"

Morgan's eyes bugged.

"What are you talking about? Why is she on her way to Grand Rapids?"

"I'm sure Trent told her to get in her car immediately and start driving! She ran out of here like her butt was on fire!" Luke screamed.

"Where is she headed, Luke?"

"I don't know! She stepped away from me! Trent sent her something that spooked her! She looked like she was going to be sick!"

"I'm getting in my car! Are you on 131?"

"Oh no! I lost the watch signal for a second... wait, it's back!"

Morgan sucked in a breath, he had to sit down, he felt sick with fear.

"Don't you lose her Luke! You are our only chance right now!" Morgan exclaimed.

"Meet me at Gerald R. Ford Airport... that seems to be the direction she is heading."

"I'm heading out the door now! Stay on her Luke!"

Episode 28 Flight Plan

When Morgan and Luke got to the airport in Grand Rapids, they quickly realized that they had a very big problem on their hands.

Luke stood at the counter arguing with the lady.

"This is life and death lady! We need to know where she is going!"

"Like I told you sir, flight plans are private, personal information. I can neither confirm, nor deny, if a passenger is on a flight."

Morgan was on his cell screaming at Grady about the warrant.

Morgan's phone pinged; the warrant came through.

Morgan turned his phone towards the same lady that Luke was arguing with.

"Here is our warrant! Give me the information that I need to save that woman's life!"

The woman behind the desk, turned to her boss; he nodded for her to give them the information.

"It says that she boarded a private plane that will take her straight to... hmm... Municipal Airport... in... odd, this is so odd."

Morgan practically vibrated.

"Where? Where is she going?" Morgan demanded.

"Well, it seems that she is on a straight, private flight, to Nebraska City."

Luke looked stumped.

"Why would Trent be meeting her in Nebraska? That doesn't make any sense at all!" Luke exclaimed.

Morgan went still. Morgan thought back to the conversation that he had with London. Something about a town with only one resident.

Morgan turned back towards the airline worker.

"There is a small town in Nebraska, I can't remember the name. It only has one person that is the caretaker for the town... I think the name of the town started with an M."

The airline worker grinned.

"Monowi... it's Monowi. It's a ghost town. The one resident that resides there is the caretaker. She opens the pub daily. It's about four hours from Nebraska Municipal Airport. You have to rent a car to get to Monowi from there."

Morgan turned towards Luke.

"I know what Trent is doing, Luke. He's taking London back to the spot where he hurt her, where he dug her grave! He truly is insane!"

The airline worker gasped, hearing what Morgan said.

Luke gaped at Morgan.

"We have to get there, Morgan! We have to save her!"

Morgan turned back towards the airline worker.

"What's your quickest flight out of here for the two of us that will take us to Nebraska Municipal Airport?"

She taped a few keys, then she picked up a phone.

"Hold that plane! Hold it, I say! I have a police officer and his sidekick that have to make this flight!"

"The plane is being held for you. Run! It's the last terminal up that ramp to your left! If you make this flight, you won't be too far behind her! Good luck! Please! My name is Gwen Wilson, can you please get ahold of me, so I know how this all ends?"

Luke grinned.

"We sure will Gwen and thank you!"

Morgon and Luke raced up the left ramp, to the back of the airport. Morgan had to check his gun; he couldn't carry on the plane. Soon they were seated and in the air.

Morgan glanced at Luke.

Luke gripped his arm rests till his knuckles shown white.

"Problem Luke?" Morgan asked.

Luke's eyes were glued shut.

"I'm fine. Why do you ask?"

"You're sweating, your eyes are slammed shut, and you are about to rip off your arm rest."

Luke peeked at Morgan.

"Uh... I have a bit of a problem with heights." Luke gulped.

"Dude, riding in a plane is like riding a bus." Morgan stated.

Luke glared at Morgan.

"Do buses fly way up high off the ground? No, they do not!" Morgan leaned in closer towards Morgan.

"Dude, if we plumet to our deaths, we will be like a bug hitting a windshield! A completely, flat bug!"

"Mommy, are we going to crash like a bug and die!"

Luke and Morgan's eyes went wide. Simultaneously they turned to look behind them. Peering through the crack in the seats, they could see a little girl, maybe five years old.

"No Mara, we are not going to crash; we are fine."

Mara's mom glared at Morgan and Luke.

"Nice move you two! Now look at what you did! You have no idea! Mara is like a dog with a bone, she is going to worry during this entire flight! Stupid men!"

Morgan and Luke unbuckled their seatbelts, they stood up and turned towards the cute little girl.

"Hi Mara, my name is Sheriff Morgan, and this is Luke. He was kidding about crashing. We are not going to crash!" Morgan said a bit louder than he intended.

Mara had long, dark pigtails, she had big, dark eyes and currently her lip was sticking out.

"I don't believe you! We are ALL going to DIEEE!" Mara screeched.

Luke gaped at the little girl.

"Uh... Morgan does she know something we don't know? She seems awful sure that we are going to crash." Luke looked very nervous while chewing on his thumb nail.

Morgan shook his head in disgust.

A man in a business suit stood up towards the back.

"What's going on up there? Is there a problem with the plane? Someone said the word CRASH! Plus, you look like a law man, is that guy your prisoner?"

A very large woman stood up waving her umbrella aggressively.

"I didn't sign up to have no criminal on my flight! Why isn't that man cuffed? He looks very shifty to me!"

The same woman's eyes went wide.

"I bet he's a master criminal, and he's going to make the plane crash to make his getaway!"

Everyone started talking at once. Women screamed, babies fussed, men shouted.

Mara let out a long, piercing scream.

Morgan was sure he could see her tonsils.

While Mara continued to scream, Luke's one eye started to twitch. Luke plugged his ears, slamming his eyes shut. Luke figured if he couldn't see or hear what was going on, it wasn't really happening.

Morgan growled at Luke.

"You started all of this; face this mob like a man!"

Luke shook his head NO. He kept his ears plugged but opened one eye.

Morgan stepped into the aisle.

Morgan couldn't believe what he was seeing and hearing. The entire plane was mayhem; people were sobbing and screaming.

Two men were wrestling in the aisle fighting over the last bag of nuts.

The men took turns swinging at each other, they were mostly sweating because neither one could land a punch.

"How dare you try to take my nuts! If we crash that might be the only thing between life and death for me! It's not my fault that you pigged down three bags of nuts! These are mine!"

"What are you, the nut police? Hand em over or else!"

Both men put up their fists, they were about to attack, again.

Morgan let out a long, loud whistle.

The entire plane went silent, except for Mara.

Morgan glared at Mara.

Mara glared right back, while continuing her piercing scream.

"Stop screaming Mara!" Her mother demanded.

Mara sucked in a breath to let another scream loose.

Morgan placed the palm of his hand over Mara's mouth.

"Listen up kid, don't make me take you to jail." Morgan said through gritted teeth.

Morgan was nose to nose with the kid. Morgan looked grimly down at the girl. The eyes looking back at him, over his hand, glinted dangerously.

"If I take my hand away, are you going to scream?" Morgan asked.

Mara glared daggers at Morgan and nodded her head yes.

Morgan sighed.

"Ok lady, what do you normally do to shut this kid up? You got any ideas?"

"My name is Brenna, nice to meet you. Usually, I would take her in the bathroom and spank some sense into her, but nowadays people get all upset if you look at your kid wrong."

Morgan nodded at Brenna.

"Go ahead, take her back there and spank her. I'm the sheriff, so if I say you can spank her, you can spank her!"

Mara's eyes went wide.

Morgan let go and Mara screamed with rage. Morgan had to admit that Mara had a nice set of lungs.

Morgan raised his voice.

"Can I get a show of hands here? How many of you all think that Mara needs a good old-fashioned whooping?"

One man stood up looking disgusted.

"Please! Spank her! Shut that kid up! I swear she is going to make my ears bleed!"

An elderly lady on the plane stood up.

"That's what's wrong with this generation! Tan that girl's backside! Spank her! Spank her! Spank her!"

"Spank her! Spank her! Spank her!" Now the entire plane chanted along with the old lady.

Brenna stood up; Mara gaped at her mother.

"You brought this on yourself sweetheart. I kept telling you to stop and you wouldn't, so let's go!"

Mara dug in her heels; she screamed all the way down the aisle to the restroom.

Everyone kept chanting, *"Spank her! Spank her! Spank her!"*

The chanting only stopped when Brenna shut the bathroom door. Then, the plane went silent, because everyone was trying to hear what was going on in the bathroom.

Mara could be heard arguing with her mother.

"If you spank me, I'm going to tell the police!"

"They are the police darling; they told me to spank you, dear."

Whack! Whack! Whack!.... Whack! Whack!

Snickering broke out on the plane.

Morgan grinned.

Luke and Morgan watched the two men that were fighting roar with laughter. They laughed so hard that they had to lean on one another.

"Hey dude, I don't think we are going to crash; I'll share my food with you."

"That's ok, I'm quite full, but thank you! My name's Bob, nice to meet you!"

The other man gasped.

"My name is also Bob! Maybe we are related!"

The two men sat back down to discuss their Bobness.

The airline stewardess clapped her hands to get everyone's attention.

"Alcoholic beverages are free!" She shouted, with a big smile on her face, arms thrown out with joy.

Everyone started clapping and cheering.

Luke raised his hand high.

"I'll take a Bloody Mary!" He shouted.

Morgan arched an eyebrow at Luke.

Luke shrugged.

"What? It has tomatoes, that's fruit. It has celery, that's a vegetable. The liquor is my... fortification."

The stewardess handed Luke his Bloody Mary.

"Listen up cutie, you caused all of this. I'll be putting your name on a list! In the future you can fly with our airline, but you are hence forth red flagged."

Luke's jaw dropped.

"What does that mean, exactly?" Luke asked.

The stewardess pinched his cheek, wiggling it back and forth.

"When you get on one of our planes you will be the first one to be offered free alcohol. We want to get at least one drink in you before we take off in the future. You mess a plane up

194

like this again... your red flag turns into banishment."

The stewardess turned and walked away.

Morgan snorted with laughter.

Brenna escorted Mara back to her seat.

Mara was very quiet.

Morgan leaned in close to Luke.

"Don't make eye contact, sit down quickly Luke."

Morgan and Luke sat down. All throughout the flight they could feel those big, brown eyes, boring in the back of their heads.

"I swear I can physically feel her eyes drilling into the back of my head, like laser beams, Morgan." Luke complained.

"Hush up Luke. Do you really want to get that demon child screaming again?"

Luke shivered.

"Now do you see why I hate flying Morgan; too much drama!" Luke huffed.

Morgan rolled his eyes, crossed his arms, and sighed.

The stewardess picked up her microphone.

"We regret to inform you that due to a small electrical malfunction, we will be landing at Des Moines International Airport."

The stewardess had a plastic smile plastered across her face.

"There is no reason to panic." She said in a sing song manner.

The entire plane panicked.

Mara sucked in a breath and let rip her scream of death.

Luke's eye twitched something awful, he was back to gripping his arm rest, sweating, and requesting another Bloody Mary.

"Sorry sir, no more alcohol is available at this time, due to our sudden, unexpected landing."

Luke's eyes went wide.

"But I'm RED FLAGGED! It's my medicine when I fly!"

Morgan glared at Luke.

"Shut it, Luke! Now we have to take another flight, I'm praying we don't have a long layover! We need to get to London, before that maniac... hurts her or worse."

Luke gave Morgan a sympathetic look.

"We will make it Morgan, I'm sure of it."

Morgan felt sick; Morgan's radar was screaming in his head.

Something bad was coming.

Mara hit a particularly high note.

Morgan tilted his head, one eye closed part way. Maybe it wasn't his radar screaming in his head. Maybe, it was Mara!

Episode 29, Back to the Scene of the Crime.

When London got off her private flight a rental car awaited her.

London had a four-hour drive ahead of her.

London set the GPS, that would take her right to Trent.

It was starting to get dark, the closer she got to her destination.

London shivered as things started to look familiar.

London stopped the car on the side of the road. She felt sick! She realized that Trent was taking her back to where he had dug her grave!

London felt tears gather in her eyes, she leaned her head back sucking in precious air.

"You can do this girl! You have to! He's just a man!"

London rubbed her hand across her brow, she realized that she was sweating. London continued to talk out loud.

"Okay, yes, he is just a man... a very dangerous man... a murderer... who is intent on killing me! But I got this! That's right girl! You are fierce and strong, and you don't quit! You fight right up until your last breath if you have to!"

London continued driving.

When she pulled up to the spot where Trent took her last time, the spot where he violated her and dug her grave, she thought she was going to hyperventilate.

Trent stood alone; he had a big grin on his face.

London was thankful that she was wearing her spandex pants, her sports bra with a t shirt over the top of it. She had gotten in the habit of dressing in her fighting clothes just in case Trent's goons jumped her. London also had on her best pair of running shoes, strong and sturdy.

"Welcome home sweetheart." Trent cooed.

"Cut the crap Trent; we both know why we are here."

"Do tell wife."

"I'm not your wife! We are divorced! Thank goodness!"

Trent shook his head.

"No, I'm afraid you have that all wrong. I've been saving this little tidbit of information for a day like today. We are not divorced darling."

London shivered.

"We are divorced! I have the paperwork to prove it!"

Trent roared with laughter.

"You think I can't buy people to make that stuff look real? Didn't you ever wonder why I made the divorce so easy? Because it never took place. You are still, and always will be, my wife."

"Doesn't matter Trent! If I'm not divorced today, I will be soon, and you will be in jail!"

"For what? All I've done is ask you to meet me somewhere quiet so we can talk. I even brought a picnic basket."

London saw that Trent spread the blanket on the ground where her grave used to be. There was a picnic basket also, set off to the side.

"Let's eat dear and talk. Maybe if you are very nice to me... I'll continue to be nice."

London looked back over her shoulder, the area was so desolate, she felt so alone.

London lifted her chin, she started towards Trent, showing not one ounce of fear.

"By the way London, I know what that watch does. My dad's company makes those, take it off!"

London froze. Trent's gaze turned deadly. When she saw his fist curl she unclasped the watch, tossing it to him.

Trent placed the watch on a good-sized rock and smashed it to pieces with a smaller rock. The watch was toast.

"Good, now it's just the two of us. Come and eat wife, I don't know about you, but I am starving!"

Trent sat down, rummaging in the picnic basket.

"I brought all your favorite dishes, London. Fried chicken, potato salad, pistachio pudding, and blueberry pie."

London huffed.

"Those are your favorite dishes Trent, not mine."

Trent went still, he slowly turned his head, leveling London with his ice-cold stare.

"London, sit down!"

Trent stood up; London took a step back.

"If I were you sweetheart, I'd watch my mouth. Now... how about some appreciation for this wonderful meal I've provided. Sit down! Now!"

London sat down carefully, keeping her eyes trained on Trent.

Trent seemed to calm down, he sat back down on the blanket, continuing to unpack the food items.

"It's getting late Trent. It'll be dark in about an hour... are we really going to sit here in the dark and eat?" London asked.

Trent smiled.

"I would think that this could be considered romantic, don't you? But not to worry, I set up tiki torches all around us."

London looked around, she hadn't noticed those before, she had been so focused on Trent.

"They are solar, when it starts to get dark, they automatically turn on. What's cool is that my dad's company makes those too! Not only do they light up, but they give off a signal to deter bugs. I do hate bugs when picnicking."

Trent held out a plate to London. London hesitated but then she reached for it. London was so pleased to see that her hand wasn't shaking one bit.

"How do I know you haven't drugged my food, Trent?"

Trent leaned close to London, too close. Trent stabbed his fork into a chunk of her chicken and took a bite. He also scooped up some potato salad. Trent took a bite of everything on her plate, showing her that the food was fine.

London picked at her food. She hadn't had much to eat or drink today, she worked on the chicken a bit, to get some protein into her.

"Why Trent? Why are you this way? It's just you and me here, out in the middle of nowhere. What made you... kill your mom, my aunt, and who knows how many others? Do you even know how many?"

Trent finished chewing a bite of food, while waving his fork around. He seemed to be trying to figure out a number.

London was floored.

"You have to think about it, Trent? You seriously have to sit there, and try to figure out in your head, how many people you have killed? What is wrong with you?"

Trent took another bite, but his eyes never left hers, then he smiled. It was his eyes that gave him away. There... in his eyes, she could see the madness, the insanity.

"I'm waiting Trent, how many?"

"Roughly... fifty... give or take a few. Does it really matter?"

"You told me that you pushed your mom down the stairs, but you never really told me why."

Trent's face turned serious.

"My mom... she was perfect you know. She didn't beat me, or starve me, she read to me at bedtime and spent time with me. We swam together in our pool almost every day. You know, most wealthy people send their kids off to boarding school as young as four, but not my mom. My mom truly loved me and fought with my dad to keep me home with her. I loved her for that, I really did."

London gaped at Trent.

"Then why kill her?"

Trent considered her question.

"It was because I loved her that I killed her. She was going to love me so much that she was going to make me soft, weak. I loved her so much that the thought of losing her... would give me nightmares. I had to make all that stop. By taking her out of the equation, I was free."

London's mouth hung open.

"You really are insane." London whispered.

Trent huffed.

"Who in this world is normal, tell me that. I choose to remove obstacles from my path. If I start to care about someone or something, poof! Gone!"

"So... are you saying you care about me because you hurt me over and over and then tried to kill me on this very spot?"

Trent nodded.

"See, now you are starting to understand. Last time we were here, I enjoyed the time we spent together but you had to go."

"You raped me! You pig! How dare you sit there and say those things to me! You dug my grave!"

"Yes... yes, I did. You shouldn't have left me... I lost my temper. I did some bad things, I admit that, but I want to change that. I want us to go home and be together again. I got you pregnant once, we can do it again."

London stood up.

"That's never going to happen. Remember how you treated me, Trent? You starved me! You beat me! You raped me! I came here today to end this fiasco! Stand up and fight me!"

Trent went still. Darkness descended while they talked. There was no moon tonight. The torches lit up while they talked, giving them a large circle of light to see by.

Trent stood up, he packed the picnic away and folded the blanket. Trent stepped back into the lighted circle. London noticed that he still walked with a limp. His right side was vulnerable, she could work with that.

Trent removed his shirt, standing bare chested, feet planted wide apart. Trent's face filled with hate.

"You know, London, it didn't have to be this way. But, once again, I find myself wanting you too much. If something becomes a weakness... you snuff it out."

Trent started to laugh; he even tossed his head back.

"Just back there, about a quarter of a mile in? Your grave is already dug and deep; no shallow grave for you my dear."

London felt herself starting to shake but instead of giving into those fears she decided to channel them. So, she began to talk and to taunt Trent in the hopes that anger would make him sloppy.

"Just so you know Trent, you were horrible in bed. Morgan kissed me one time and there was more promise of fulfillment in that one kiss, than any kiss you ever gave me."

Trent snarled; his breathing picked up. Trent was shaking with rage.

"Here I was planning on just killing you this time, but now you are challenging my manhood. I might just have to make you pay for that."

Trent started towards her.

"I wasn't finished!" London exclaimed.

Trent stopped.

"I think your story about your mom is bull! You didn't kill her Trent! Your poor mother saw what you were, she leaped down those stairs to get away from you! She saw what a whacked out, piece of trash, she had birthed, death was preferable to her, rather than sticking around a beast like you!"

Trent roared and made his move.

Trent was so mad that his fists went wild. He lunged and swung but London was controlled, calm, and deadly.

Trent stepped forward with his right leg. London stomped on his bad foot, quickly stepping out of his reach.

Trent screamed in pain. He shook with the force of it, spittle running out of his mouth, tears streaming down his face.

Trent circled her, he grunted from the pain.

London stopped long enough to whip her t shirt off. She needed more freedom of movement.

Trent lunged trying to grab ahold of her but what Trent didn't know was that London made a stop at the local party store before heading this way.

London pulled over and covered her arms and neck with petroleum jelly. No matter how hard Trent tried to grab ahold of her she just slipped away.

Trent screamed in frustration.

"Aww poor Trent... what's the matter Trent... you can't catch me?"

London's eyes glittered with hatred. "I'm not going down today, Trent; you are!"

London surged forward, she hit him with a right, left, another right. Trent staggered back.

Trent took a swing with his right fist, but she ducked. He followed with his left, she raised her right arm, blocking the punch. London made a straight punch to his nose. London did not let up, she just kept hitting him until he was flat on his back, not moving.

London heard a car, but she didn't turn around, she wasn't about to take her eyes off Trent, not for a single second.

Morgan and Luke shouted; she could hear them coming.

When Morgan and Luke got to the edge of their circle, Morgan started to rush forward.

Luke shot his arm out, stopping Morgan.

"What are you doing man? Let me help her!"

"She has to do this herself Morgan; otherwise, she will be afraid forever."

London took one step towards Trent.

She could see in her mind what he would do; Trent was that predictable.

"London! Be careful!" Morgan shouted.

London continued forward, one measured step at a time.

Trent appeared to be knocked out, but she knew better. He was playing opossum.

London was ready for him when he opened his eyes to lunge at her. London dropped to her knees, right on top of Trent. London jabbed both her thumbs into his eyes. *After all, if you poke it in the eye... how scary can it really be?*

Trent's eyes watered, he screamed grabbing both of his eyes, thrashing back and forth. London took advantage of that fact and punched him in the nose, again.

By now Trent was writhing on the ground, screaming, and crying in pain.

London stood up, she was sure he was well and truly done.

London started to turn away; her face turned to stone.

If you think he's all done in? Don't believe it! He will try one more time to win!

London whipped back around. London brought her very sturdy running boot down onto Trent's man package.

Trent sucked in air, gasping like a fish on the bank of a river. He cupped his man parts, while rolling onto his side.

Morgan and Luke both jumped.

"Oh dang! It's like I felt that shot... whooee Morgan!"

"You and me both Luke! I am literally sweating right now!"

"I threw up in my mouth just a little bit, even." Luke stated.

"I admit I'm feeling a bit queasy also." Morgan moaned.

London finally looked towards Morgan and Luke.

London raced across the clearing, wrapping her left arm around Morgan and her right arm around Luke.

"I'm so happy to see the two of you." London sobbed.

Luke hugged London but then he pulled back.

"Uh... London you feel like one big ball of grease! What in the world?" Luke murmured.

"I rubbed petroleum jelly all over me so he couldn't grab me, Luke."

Luke grinned.

"Now that, is a fantastic idea! Where did you come up with that one?"

London shrugged; she saw it on a movie, but she couldn't remember which one.

Morgan eased back.

"I'm so happy to see you too darlin. I'm pretty sure you made me age ten years when you took off like that. Just so you know... we will... be having a discussion about that!" Morgan promised.

Luke stepped back peering at Morgan's hair.

"Oh dang! You have grey hairs Morgan! London literally gave you grey hair!"

"I do not have any grey hairs!" Morgan groused.

"Hmmm I guess it could be the lighting, but dude maybe you should get some of that hair darkening stuff for men."

"Luke! I'm trying to hold this woman, comfort her and maybe even kiss her! You go watch the criminal while I get to it!"

Luke saluted Morgan.

"Sir! Yes sir! At your service, my.... Sheriff!"

Luke marched away to glare at a still crying Trent.

Morgan pulled London in for a hug, but she resisted.

Morgan let go.

"I... just want to get out of here Morgan, I can't be here anymore."

Morgan's brows drew together.

"Did he... hurt you again?"

"No... I hurt him... but... I need to leave."

Morgan nodded.

London headed for her rental car; Morgan dialed the local police.

"London! Will you just sit in your car? The local police are going to want to talk to you. I don't have jurisdiction here. We can't let him get off on a technicality."

London sighed, she nodded.

"Ok, I'll wait in the car." London turned away.

Morgan cuffed Trent.

Luke looked concerned.

"Is she okay? She's acting a bit odd." Luke murmured.

"I'm not sure what is going on, but she will tell us, eventually." Morgan stated.

Episode 30, I'm Fine... I'm Fine!

Trent wasn't even arrested!

Morgan tried to talk to Grady, but Grady informed him that he had been directed by his client, that she wanted to enforce confidentiality.

Morgan was shocked. Morgan then tried to talk to London, but she wasn't talking either.

Morgan walked into Luke's gym; he was going to try again to reach her. Morgan spotted London working the bag. London seemed to pause, like she knew it was him, but she didn't look in his direction. Morgan noticed that she started working the bag a lot harder.

Morgan glanced toward Luke; Luke shrugged. Neither one of them had a clue what was going on with London. She wasn't talking and she wasn't letting any of them get too close.

Morgan headed towards Luke.

"How is she doing today, Luke?"

Luke sighed.

"She's stronger than she's ever been. She's not acting right Morgan, she's so calm, focused, but if I try to question her, she shuts down. I'm wondering what exactly went on with her and Trent before we got there, but all she says is, *"I'm fine."*

Morgan nodded. "I'm getting the same from her as well. I can't get close to her, at all. Maybe she just needs time."

London finished up, she glanced at the two men, slowly heading towards them.

Morgan smiled at London.

"Hey there London, how are you today?"

"Fine."

Morgan and Luke glanced at one another.

"Can I talk to you for a minute, London?" Morgan asked.

London seemed to frown a bit but then her *"I'm fine mask"* came back.

"Sure."

Morgan led London to one of the sitting areas.

Morgan took off his cowboy hat, twirling it.

"So... I know you keep saying that you are fine, but everyone is worried about you."

London sighed.

"Why? I'm fine. I faced my fears, beat up... my... Trent. Life is good."

"Wait, you said... *My*? What were you going to say?" Morgan questioned.

London's eyes glittered with anger, and it was all directed at Morgan.

"I need you to back off Morgan! Just let me be! I need space right now and I need everyone to give it to me!"

"What happened?" Morgan shouted.

"Nothing!" London shouted back.

"Something happened because you came back from, all of this, very different! We are all worried sick about you, and I can't get close to you!

London stood up; Morgan followed. They were both breathing hard, glaring at each other.

Luke stepped between them, trying to push them back and away from one another.

"Okay you two, you look like you both are about to throw down. Why don't you two kiss and make up? Hmm... what do you say to that?"

Morgan grunted while pushing on Luke a bit. Luke bounced off London, back over to Morgan. Luke tried to wiggle closer to London, but she shoved him bouncing him into Morgan. Back and forth the poor guy went, like a ping pong match. Luke yelped and grunted every time he got shoved or bounced.

London glared at Luke, then back to Morgan.

"I'd rather kiss a cactus! I am out of here! Everyone just back off!"

Morgan growled, slamming his hat back onto his head.

"Fine! I'll have the florist shop deliver a nice big cactus to your apartment! Kiss away!"

"London grabbed her stuff, slamming the door on her way out.

Morgan began to pace back and forth. Morgan noticed that Luke was looking a bit rumpled.

"What's wrong with you, Luke?" Morgan groused.

"What's wrong with me?" Luke growled softly. "I'll tell you what's wrong with me! You two are going to be the death of me! You can't be in the same room right now without screaming the place down."

Luke sat down heavily. "I can't take this anymore. All that girl does is go to work and come over here to train. Honestly, that girl is lethal, she really doesn't need me anymore. Heck, I think she could teach me a thing or two!"

Luke waved at Morgan to sit down and stop storming around.

Morgan sat.

"I don't know what to do! I can't reach her! She's closed herself off and I don't know why. I thought her facing Trent, one-on-one would be healing, in some way."

Luke handed Morgan a fresh coffee.

"I wish I could sit down with that clown! That man loves to talk, I bet I could get it out of him!" Luke ranted.

Morgan nodded. "I can't believe they didn't arrest him! That man is dangerous." Morgan stated.

"Well... I mean it's crazy, but she didn't have a mark on her. She beat him up good! It was touch and go there for a bit. For a second, I thought she was going to be the one to be arrested!" Luke exclaimed.

Morgan took a sip of his coffee.

"Yeah, I mean I can't blame the local law, Luke. They had no idea what the real deal was. Plus, when the police asked Trent if HE wanted to press charges, he said no. I swear that man lives under a magic star!"

Morgan's face turned sad.

"Maybe... I'm a fool, Luke. Maybe she really doesn't care for me the way that I care for her... maybe, this is her way of pushing me away but I'm too stupid to get the message."

Luke shook his head no. "I think that she has feelings for you... I mean she's never really said for sure."

Morgan rolled his eyes.

Luke patted him on the back in sympathy.

"Don't give up man, she's worth it." Luke stated.

Episode 31, Lies or Truth?

London didn't want to make this call but there was no way around it. The phone rang twice, Trent picked up.

"Trent... this is London, we need to talk."

"Yes, we do."

"My lawyer has been in contact with your lawyer. I want a divorce, Trent. You and I can just walk away from each other. I want nothing, no money, no alimony, nothing from you."

"I really hate discussing these things over the phone. Meet me for dinner at... isn't there a

steak house right there on main street in your quaint little town?"

London fumed, that was the spot that Trent hurt Grady.

"Exactly how are we going to have dinner when you are so far away?" London questioned.

"Sweetheart, I'm staying at the Shack in Jugville. I must say this place is beautiful."

"You're here?" London gasped.

"I'm here to discuss terms London, in person, that's the only way that this is going to happen, but don't worry, you never have to be alone with me."

London considered Trent's proposal. She had no idea what Trent's end game was here, but she felt like she had no choice but to meet up with him.

"Okay, I'll meet you there at six pm."

"I'll be there, wife."

London hit the off button on her cell phone. She wanted so badly to ask Morgan and Luke for help but once again, Trent proved that he was untouchable.

When London told the police in Nebraska that Trent dug her grave about a quarter of a mile, straight back, they looked. No grave was found. Trent only said that to shake her up. Trent told the police that that spot was special to them, that he owned that land, and he was trying to convince her to come back to him. The police bought every word he said.

She would get her divorce, she would! The problem was, she now knew that she was going to have to be civil and try to reason with Trent.

"This ought to be fun." London said out loud.

Due to it being Friday, the *T-Bone Steak House* was beyond full. London wasn't sure they were going to be able to get a table.

London stood by the door. Debbie Yarrow was greeting people and seating them.

London was up next.

"Hi London, your table is ready." Debbie announced.

"It is?" London looked confused.

"Your table was booked ahead of time, about a month ago, which I thought was a bit odd but oh well."

London was floored. *Trent booked this table a month ago. How could Trent be this many steps ahead of her? What did he do, book the table right after she beat him up?*

Debbie took her to the back of the restaurant, it was very private, probably the nicest table in the whole place.

"Here we are, your server will be right with you to get you started."

"Thank you, Debbie."

"My pleasure." Debbie went back up front to greet the next patrons.

London wore a silk dress tonight; it matched her dark blue eyes. She left her long, blonde hair down, letting it flow to her waist. Her makeup was a bit more dramatic tonight, she usually wore her makeup lightly, but tonight when she applied her makeup, she almost felt like she was putting on armor.

London had no idea how incredibly beautiful she looked tonight. Many eyes turned her way, but she had not a clue.

London saw Trent walk in, he smiled at Debbie, being his most charming self. London had to admit that if she didn't know Trent and what he really was, she would probably be just as fascinated by his charm and good looks as every other woman in the place.

Trent made his way towards her. Trent sat down, smiling at London.

"I must say, London, you look stunning tonight. You literally are taking my breath away."

"Thank you? You... um... look very nice also, Trent." London said awkwardly.

"See... isn't this nice? You and me being cordial to one another?"

"I keep waiting for you to tie me up, kidnap me, or hurt me, something like that."

Trent laughed.

London let out a hysterical giggle.

"I'm not going to hurt you, London; I promise. Let's just have a nice meal and talk."

London had to admit, she was stumped. London was sure that the real Trent would soon appear, she just had to wait five minutes.

Trent had a serious look on his face, as he eyed London.

London worked hard not to squirm.

"I wanted to tell you... London, I'm glad you agreed to meet with me."

"I didn't have much choice if I want my divorce, and I do want a divorce Trent, that hasn't changed."

Trent nodded thoughtfully.

"I didn't really kill my mom, London." Trent whispered.

London's eyes rounded in shock.

Trent sighed.

"I would never hurt my mother. I said that to scare you. I'll take a lie detector test as soon as you can set it up, to prove to you that I'm telling the truth. I'm not a serial killer, I lied about that too. Your aunt died of natural causes London, you have my word, but again, I'll take the test."

London was unable to even form a sentence.

Trent leaned forward putting his arms on the table.

"When my mom fell down the stairs, I was there. I stepped out of my room, she turned and looked at me. She smiled so softly and waved at me. I waved back at her. I was about to run to her... when... she leaped. My mom spread her arms out, like she could fly... and she jumped."

London gasped, her hand flying to her mouth.

"How can I believe anything you say Trent? Can you see that I would have a problem with anything that comes out of your mouth? Remember, you did hurt me, repeatedly. You dug my grave, Trent." London whispered.

Trent looked wrecked.

"I'm sorry... so very sorry. Let me continue, tell you the rest, then I'll give you your divorce. You will never have to see me again."

London was about to say something, but their waiter showed up with their order.

London looked surprised.

"I ordered for you; I hope you don't mind." Trent said.

London looked down; Trent ordered her favorite fish and shrimp dinner.

"That's fine, thank you." London said quietly.

London couldn't believe she was hungry, but she managed to eat at least half her meal before she asked her next question.

"So... you never killed anyone, that is what you are saying here."

Trent nodded.

"Seeing my mom commit suicide... changed me. I heard someone screaming that night. It went on and on, then I realized that it was me that was screaming. I felt dead inside, no emotions. I always felt like I was standing outside of my body, watching myself be... awful."

"That doesn't excuse everything you've done, Trent!"

"No, you are right. I'm just trying to make you see why I am the way that I am."

London sighed.

"Again, how do I know this version of events is the truth?"

Trent grabbed London's hand, she snatched her hand away, shaking her head no at him.

"Sorry, I won't do that again." Trent fiddled with his fork, moving his food around.

"My dad sent me to several therapists; nothing worked. They medicated me, changed my meds, at one point I was hospitalized. My father authorized them to fix me by any means necessary."

Trent's face lost all expression.

"Doctor's can be fooled fairly easily, London."

"What do you mean, Trent?"

"I finally realized that the only way to make it all stop was to... act happy, smile, play with toys, draw happy pictures. I had to play their game, do things their way, conform to their rules of right and wrong."

Trent huffed out a laugh.

"What? What's so funny?"

"One doctor was showing me these cards with blobs on them. She would hold it up and say nothing. I had to eyeball that thing and tell her what I was seeing.

"I said the usual things but this one card... it looked like a face... I saw my mom in that card. I thought that if I admitted that, they would lock me up for the rest of my life... but... I couldn't say dog, or cat, or tree... it swirled like her hair, almost a profile of a woman. Well, that's what I saw." Trent seemed embarrassed.

"So, what did you do?"

"I looked her straight in the eye and said, *"That... looks like my mom."* I started crying so hard that I couldn't stop. The doctor handed me the card to keep and had me escorted to my room. My dad picked me up the next day."

London grabbed her wine; she took a quick gulp.

"Even though I dealt with the loss of her, I never really got over it. My father and grandfather sent me to an elite boarding school, then college."

"How old were you when you went to... away to boarding school?" London asked.

"Six."

London was floored.

"How old were you when you saw your mom die?"

"Five."

London sat back, slumping in her chair.

"If this version of events is true... then, I'm sorry for you Trent, but I still want a divorce. That's all I want, I don't want your money, nothing, just a divorce."

Trent nodded.

"Everyone leaves me... my mom, my dad, my grandfather. I never had a lot of friends. Except in college, people that wanted to be my friends because they wanted something from me."

"We all have something in our past that can affect us in the here-and-now, but you went too far. You locked up our food, and drinks, you hurt me, you hurt me some more, and dug my grave, you were going to bury me there!"

Trent had unshed tears in his eyes.

London never saw Trent cry before, but she wasn't falling for it.

"I am sorry... I can see myself doing all of that, but again... I was on the outside looking in... I can't explain it any better than that."

London nodded.

"You need help Trent. As an adult, therapy will be far different from when you were a child."

Trent nodded.

"I'm going in for treatment next week. It's an inpatient program. I'll be there for a couple of months... or more."

London's jaw dropped open, she had to admit that she was shocked.

Trent pulled out some paperwork, he slid it over towards London.

"Have your lawyer look at these and get back to my lawyer. You won't see me again. I'm done hurting you London." Trent assured her.

"I don't know what to say, but if you are being sincere... then, I hope you get the help you need. I hope you fall in love and have lots of babies, true happiness Trent."

Trent smiled softly at London.

London's smile was small, but it was there.

Morgan chose that moment to walk in, with Luke and Alden.

Morgan couldn't believe what he was seeing.

Luke's mouth literally hung open, while Alden put an arm across both of their chests.

"Keep your cool guys, we don't know all the facts. Let's just go... turn around and walk out."

Morgan turned back the way they came in, he took two steps, then he spun around, making a beeline for Trent and London.

"And he's gone, that man never listens! I'm left here talking to you!" Alden exclaimed.

"This is going to be bad!" Luke started forward to chase down Morgan.

"And he's gone too! I feel like a babysitter! Great! Now I'm talking to myself!" Alden raced after both men.

When Morgan reached the table, London gasped.

Luke and Alden stepped up as well.

Morgan was angry.

"Please explain to me what is going on here? Why are you with this man, eating in a restaurant like you are buddies?"

Debbie raced over to the table.

"Excuse me gentlemen but this is a public place. You are ruining the ambiance. Take it outside please!"

London stood up, tossing down her napkin.

"You don't know what is going on Morgan, you need to leave! Stop this now!" London demanded.

Morgan leaned in close towards London.

"Do you know why I don't know what is going on here? Because all you say is, *"I'm fine."* You haven't told me squat! Well, prepare to talk woman!"

Morgan grabbed London, spun her around and cuffed her.

London huffed at Morgan.

"What am I being arrested for? This is abuse of power! Let me go this minute and I may not press charges, Morgan!"

Trent stood up.

"I'll bail you out, no worries there." Trent assured London.

Morgan's fist curled; his eyes slid towards Trent. Morgan pulled back his arm to slam his fist into Trent's face, but Alden and Luke tackled his arm, pulling it down and away from Trent.

Morgan never let go of London.

When Alden and Luke towed Morgan away from Trent, London was pulled with them.

"I cannot believe you Morgan Dun! You are going to pay for this!" London cried.

"Threatening the sheriff aye? Well, that right there gives me good reason to arrest you, London." Morgan whispered softly.

London gaped at Morgan. London brought back her foot and kicked Morgan in the shins as hard as she could. While Morgan jumped around on his one good leg, she aimed for that one too. While Morgan roared with pain and anger; London started to run away, still cuffed.

Morgan lunged at London, he picked her up, tossing her over his shoulder, marching out of the *T-Bone.*

"Attacking the Sheriff is not a good idea, London! Let's add aggravated assault, and resisting arrest, as well!" Morgan grunted.

Alden and Luke chased after Morgan.

"Dude! You are taking this a bit too far! You need to calm down man." Alden begged.

"What exactly is your plan here, Morgan; are you really arresting London? Stop, take a breath, and think!" Luke chimed in.

Morgan tossed a screaming London into the back of his police car. Morgan slammed the car door, turning towards his friends.

"I am calm, go have dinner. I have a criminal to question." Morgan stated calmly.

Alden and Luke's eyes rounded.

Alden laid his hand on Morgan's shoulder, looking him dead in the eye.

"Remember when I told you that you would end up living above my garage, with Jonas as our new Sheriff? You would become a pariah in the community, a drunk that never showers? Dude! You are heading in that direction!" Alden ranted.

"So be it! Get out of my way!"

Morgan swung his door hard, making the two men jump back quickly. Morgan got in the driver's seat driving away.

Luke threw up his hands in disgust, spinning in a circle.

"That man is so hardheaded! What are we going to do, Alden?"

Alden had his hands on his hips, head slightly tilted, eyeing Morgan's taillights.

"I guess we are going to have to save him from himself. Get in my SUV man, we have a cop to catch up too."

Luke jumped in smiling from ear-to-ear.

"Isn't this exciting? You and me, going on an adventure together! I feel a real connection here between us… bro!"

Alden rolled his eyes, snickering.

"So, if I'm your bro, that would make me your older brother; you have to do as I say, at all times."

"Now you get it! I'm like the brother you never had, Alden."

"A younger, annoying brother."

Luke smiled.

"Yep, that's me, that's what I do best!"

Alden hit the gas, racing after Morgan.

"He got a bit of a head start but maybe he won't realize we are tailing him." Alden stated.

"Check us out! It's like we are the cops, and he is the criminal! I've got goosebumps man!"

Alden chuckled.

"You are such a nerd."

Luke huffed and crossed his arms, then he quickly turned back towards Alden.

"Aww man! I can't stay mad at you! I wish we had snacks and drinks! If this turns into a stake out, we should have big cups of java, maybe cigarettes littering up the ashtray, or cigars!"

"We don't smoke, Luke."

"Hmm yes, true… but snacks and java sound good! Can we stop and get some? We didn't get no dinner."

"I'm following Morgan at a discreet distance to see where he's taking London." Alden huffed and rolled his eyes. "I mean, I highly doubt he is actually going to arrest her."

"Uh… Alden? He just pulled into the police station. I think… now this is just me thinking outside the box here… he is for sure arresting her!" Luke exclaimed.

Alden couldn't believe what he was seeing. Morgan had the back door of his police car open, trying to wrestle a resisting London out of the vehicle.

Alden roared up next to Morgan, Luke and Alden raced over to a very sweaty, angry sheriff.

Alden stepped between Morgan and a kicking London.

"Dude! Stop! You are not arresting her! You are going way too far with this, because basically, you are losing your mind." Alden explained.

Luke nodded vigorously.

"What he said Morgan! You are losing it big time! Remember how I taught you those breathing exercises? Now would be a good time to suck in some air and slowly blow it out... like blowing out a candle... softly... sweetly."

Alden and Morgan both turned to watch Luke suck in a deep breath; then, he puckered his lips, blowing softly with his eyes half closed.

Luke opened his eyes and smiled big.

"Oh! I feel so much better! You all really need to give this a try!"

London giggled from the back seat.

Morgan scowled, whipping his eyes back towards London.

Alden braced himself against Morgan to keep him from lunging at London again.

"I hate to do this big guy, but you've lost your marbles." Alden stated with a grim look on his face.

Alden brought back his fist and slugged Morgan in the jaw. Morgan staggered backwards, falling on his butt. Morgan sat on the grass strip alongside the parking lot.

Morgan's eyes were a bit glazed over.

"Happy Pet Appreciation Day!" Morgan stated with a bit of a slur.

Morgan promptly fell backwards unconscious.

"Ohhh! You are in so much trouble Alden! You punched the sheriff!" Luke exclaimed.

"I didn't punch the sheriff... I punched my best friend that is trying to ruin his career!"

London finally struggled to the edge of the back seat, towards the open door. London gaped at an unconscious Morgan.

"Is he ok? Oh, my goodness, call a doctor, or an ambulance! Do something you two morons!"

Alden grabbed the cuff keys, while Luke stood over Morgan with a thoughtful look on his face.

Luke bent down; he straightened out Morgan's head, so his head wasn't bent.

"Poor guy is going to have a crick in his neck if we leave him like that." Luke stated with a smile.

Luke turned, grinning at a gaping Alden and London.

Luke grabbed Morgan's left and right arm, placing them on his chest.

"See! He looks much more comfortable, and so peaceful!" Luke assured them.

Alden uncuffed London, but he didn't let her anywhere near Morgan.

"He won't be down for long, London! We have to get out of here!" Alden explained.

"But... he needs help!" London cried.

Alden waved his hand at London shaking his head no.

"That man has the hardest head I've ever seen! He's more than fine! Let's go!"

Luke frowned.

"I do not want to be here when Morgan wakes up, no way!" Luke exclaimed.

Luke raced for the SUV.

London looked concerned but she quickly agreed. London speed walked to the SUV.

"Let's go guys, he's fine!" London screamed.

When the three of them were in the SUV, Alden turned around to look at London.

"Where are we going to stash you woman? I can't take you to your apartment, that's the first place he will look." Alden stated.

Luke smiled.

"I know where we can stash her!" Luke exclaimed.

Luke told them his plan.

Alden nodded.

"Good plan baby bro, you are so smart! You must get that from me!" Alden insisted.

Luke laughed out loud.

"For sure big bro, I learned everything from you! Has anyone ever told you how incredibly smart you are, man?"

Alden eyed Luke.

"You know, mostly I just get yelled at; pretty much all the time, in fact!"

Luke gasped.

"That is so wrong! I got your back, man!" Luke exclaimed.

London sighed.

"Bro? Brothers? You two aren't even related! When you guys are done with your BROMANCE; we need to leave! Morgan is waking up!" London shouted.

Alden and Luke let out girlie screams as Alden floored the gas pedal.

Episode 32, Westman Crazy Train

Morgan pulled up to Alden's place. Morgan looked everywhere but he couldn't find London. Morgan was worried that she really had skipped town. He couldn't blame her, after all, he had acted a bit nutty.

Morgan no sooner slammed his cruiser door than the front door burst open. Morgan gaped at the stream of people exiting the house. Alden and AJ were front-and-center but the rest of the Westman boys were right behind them.

Stella flew out the door after them, waving a... toilet brush?

"You all better get your backsides back in this house or you will starve to death because this woman won't be cooking one darn thing!"

Alden Senior reached Morgan's side.

"Save me man! Save me from that crazy woman that I call wife!"

Morgan noticed that Stella's hair looked wild and greasy, all-at-the-same time. Her shirt was covered with… he didn't know what, but the worst thing was that she had two, huge, wet circles, right where her very large, breasts rested.

"What is wrong with her shirt, Alden?" Morgan squeaked.

"Dude! She produces enough breast milk to feed a small, war-torn country! I have seen the babies choke Morgan! Those girls are trying to feed, and they can't suck fast enough. She takes a baby away from her breast and milk shoots across the room! I told her to pump them things before she tries to feed them girls. Stella leaks like a faucet that's busted." Alden cried.

Morgan's face turned beet red.

"Maybe I should go! Yes! I'm sure I'm needed… somewhere!" Morgan exclaimed, while trying not to look at Stella's breasts.

Alden held onto Morgan so tightly that Morgan couldn't run away, even if he wanted to.

"You are not leaving me man; we are best friends!" Alden begged.

Alden held onto Morgan's shirt with a death grip; he even ducked down a bit, hiding behind Morgan's shoulder.

Meanwhile, the boys all stopped. They stood quietly while their mother waved the toilet brush around. They were getting chewed out royally.

Caleb grabbed his throat, pretending to choke. It was all very dramatic. Caleb fell backwards, holding his throat, gasping for air.

"Caleb Westman! Stop pretend choking! One of these days you are going to choke for real, but because you keep doing this all the time, we won't know if you are really dying! Get it? Stop crying wolf!"

Caleb sat up abruptly.

"What does a wolf have to do with me choking to death, Ma?" Caleb mocked.

David shrugged. "Yeah Ma! What's all this about a wolf?"

Stella pointed the toilet brush at Caleb and David.

"This is what I'm talking about! We talked about this you guys, more than once! Remember the story about the boy that kept lying... he came to a very dastardly end, he got eaten! You two never listen to a single word I say!

Stella re-educated the twin boys about the wolf story, including the moral of the story... again! Then she made them repeat it back to her, just to make sure they were listening.

After that Stella went back to ranting about ungrateful children.

Alden was completely hidden behind Morgan now.

"What exactly has Stella so upset? What did you guys do?" Morgan whispered.

"We pee standing up... we are barbarians... according to Stella, the list is long."

Morgan wasn't sure what to say to that.

"Uh... don't all men pee standing... up?" Morgan questioned.

"Stella says no."

Morgan gaped at Alden.

Alden looked stressed and a bit panicky.

"Morgan, is it weird that I feel guilty when I pee standing up, now? I'm starting to have performance issues! I can't pee because I'm sure somehow, she knows!" Alden exclaimed.

Stella's voice went higher, catching their attention.

"How can you all miss the toilet bowl? The opening is the size of a very large watermelon!

There is no excuse for this kind of behavior! You are not firemen and that thing you pee with is not a hose that you spray wherever you wish! Your penis is not a toy! Do I look like your maid? Don't answer that! You should be listening, not talking! Do you all really believe that I should be down on my hands and knees cleaning up your DNA, after a very long night with the girls? Don't answer that! Did I say you could speak? You all need to listen to the words that are spewing out of my mouth, and by golly you all need to straighten up and fly right!"

Stella began to march back and forth, her toilet brush wasn't dripping, thank goodness! As she stalked back and forth, Morgan blushed when he realized that Stella's milk circles were much larger. Her milk circles now resembled large, eggplant shaped stains, that now reached her belly. Morgan thought that Stella's breast milk was flowing hard, partly due to the fact that she was marching back and forth, her breasts bounced around fiercely.

"Uh... Alden." Morgan whispered.

"What?" Alden whispered back.

"Um... your wife's leaking is getting... worse." Morgan choked.

"You have no idea, man! Sleeping with her is like sleeping on a waterbed. I've been sleeping on the couch for a while now."

Alden jumped when the passenger door opened on Morgan's cruiser; Luke stepped out.

"What's he doing here?" Alden questioned.

"It's his day off, he said he wanted to ride around with me to try to locate London."

Alden gulped. Alden stood beside Morgan trying to look serious. He had one hand resting on his chin, the other on one hip.

"Is that so... hmm... any sign of her?" Alden's voice was high and squeaky.

Morgan glanced at Alden.

"I can't tell if you are feeling guilty for peeing standing up, or if you feel guilty because you punched me in the face. You stole my prisoner, and you are being awfully quiet about her whereabouts! That's why I'm here, to question you about that."

Alden waved his arms around dramatically.

"Dude! Can't you see I'm on a Westman Crazy Train right now? I don't have time for your problems! I have enough of my own!"

Luke wandered towards Stella; he had his hands out like he was trying to quiet a spooked horse.

"Hey there Stella. I must say, motherhood looks good on you girl."

Stella smiled softly; she blushed a bit.

"Oh, hi, Luke... I had no idea you were here." Stella stated.

Luke gently took the toilet brush from Stella.

Luke turned on the boys.

"Take this toilet brush, you guys all need to break up into three teams. Each team needs to pick a bathroom, I want them to shine like the top of the Chrysler Building, you get me?"

The boys all gaped at Luke.

Luke's voice turned to steel.

"Move! Let's get it done!" Luke roared.

All the boys crashed into one another while trying to race into the house. They all liked Luke, but they also knew that he could hurt them all, if he really wanted to.

AJ didn't run but he did walk up to his mom giving her a soft hug.

"Ma, dad and I will watch the girls while you sit and relax. We have frozen breast milk, we got this."

AJ turned, yelling for his father.

"Dad! Stop hiding behind Morgan and let's get going!"

Alden sighed. "Aww Man! See you later Morgan."

Alden kicked a couple of stones, while keeping his eyes lowered as he went past his wife.

Just as Alden started to ease past Stella, she scowled fiercely. Stella threw out her arms, stomping in Alden's space.

Alden jumped with fright, racing into the house quickly.

Luke sat Stella down on one of the porch chairs.

"I can see that your boys... and your... man, are making your life a bit difficult. You go on inside and take a nice, long, hot bath. You stay in that bath as long as you want. I will stay right here, directing the boys. I am also going to make all of you the best meal you have ever eaten."

Stella's eyes filled with tears.

"That's so nice of you, Luke! I don't know what to say! *Sob*."

"You go on now, I got this." Luke assured her.

Stella went to hug Luke, but he nodded at her chest.

Stella looked down and sighed.

"I swear these things never stop! How do you know so much about women and yet you are still unmarried, Luke?" Stella sniffled.

"I grew up in a house full of women, five women, counting my mom. I am the oldest by the way."

Stella's mouth dropped open, in shock.

"I had no idea that you had four sisters!"

Luke nodded wisely.

"A lot of people don't know this, but women that live together... cycle together... I'm not talking about bikes here, Stella."

Stella blushed then she laughed out loud.

Alden opened the door when he heard his wife laugh.

"Honey, it is so good to hear you laugh like that." Alden said softly.

Stella's eyes filled with tears, again.

Stella stood up throwing her arms wide, tears pooling in her eyes.

Alden stepped back outside to fold his arms around his wife. Alden held on to her, gently stroking her back.

"I'm sorry I pee standing up honey, I'll work on that. I'll try not to be such a barbarian too. I promise to get after the boys more about... everything!"

When he stepped back, Stella sniffled some more, she giggled a bit.

"You might want to change your shirt, Alden. I seem to have... messed you up a bit." Stella said.

Alden looked down, seeing two, very large, wet spots on his chest. Stella's milk leaked over onto Alden during their hug.

Alden shrugged.

"Not the first time that's happened. I must say honey, you could win a wet t-shirt contest, right now."

Stella sighed, laying her head on Alden's chest. Alden kept holding his wife, comforting her; even though his wife leaked like a busted pipe.

Alden turned towards Morgan, but his heart sped up when he realized that Morgan was eyeing the upstairs apartment.

Luke noticed also; he froze like a deer facing the headlights of an oncoming car.

Morgan glared at Alden and Luke.

"Is someone living up there? Because I just saw a curtain move." Morgan said.

Morgan charged towards the doorway to the upstairs apartment, he knew for a fact that that had to be London.

Luke hustled Alden and Stella into the house.

"Why don't you get your wife into the tub Alden, and I'll start dinner!" Luke sounded a bit nervous as he shut the front door. Luke came back to the closed door, peering out, a loud click could be heard as Luke locked the front door. The blind that covered the window, on the door, was slowly lowered down.

Episode 33, Do Tell All Please!

London had the door open, standing off to the side when Morgan got to the top of the stairs.

"Oh! So, you aren't going to hide like the criminal that you are?" Morgan mocked.

London rolled her eyes, ushering Morgan inside.

London went into the kitchen; she came back with two colas. She placed one in Morgan's hands; then, she dropped onto the couch.

Morgan sat down, opened his pop, and took a swallow.

"So, London, I need you to tell me everything, and if you don't... let's just say, I am so done with all the crap that you are putting me through! Start talking!"

London got up and grabbed the thick documents from her purse. London handed them to Morgan and sat back down.

"Trent insisted that I meet him for dinner because evidently we are still married." London crossed her arms looking grim.

Morgan sucked in a breath. Morgan opened the paperwork and went over it. When he was done, he sat back, sighing.

"Please tell me everything, London." Morgan's voice was calm now. Calm and gentle.

London crossed her arms, wrapping them around her middle, leaning forward on the couch.

"Let me get all of this out. Don't interrupt me, Morgan. I'm happy to answer any questions you have when I'm done, okay?"

Morgan nodded.

"I didn't tell you this before, but Trent told me that he killed his own mother and my aunt. He claimed that he has killed maybe fifty people or more, he isn't sure of the exact amount."

Morgan looked like he was going to start shouting but London gave him the evil eye.

"Trent acts like he's two different people! One minute he's that nice guy I met, then he's abusive and trying to kill me! He says awful things that give me nightmares. At dinner that night, he said that he made it all up, that he didn't kill his mom that she instead committed suicide, in front of him when he was five. He said that at the age of six he was put into a psych ward and that they did all kinds of treatments on him. He handed me the divorce papers; he told me he was going to be unreachable because he was going into a facility for treatment. He seemed... sane! He seemed reasonable and kind. Morgan... he had tears in his eyes as he apologized to me. I just don't know what to think about all of this."

Morgan wiped his brow; he had a headache coming on.

"Which versions of his stories are you thinking may be true, London?"

London shook her head at Morgan.

"I've seen true evil from that man... then, I saw someone else at the T-Bone. Trent's personalities change like the weather."

"There is something I can do, London."

"What? What can you do?" London looked hopeful.

"I can investigate the death of his mother and your aunt; I can do it quietly."

London smiled. London stood up rounding the coffee table to hug Morgan.

Morgan stopped her; she looked hurt and confused.

"My feelings for you haven't changed, London. But..."

"But what, Morgan?" London whispered.

"You, darlin, are a married woman. I would never pursue someone that is even technically married."

London smiled.

"I can see that. You are a very honorable man, Sheriff Dun."

London placed her palm on Morgan's cheek.

Morgan couldn't help placing his own hand over hers but then he quickly pulled away.

"So, this thing here... professional all the way, London. That means no tempting me. I'm just a man; I have feelings. Don't walk all over them, London."

London nodded.

"I'm still going to therapy, working on my issues. I care about you too Morgan. I think... you are the best man I've ever known. I respect you. I trust you with my life, Morgan."

Morgan fiddled with his cowboy hat, then he placed it on his head, showing that it was time to go.

London walked him out.

"I'll text you my aunt's information. Please, let me know what you find out. I'm living here now. I'm not working at the library anymore and I'm moved out of the apartment that I was in."

Morgan looked a bit thoughtful.

"In your divorce papers I see that Trent gave you a pretty large sum of money."

London shook her head.

"I don't want his money; I never did! The check came and I deposited it, but I haven't touched it. The divorce won't be final for quite a while."

"I get that but... that man was your husband, and that money can get you on your feet. He took an awful lot from you. It should be used for good. Use it, London. It's better to take that money and let it help you to become strong and independent. That way if ever you have to face Trent again... you are in a better position to fight him. It's just a thought. I want you to really think about that."

Morgan tipped his hat and left.

Episode 34, Special Gift

Winter arrived with a vengeance.

London stomped her feet while knocking on the Westman's front door.

Stella opened the door glaring at London.

"Just come inside! I've told you to just come on in, girl! You are family!"

London hugged a squeaky, clean Stella. Stella must be getting more sleep because she was clean, she smelled great too. Her long, beautiful hair fell almost to her waist.

"Woman! You look amazing! How can a woman have eight children and look as fantastic as you do?"

"I'm tall, I can carry a lot more weight; doesn't mean I want too though!" Stella huffed.

London eyed Stella.

"Maybe it's your... upper body? It's... large... and those things make the rest of you look small."

Stella roared, then she slapped her hand over her mouth and listened.

London listened also.

Stella sighed with relief, sitting down to drink her dreaded decaffeinated coffee.

"I can't figure this out, London; the girls just don't sleep well! They fuss all night long."

London thought about that.

"I'm no expert, but the other day when I was here, you were literally vacuuming the floor, and your dog Ernie was doing his blood-hound bark. The boys were fighting, and the girls slept right through it all. I think the house is just too quiet at night." London stated.

Stella's jaw dropped.

"Sweet goodness! I've been shushing everyone to be quiet! Those girls are used to mayhem! I'm going to put a box fan in their room and maybe turn on the radio. What was I thinking?" Stella twirled her finger around her own temple, basically say, "I'm nuts."

London grinned while sipping her coffee.

The door burst open and in walked... everyone.

Alden and AJ looked like they were part snowmen. Ben, Caleb, and David made a beeline for the refrigerator, tracking snow across the whole house.

"Boys! Get your snow stuff off and put it where it goes! We go through this every day!" Alden growled.

Alden corralled the boys, then grabbed the mop and cleaned up.

Franny stopped by her mom; she was wrapped up like a mummy. Franny's light, blue eyes sparkled between her scarf and her hat. Stella helped unwrap her daughter like the perfect gift.

"When only your eyes show like that Franny, I could stare at you all day long." Stella promised.

Franny smiled. Her two front teeth were missing, so her smile was beyond adorable.

Elijah walked up to AJ and handed him a gift-wrapped box.

AJ looked surprised.

Everyone looked surprised.

"You got me a gift little bro? What's this for?" AJ asked.

Elijah smiled softly and shrugged.

"You can open it now or when you are alone, that's up to you, AJ." Elijah announced in a very adult tone.

AJ looked around, he sat down, while ripping the paper off. The box underneath was plain brown, about the size of a small loaf of bread.

Everyone gathered around, wanting to see what Elijah got AJ.

"Did you and dad know anything about this gift mom?"

"No, not at all. I'm just as curious as you are." Stella said.

AJ shrugged and opened one end. He pulled out the white Styrofoam insert gently. Alden handed AJ his pocketknife to gently cut the tape that held the Styrofoam together.

AJ lifted the lid and froze.

Inside the Styrofoam, was a rectangular glass picture. Not a normal picture, but solid, thick glass. AJ pulled it out carefully.

Alden leaned over AJ's shoulder. When AJ's hands started to shake, Alden gently took it from him.

"Let me hold that for a second son." Alden said softly.

Alden held up the clear glass. Inside the glass was a 3-D image of Bud No and AJ. Bud No got his name because when he was a pup they were always yelling, *"Bud No!"* As he got older, they called him Bud, unless he was being bad, then it was back to Bud No.

Bud was their dog that had to be put down. Bud had a heart attack, there was no saving him. AJ and Bud were the best of friends, they grew up together. Bud went everywhere that AJ went. When Bud got older and moved slower, AJ moved slower to accommodate the dog.

AJ reached for his gift again, after hugging Elijah.

"Thank you so much Elijah, this is the best gift ever!" AJ said.

"How did you pay for this Elijah?" Alden questioned.

"I save all my money." Elijah said.

Everyone just nodded; that made total sense.

Everyone gathered around, peering into the glass. Inside the glass it showed Bud No, and AJ sitting on the front porch. AJ and Bud were both looking straight at the camera. AJ had a big smile on his face and everyone that had ever seen that photo swore that Bud No was smiling too.

When you turned the glass the boy and dog seemed to move too. It was astounding!

When the gift finally ended up in her hands, Stella cried like a baby.

"I remember how Ernie kept coming up missing." Stella gulped. "He would go out to Bud No's grave and lay there with him."

Alden huffed.

"I remember just before you had the girls that you were as big as a... uh... you were big... but beautiful!"

Alden changed his wording when his wife glared at him.

"We all found you sleeping with Ernie on Bud's grave. You almost gave me a heart attack woman." Alden groaned.

"All I remember is I had to pee so bad! You guys were standing there trying to figure out how to get me up! I finally had to get myself up!" Stella told London.

London laughed out loud.

The door opened again. In walked Alden's mom, Grandma Nettie looked... furious.

Alden smiled cautiously at his mother, hugging her.

"Where's Dad?" Alden asked.

Nettie scowled.

"He... fell... in the snowbank."

Alden gasped, heading for the front door.

"He's fine Alden; he needs to cool off anyway! That man had the nerve to tell me on the way over here that I was gaining weight! I'm wearing snow gear! It's dang cold out there! After I told him that, he suggested that perhaps we should stop and buy a measuring tape, maybe keep a journal! Why, I never! That man is going to get a punch in the eye one of these days!"

Alden and the boys ran outside to save Pop.

Stella stood up.

"This I must see! Come on London!"

Everyone crowded outside onto the front porch.

Stella gasped, along with London.

Stella glanced back into the house. Grandma Nettie sat, calmly stirring her coffee, without a care in the world.

Stella whipped her head back towards Pop.

Pop was upside down. When he fell, he fell over the snowbank, his head was lower than his feet. He couldn't roll because he too was decked out in snow gear.

"Dag blasted woman pushed me! That's assault! Call the sheriff!" Pop hollered.

Alden and AJ each took an arm. With all his snow gear, and being upside down, they couldn't budge him.

"We must spin him, AJ; that's the only way we are going to get him back on his feet."

Pop roared with disapproval.

"I'm not a clock, or a compass!"

Alden peered down at his father with one eyebrow up, his head slightly tilted.

"Have you put on weight dad? You look a bit more... beefy." Alden said slyly.

"Why I never! I weigh the same as I did when I was... thirty... ok, maybe forty."

Grandma Nettie could be heard yelling, "Hah! I don't think so, fatty!"

Alden crossed his arms, waiting for his dad to be honest.

"Fine! Sixty, but not a day over! Spin me boys! Spin me and get me up!"

Elijah had the video recorder running; he didn't miss a second.

"Boy! You and that thing need to go away!" Pop roared.

Elijah just grinned and kept recording.

Pop's face softened a bit.

"I must say, when I see this side of Elijah... I find myself feeling so much pride for the boy. Problem is he came out of his shell, and there's no stuffing him back in there."

During the birth of the twin girls, Elijah recorded the entire event by taking at least a thousand pictures. The boy took pictures of EVERY aspect of birth! At one point his dad passed out, he got loads of pictures of that. Also, his brother Ben passed out after the girls were born, those pictures are still hidden and brought out only by Stella. Ben hates those pictures but there is no way that those pictures will ever go away.

Pop's face turned red with fright. Pop tried to get up on his own, waving his arms around, frantically.

"Dad! What are you doing? Hold still!" Alden exclaimed.

Pop started pointing frantically while gulping and gasping with fright.

"Ca... Ca... Ahhh! CATS There!" Pop screamed.

Alden realized that while they were talking their two one-eyed-cats sat themselves on the highest point of the snowbank. Skit is a very large, lilac tipped, Siamese cat, with one big blue eye. Skit lost his eye in a cat fight with their other cat Mason. Alden was sure that Skit had some type of big cat in his genetics, but he wasn't sure what, he was that big! Meana was his opposite in every way. Tiny, a mostly black cat with one seafoam eye that blinked at a now thrashing Pop.

So many cats were dropped off on their property that Stella got mad one day. She painted a sign that said, *Stop dropping off cats! I only take one-eyed cats!* Someone took her seriously and that's how they ended up with Meana.

Stella took the sign down right after that whole fiasco.

"Dad! Those cats would never hurt you! Why in the world do cats scare you so much?" Alden asked.

Pop's face turned practically purple with rage.

"None of your darn business! Get me up! Hurry up!" Pop hollered.

Pop glanced behind Alden; Pop looked so nervous.

"Look at them! They are licking their chops! I'm a goner!" Pop sobbed.

Alden and AJ glanced at the cats.

"Dad, they are bathing themselves; that's what cats do." Alden rolled his eyes.

AJ snickered.

Pop gulped, still pointing at the cats.

"But... they are sitting side-by-side. Because they each have only one eye... it looks downright monstrous! They keep staring at me and licking their chops!" Pop cried.

"They are staring at you Pop because they are trying to figure out why you are such a big scaredy cat. Hah! Get it Pop? Scaredy... CAT!" AJ laughed.

AJ hooted and slapped his leg.

Stella and London watched with smiles on their faces, trying not to giggle out loud.

"Very funny grandson! You are out of my Will!" Pop fumed.

AJ laughed even harder.

"Dad, we are going to spin you on three." Alden announced.

Alden started counting.

"One… Two…"

AJ stopped suddenly, dropping Pop's arm while standing up.

"Wait! Dad, are we counting one, two, spin as soon as we say three, or do we say, one, two, three, then, after three… we spin? I'm confused, Dad."

Alden looked stumped also, dropping his dad's arm. Alden stood as well, considering AJ's question.

"Hmm… good question son."

Stella's jaw dropped.

"What is it, Stella?" London asked.

"They did this exact same thing when I was stuck on my butt at Bud's grave. Some things never change! I take comfort in the fact that my men are so good looking because sometimes, I worry that's all they have going for them."

London snickered.

"It's true, the hotness in your family is off the charts, Stella."

Alden pointed his finger at AJ.

"Ok, we say, one… two… and as soon as we say three, we spin."

AJ nodded, he smacked his glove-covered-hands together with some force, and said in a deep, growly voice, "Let's do this!"

Alden and AJ took ahold of Pop and did their count. When they spun Pop, he didn't holler, it was more of a squawk.

"How are you doing Dad?" Alden asked.

"Oh... peachy... I've never been better! Wait till I get my hands on your mother, Alden!"

London went still, a glimpse of fear entered her eyes.

Stella hugged London.

"No worries, Pop adores Nettie. Pop would never harm a hair on her head."

London nodded, smiling softly.

Pop was finally standing, he heard Stella's last comment.

"Hurt my Nettie? Never! But I might steal her coffee! I'm freezing!"

Pop started ambling towards the house.

"Nettie! I'm sorry I called you THICK, honey cheeks!"

Pop shivered as he opened the door.

Nettie was already standing at the door with a fresh cup.

"Here you go my darling. I forgive you, but don't ever bring up my weight again!" Nettie growled.

"You have my word THUNDER THIGHS!" Pop cackled and slapped his own leg, loving his own joke.

Nettie snatched Pop's coffee back, storming away.

"Kidding PORKY! The truth is, I love a little more meat on my woman. FAT looks good on you!"

Nettie looked ready to chuck something at Pop.

"Sweetums, when I say... FAT... I mean ROUNDER. When you do Jumping Jacks... whooeee! You make my day!"

Pop tried to hug Nettie, but she gave him a shove.

Pop flew backwards, landing on his back.

Nettie stood above her husband with an evil grin on her face.

"Oh! Sweetie! I don't seem to know my own strength! Must be on account of my big, beefy arms!" Grandma Nettie exclaimed.

Alden and AJ raced back over to Pop.

"Are you hurt Dad?" Alden asked.

"No! But when I get up, I DO NOT want to sit by her!"

Alden glanced at AJ.

"Same as before son, lift on three."

"Got it Dad! Let's do this!" AJ clapped his gloves together again.

Once again, Pop was on his feet. This time they placed him directly on one of the dining room chairs. Pop was at one end of the table, Grandma Nettie at the other end.

They glared at one another.

Pop was about to open his mouth, but Franny slammed her pointer finger over his lips.

Franny is the only red head in the family with light blue eyes. She looks one hundred percent like the Westman's, but her coloring was gifted to her by her great, great aunt. Franny's hair is full of corkscrew curls that seem to have a life of their own. Franny's hair bounces right along with her personality.

"No Pop, not a good idea!" Franny lowered her voice whispering loudly.

"Grandma will get even with you... you won't know when... it could be years! Then... BAM!" Franny thumped the table loudly.

Everyone jumped.

"She will get yah!" Franny's eyes were squinty and mean. With Franny's two front teeth missing her grimace was fierce.

Elijah being Elijah snapped a picture of that to go in the album.

Franny looked around, still whispering for all to hear.

"Remember Pop... she pushed you... twice... TWICE POP!" Franny nodded at Pop, letting him know that that could happen... AGAIN. Franny held up two fingers on her hand, shoving them in her Pops face.

Pop looked a bit unsure, he glanced at Nettie, he gulped and shut up.

Stella placed a cup of coffee in front of Pop, he grabbed it thankfully.

London was chewing her cookies fast while slamming back her coffee.

Stella patted London on the shoulder.

"You okay over there, London? You seem to be power-eating and drinking."

"This family is so nuts! I think I need popcorn! Ya'll are like this big ol train wreck, that is horrible and bloody, but no way can you look away!"

"London... ease up on the coffee girl. You seem a bit... jittery." Stella giggled.

"I feel great! I am so stoked! I feel like I could run five miles." London squealed.

Everyone glanced out the big picture window; the snow was coming down hard.

London looked out the window, also.

"Ok, no running out there today." London shrugged. "Maybe I should switch over to decaffeinated coffee." London stated.

Everyone laughed.

The happy laughter woke up Gracie and Hannah. Franny squealed with happiness; she loved scooping her sisters up after nap time.

"Wait for me Franny! I want one too!" Grandma Nettie yelled, as she raced Franny to the baby's bedroom.

Episode 35, I Miss Him!

Stella waved the kids off, as they trekked down their very long driveway, to get on the bus.

It was a crisp Winter morning; the sun was shining, and the air felt good.

Stella was getting ready to turn back, to head inside but she heard something. Stella listened intently.

Thwack! Thwack!... Thwack! Thwack! Thwack!

The noise was coming from the garage. Stella headed that way, the girls were still asleep, the fan and radio noise seemed to be doing the trick. The girls, now over a year old, were finally sleeping through the night.

Stella peeked through the window of the garage door. Inside she could see... London? London was beating the crap out of a punching bag, that was hanging from the rafters.

Stella's eyebrows shot straight up.

Whooeee that girl looks lethal! She's toned, and fit looking. In fact, I don't think she's ever looked this good! Stella thought.

Stella stepped inside. London didn't notice her right away.

London grabbed the bag, she held it with both hands, while raising her right knee, repeatedly slamming it into the bag.

What really caught Stella's attention was the fire in her eyes.

"Die, scum bag! That's right! I'm your worst... *Thwack! Thwack!*... nightmare!"

London dodged and weaved, still whacking the bag.

Stella figured that had to be one dead bag.

"You uh... seem to have some deep... deep... anger issues going on here, London."

London screamed and grabbed her chest.

"Oh! Stella! You scared the life out of me! Don't sneak up on me! I could have turned my mad skills on you by accident." London huffed, trying to catch her breath.

Stella held up her hands in surrender.

"Please no... don't hurt me... crazy lady." Stella's voice was all one level, monotone. Stella had a big grin on her face.

London huffed out a laugh, while sucking in some deep breaths.

"Who exactly are you beating up, London?" Stella questioned.

London scowled, she ripped her gloves off, flinging them across the garage.

"Sometimes Morgan... sometimes Trent... sometimes even, myself."

Stella patted London on the arm.

"Come have a coffee. My house is eerily quiet after the kids leave for school and the twins are still out. Thank you by the way, for the advice about the fan and radio. That trick is working like a charm."

London grinned. "My pleasure."

Together they walked to the big house.

After a couple of very needed sips of coffee, Stella questioned London again.

"So... what's going on with you? You looked amazing but downright hostile back there."

London sighed, propping her chin on her hand.

"I miss him."

Stella smiled softly.

"Who do you miss exactly?" Stella teased.

London sighed again; her chin still propped on her hand.

"Morgan."

"Ah! I see."

London seemed to wake up, she dropped her arm, scowling at Stella.

"You know you could be a bit more supportive! I'm so sad, and mad, and... I don't know exactly what I am, but I'm something!"

"You sweetheart are a woman in love. I'm so happy for you girl!"

London spluttered and tried to deny it, but she couldn't.

"You may not know this about me Stella, but I have... intimacy issues." London's face flamed.

Stella nodded.

"That's to be expected but you said the other day that therapy is really helping you."

London sighed, "I can talk about everything now, probably because I've repeated what happened to me so many times. It seems that the more I talk, the less it hurts. My therapist is working with me with something called, *Lights & Eye Movement.*"

Stella looked stumped.

"What's that?" She asked.

"I watch these lights go back and forth, while I talk about my trauma's."

"How does that help?"

"From the research I've done, the brain stores our traumatic memories in a way that doesn't let us heal properly. Like an actual physical wound that won't heal. My brain hasn't gotten the message that the danger is over. Accessing those memories in this way is supposed to help me reprocess the event and repair it. I will still remember what happened to me, but I won't continue to relive it."

Stella looked stunned.

"My goodness! That sounds so amazing! Do you feel like it's working?"

"I do! I'm not as jumpy as I used to be. I seem to be able to focus better and I'm sleeping without waking up screaming, like I used to."

Stella stood up; she ordered London to stand.

London looked bewildered until Stella wrapped her arms around her. While Stella sniffled, London smiled and hugged Stella back.

"This is the most emotional family I've ever met, but I love it... and I love you, Stella." London whispered.

Stella's tears almost dried up until London said that.

Stella stepped back.

"I love you too girl and I am here for you, always." Stella stated.

"I'm here for you too. Now, back to my Morgan problem." London sighed.

Stella grinned.

"He is hot! I've never seen actual turquoise eyes before! His eyes are quite mesmerizing. Exactly how do you resist that?" Stella questioned.

London dropped her forehead onto the table.

"I'm finally feeling like I can move forward with him, and I'm still married!"

Stella gaped at London.

"What do you mean you are still married? I thought you got divorced?" Stella questioned.

London filled Stella in, completely. She told her about Trent being a possible serial killer, but then he said he made it up. She also told her what took place when she met Trent for dinner.

Stella sat back, looking stunned.

"Maybe he's lying about the two of you still being married." Stella stated.

London shook her head no.

"Grady is on it, and he says, "*No divorce papers were ever filed.*" Trent faked the documents. I never questioned why the man gave me the divorce so willingly. I just wanted out of that situation."

"If anyone can fix this situation, Grady can."

"Grady wanted to file charges against Trent but... I told him that I thought Trent would cooperate more with the divorce if I asked for nothing and no charges. Trent sent me a check for a million dollars."

Stella choked on her coffee, spewing it across the table.

London jumped up thumping Stella on the back.

Stella couldn't stop coughing until all the inhaled, burning, hot coffee was coughed out.

When Stella was done, her eyes were watering, and her voice sounded a bit deeper.

"Do not be dropping that kind of bomb on me girl! Next time say that a bit slower! Maybe play charades with me! Egads, I think I burned my lungs!" Stella complained.

London giggled.

"What are you going to do with a chunk of money like that?" Stella questioned.

"Morgan says I should use it to get myself on my feet. That way if Trent ever tries to come back into my life that I will be stronger."

"I think Morgan is right. Figure out what you want to be, what you want to do with your life. You deserve that money; I say go for it."

London nodded.

"I've been taking online classes to finish my law degree. I hate lawyers!" London fumed.

"Then, why would you want to be a lawyer?"

"Because I want to be a good lawyer, no not good... a great lawyer! A lawyer, this town needs to protect people, to help them! When I originally went to Harvard for my law degree, I had such dreams! Then, Trent happened, I began to hate the justice system. It seems so... broken. I want to do my best to fight for anyone who is being abused or mistreated. Most abusers are men but there are men out there too that are abused by women. Men don't like to confess to that, embarrassment you know."

"I'm so proud of you!" Stella said enthusiastically.

London smiled sadly.

"I've missed Morgan so much that I've finished my online classes in record time. All that is left to do is take the Bar Exam." London announced.

Stella gasped.

"That's amazing! My bestie, a lawyer! What do you think your sign will say on your office?"

London thought about that for a minute.

"I'm hoping it will say, *"Dun Law Offices."*

Stella's eyes sparkled.

"Oh my! What are you going to do; ask that man to marry you when your divorce is final?" Stella teased.

London looked serious.

"You know... I think I will."

Stella and London clinked their coffee cups together.

London wanted to see Morgan, but she had to respect the man for his firm convictions. His moral character, his dedication, all of it, made Morgan even more special to her.

"I'm going to go and give Grady a call and see where we are at with this whole divorce... and I'm going to stop and see Morgan, find out what he has discovered about my aunt's death."

"Make sure you shower first London... you smell beastly." Stella said with a snicker.

"Uh... yes... I do believe you are right."

Episode 36, Awkward!

London hesitated before entering the station.

Why is this so hard? Just go in there and be professional! Ask what you need to know and no mooning over the man!

London opened the door, stomping her boots off on the giant floor mat.

A man behind the main desk looked up and smiled.

The officer was huge! Muscles on top of muscles, with broad shoulders. The man resembled a tank!

"Hello, how may I help you?"

London glanced at his name tag.

"Hello... Officer... Jamison? I was wondering if I could speak with Sheriff Dun?"

"Do you have an appointment?"

London stopped smiling.

Awkward! Dang it! Now I'm all flustered! I'm leaving! It's fight or flight and I'm choosing FLIGHT!

London glanced at Morgan's office. The blinds were open, but Morgan seemed intent on what he was looking at.

"Um... never mind, I changed my mind!"

London speed walked out the front door.

Morgan glanced up, just as London turned around, fleeing out the door.

Morgan hit the extension for the front desk.

"I just saw London at your front desk, chase her down, now!" Morgan roared.

The guy at the front desk stood up quickly, tipping his swivel chair over. Papers flew all over the place, but he left it all behind, pouring on speed to do as he was ordered.

When Officer Jamison got outside, he spotted London heading towards her car. He raced over to her, blocking her from getting into the vehicle.

"Ma'am! *Gasp*! The Sheriff would like you to come back inside. He ordered me to come and get you…. Please?"

London glared at the officer.

"Tell the Sheriff to take a flying leap…. Please!"

Horror crossed Jamison's face.

"Oh no miss, I could never say that to my boss… not in this lifetime! I'll never get off front-desk-duty if you don't come back inside! Please! Please, come with me!" Jamison pleaded; hands folded practically in prayer.

London crossed her arms looking very irate.

"He's not going to boss me around and you shouldn't let him boss you around either!"

"But… he's, my boss! I must do what he says!" Jamison's eyes were rounded, the whites of his eyes huge with distress.

London patted poor Jamison on the shoulder.

"Don't be a SHEEP man, be a WOLF! That's how you get off the front desk! YOU… TAKE… ACTION! Be a LEADER not a FOLLOWER!"

Jamison nodded.

"I get it! Okay then, I'll do it!" Jamison looked ready to take on the whole world.

"See! That's the spirit!" London exclaimed.

London squeezed his cheek wiggling it back and forth.

"You little go-getter-you; now you got it!" London said with a grin.

Jamison's face turned fierce. Jamison stood straight and tall, he had to be six-three. Jamison's jaw firmed until it resembled granite. When he crossed his arms and scowled, he looked deadly.

"Ma'am! I am going to have to INSIST that you come back inside! The Sheriff, my BOSS, would like a word with you!"

London looked confused for a second.

"Wait... are you trying to order me to go back inside?" London started laughing, hysterically.

Jamison crossed his arms looking firm.

"You can't make me go back in there! Now out of my way! I have places to be and more important people to see!"

London tried to step around Jamison; Jamison stepping in her path, like the brick wall that he was.

London tried to dodge the other way; Jamison dodged right along with her.

London screamed and stomped her foot.

"You, big, stupid buffoon! Get out of my way!" London screeched.

Jamison's mouth dropped open.

"Now ma'am, that isn't nice, calling people names is very hurtful."

London raised her purse and smacked Jamison hard; hard enough to make him stagger. London kept swinging, Jamison threw up his arm, to block London's attack.

"Now ma'am, I am starting to get angry! You need to stop hitting me... I am an officer of the law!"

London tried to race to her car, but Jamison got the drop on her.

Jamison whipped out his cuffs, he slapped it on her left wrist, he spun her around and cuffed her right wrist.

"You let me go! I have rights! This is abuse of power!" London railed.

"You have the right to remain SILENT... and I sure wish you WOULD! Be nice! You don't want to add resisting arrest to your long list of offences. As I was saying, anything you say and do, can be held against you. You have a right to an attorney."

Jamison paused, giving London a sweet smile.

"I hear you already have one. Grady sure is a real nice guy, he's the best attorney around these parts too."

London gaped at the man.

Jamison frog-marched London back into the police station. London was screaming and trying to kick him in the shins, but for such a big guy he was surprisingly spritely.

They stopped in the entryway for a second, because London refused to stop wrestling with Jamison.

"Do you understand the rights that I have just read to you?" Jamison questioned.

London gaped, she swiveled around to finally get a look at Jamison's face, instead of his shins.

Jamison had a card in his hand that he must have been reading from.

London was so mad she couldn't even speak... so she screamed with rage... right in Jamison's face. Well, more like his chest area, because the man was as big as a barge. Jamison turned a bit white. He leaned back a bit, very alarmed at the crazy lady going off on him. Jamison forgot to dodge her last kick. London brought her hefty boot back, kicking forward with everything she had in her.

Jamison screamed in pain, hopping around on one foot.

"Mommy! I want my mommy! It hurts so bad! I think she broke my shin bone!" Jamison sobbed.

The entire squad room erupted with laughter.

London hearing the booming laughter froze.

London glanced around the office. Officers were leaning back in their chairs or bent forward laughing out loud. One officer could barely walk; he weaved his way over to her but had to stop and rest on a desk, wheezing loudly.

London heard someone clear their throat.

When she looked towards the back, she saw Morgan framed in the doorway of his office.

Morgan arched an eyebrow. London felt her face heat up with embarrassment.

"What in the *Dunkin Donuts* is going on out here, and why is London cuffed... again?" Morgan asked.

Jamison limped over to his boss. Jamison stood on one leg while saluting Morgan.

"I did what you said, I brought her back in, but I must say boss, she is a fighter! She kicked me so hard in my shin, I'm not sure I'll ever be able to have children!"

Morgan rolled his eyes. Morgan did a double take trying to figure out how getting kicked in the shin equated to NOT having children.

"Ok, I'm just going to ask, Jamison. How does getting kicked in the shin, prevent you from having children?"

The entire place went quiet, waiting for Jamison's answer.

"Boss, I may be one fine hunk of man, but if I end up with a permanent limp... well, maybe women wouldn't want me... I'm so sad boss! What if I limp for the rest of my life? I'm going to die sad, and alone!"

Jamison dropped his head to his chest looking forlorn.

Morgan sighed.

"Jamison, we can talk about your love life later. Let's get back to London and why she's cuffed. I didn't mean that you had to CUFF her and bring her back in here! I just meant for you to REQUEST for her to return."

"I even said please boss, she wouldn't listen. She said you weren't the boss of her. Is she always this ornery boss?"

Morgan sighed; he pinched the bridge of his nose.

"Yes... yes, she is."

"Boss... I was a WOLF not a SHEEP! I... Took... Action! I refused to take no for an answer! I was a LEADER not a FOLLOWER!"

Jamison limped as he marched back and forth.

"I'm just going to be brave and ask you straight out boss. I want to be off the front desk! I'm ready!" Jamison exclaimed.

Morgan tilted his head thinking about Jamison's request.

"You know what Jamison? Anyone that can handle London like that deserves to get off the front desk. Go ask Murphy for your new assignment."

"Whoopeee! Yeehaaaa! I'm off the front desk!"

Jamison gritted his teeth with pain but limped over to London with a big smile on his face.

"It's all because of you Miss London! I couldn't have done it without you!"

Jamison grabbed London by the shoulders; he reeled her in and planted a big kiss on her cheek.

London couldn't help but giggle.

Morgan growled, stepping towards Jamison.

"Oh! Sorry boss, I didn't mean to be smooching on your... um... your girl?"

"Jamison! Take those cuffs off her, AFTER you escort her into my office."

"After boss? Why can't I take the cuffs off right here?"

"Because she's stubborn and I don't want her to get away. So, in my office please." Morgan waved at his office, practically bowing.

Morgan held open the door as Jamison once again frog-marched London into his boss man's office.

When Jamison went to uncuff London, Morgan waved his hand in frustration.

"Just give me the keys! I'll free her up after you leave, Jamison."

When Jamison left, Morgan held up the keys to the cuffs.

"Seems to me that you have been cuffed an awful lot of times in your lifetime, London."

London rolled her eyes.

"Funny! Get me out of these cuffs, Morgan!"

Morgan walked slowly towards London.

Morgan noticed that his entire staff stood still. They were all up close and personal, facing his office windows. Jamison was front and center, smiling like the goof that he was.

Morgan yanked on the blind while giving them all the stink-eye.

Morgan heard a shuffling movement outside his office door.

His entire staff seemed to have shuffled six feet to their right and were peering in his door.

Morgan growled and pulled on that blind too.

"You might just want to shut that last blind, Morgan, the herd has shifted once again." London giggled.

Morgan grabbed the last blind, giving it a hard pull, closing it.

Morgan opened his office door and roared at his staff.

"Get back to work! There is nothing to see here!"

Everyone started laughing again, but they did race back to their desks.

Morgan slammed the door loudly, storming over to his chair, sitting down.

Morgan looked stressed, he even wiped his brow, slamming his hat on his desk.

"Uh... still cuffed over here, Morgan." London said calmly, one eyebrow raised.

Morgan did a double take.

"Oh, I'm sorry; I forgot." Morgan apologized.

Morgan jumped up and uncuffed London's wrists.

"Your staff.... they don't seem super scared of you." London said with a grin.

Morgan chuckled.

"They have been a bunch of pranksters lately. I guess I should have squashed that, but crime has been way down, and they get a bit bored."

"I'm glad that crime is down, but maybe you should have a *Spring-Cleaning Day* or a *Let's Paint a Wall Day.*"

"It's Winter." Morgan told London, looking out the window, just to be sure.

London grinned.

"Hey that's the best thing about it; come Spring, this place will look amazing!"

Morgan thought about it.

Morgan walked over to his office door. Morgan yanked the door open. Just on the other side, every officer was back. They were all jammed in the doorway, with their ears pressed to the door. A couple of his officers toppled over, onto the floor, falling at Morgan's feet.

Morgan put his hands on his hips, huffing and puffing.

"That's it! You are all grounded! Get your behinds back to your desks and stay put! Murphy! Where are you?" Morgan roared.

"Right here, sir."

Murphy is a thinly built man with carrot red hair. When he gulped, his Adam's Apple visibly moved.

"I want you to make a list of chores for all these slackers! Cleaning, and painting too! I want this station to shine like the top of the Chrysler Building! Move it, now!"

Murphy went to run off and do his list.

"Oh, hey, Murphy."

"Yes sir?"

"You are on front desk duty."

Morgan slammed the door in Murphy's jaw-dropped-face.

When Morgan turned around London was hunched over, shaking with laughter.

Morgan sat back down.

"I'm so happy you are so amused, London. So... what brings you to my part of town?"

London gulped some more. When she was calm, she took a seat.

"I was wondering if you had any news about my aunt?" London's face was now dead serious.

Morgan looked grim.

"I was just about to open that file, when my department jumped on the crazy train."

Morgan reached for his computer, opening the document. Morgan read a few lines; his hand dropped to his desk.

"What? Tell me!" London pleaded.

Morgan got up, sitting in the chair next to London.

"I'm sorry London, your aunt was murdered." Morgan said softly.

London started crying.

"Trent killed her! He told me he killed her! Then he said he didn't! What do we do, Morgan?"

Morgan tried to stay professional but when London cried, he had no choice but to reach for her.

"We are going to have to go and see Grady." Morgan decided. "Grady will know what our next step is."

When London stopped crying, she realized that she was on Morgan's lap.

"How did I get over here?" London asked quietly.

"You crawled in my lap, while you were melting down." Morgan stated.

London blushed.

"I'm sorry Morgan."

"No need to be sorry, it was a big shock."

London stood up, moving away.

"Can we go see Grady now?" London looked beyond miserable.

"Yes, I'll go with you, London. I planned on going with you anyway. This is what I do for a living you know." Morgan grinned at London's watery face.

London started for the door. Morgan beat her to it, opening the door wide.

London's jaw dropped when they left his office.

The officers all had dusters in their hands.

Windows were being washed, floors being swept and mopped.

Murphy raced up with a paint chip wheel.

"Boss, I was thinking this blue would be nice."

Morgan scowled at Murphy.

"No! White, and only white." Morgan announced to them all.

All the officers let out, *"Aww shucks! Why? Come on boss we need to liven this place up!"*

Morgan sighed, rolled his eyes and grabbed the paint chip wheel. Morgan scanned it, he eyed it for a while. Morgan handed it back to Murphy.

"Rich Cream, with dark chocolate accents, with touches of blue, that's my final offer." Morgan said.

Everyone cheered.

Morgan laughed as he escorted London out the door.

London was trying not to smile.

"What? What's so funny, London?"

London buckled herself into the passenger side of the squad car.

"Ri... Rich... cr... cream! With dark... gasp... chocolate accents! With t... t... touches of blue! I'm dying over here!" London smacked her arm rest, while cracking up.

Morgan turned a bit red.

"What? I like interior decorating!"

"I can see that! You know if your career as a cop ever fizzles out, you have something to fall back on!" London giggled.

Morgan shrugged.

They both got quiet, realizing they had arrived at Grady's Law Office.

"Don't worry London, Grady will know what to do. Trent isn't in my jurisdiction. So far all I have proof of is that he took you on a very long picnic and he took you out to dinner here, in town. All his confessions were never recorded. Trust me, Grady is the right, next step." Morgan reassured her.

London nodded.

Together they walked into Grady's office.

Episode 37, Mayhem Mia

London whacked the bag a few more times, she couldn't seem to concentrate today. The news that Grady had given them hadn't been good.

Trent immediately lawyered up. Grady was working on getting Trent's mother's remains exhumed.

London sat down for a second, she tipped back her water eyeing Luke and his newest... client.

The woman was tall, black hair, pulled back into a short ponytail, her eyes, big and brown.

London did her best not to grin, but the woman was literally a train wreck. She watched as the woman headed towards the drinking fountain; she tripped halfway, falling with a thud.

Luke raced over to her... again.

"Mia! In order to learn to train, you must stay upright!"

Mia got back up; she stood only a couple of inches shorter than Luke.

"I'm sorry Mr. Luke! I've been a big ol klutz my whole life."

Mia sighed.

"Seems all I do is look up at the sky or the ceiling. By the way, your ceiling could use a new paint job." Mia's southern accent was very noticeable.

Luke looked up.

"Hmm, I'll have to get my buddy, the Sheriff, over here to give me some advice on that." Luke said.

Mia looked confused.

"Why would you call the Sheriff for that?"

"Oh, my buddy Morgan may be the Sheriff, but that man can decorate! Morgan is a genius."

Mia grinned; a giggle slipped out.

Luke looked... fascinated.

London grinned again. She figured watching these two was way better than working out. London leaned back, continuing to watch the show.

"So, have you always had balance issues? Have a seat, let's talk about that." Luke said.

Mia sat down.

"Hmm, I think we are going to have ta go back a bit to figure that out." Mia stated.

"Tell me whatever makes you comfortable. Just know that balance is the very first thing we will be working on."

"I was born a preemie, two months early. I weighed about three pounds, soaking wet. I did everything late: rollin, talkin, walkin, etc."

Luke nodded.

"That is definitely a factor, keep going."

Luke wrote furiously as Mia talked.

London noticed that Luke was leaning forward, hanging on her every word. *Uncle Luke never did that to me... hee... hee... hee.*

"When I did start walkin it seemed like I was forever fallin, bumpin my head, and scraping my knees. Biking and climbing trees were my favorite things, but then I just fell faster and harder. Broken bones became a normal part of my life, along with crutches. My family... *sigh*... they call me "Gimpy," it's a pet name, I guess... a form of endearment... but I'm so sick of falling! In my school yearbook they have a whole two-page-spread, full of me at different times in my life, with me on crutches! Pictures of me with casts on my arms and legs. Nobody ever asked me out! Nobody wanted to go to a dance with *Mayhem Mia!* Do you think you can help me Mr. Luke?"

Mia placed her hand on Luke's arm. Luke smiled a big, dopey smile, the man looked like he was in... love?

"Mayhem Mia? That is the meanest thing I've ever heard! I wish I had been there! I think I would have gotten quite violent!" Luke exclaimed.

Mia looked miserable.

"It gets worse Mr. Luke." Mia moaned.

"I told you, just call me Luke. You don't have to call me Mr. Luke, just Luke."

Mia sighed.

"They also made up a song about me; they sang it every day." Mia said sadly.

Without warning Mia began to sing; the song started out fast.

"Mayhem Mia... Mayhem Mia, she can't walk a single step!
Mayhem Mia... Mayhem Mia... watch out... you know she's going to trippp! Broken bones, cuts, and scrapes, she runs around like that every dayyyy!"

Mia's voice turned soft and sad; her big, dark eyes soft and wistful.

"Mayhem Mia... Mayhem Mia... she can't walk a single stepppp... sob... She runs around like that... everyyy dayyyyyyy."

London moved closer without realizing it, her eyes rounded in awe.

Luke gaped at Mia during the whole song; especially during the last, long, beautiful note.

Mia could sing!

When the last note faded Mia looked at the two of them.

"They would sing it a couple of times a day... *sigh*. My five-year class reunion is coming up in a year, and I want to go! I want to show those meanies that I can walk a straight line! That I am graceful and elegant! I want to look hot... I might need some help with the whole hotness part too. Uggg! It's useless!" Mia wailed.

Luke patted Mia on the arm with sympathy.

"I want you to meet a friend of mine Mia, this is London."

London sat down.

Mia smiled at London.

"Hi, I'm Mia, it's so nice to meet ya."

"I'm London, *Uncle Luke* has been training me for quite some time."

Mia looked confused.

"Uncle Luke? Uh... he doesn't look old enough ta be your uncle."

London grinned.

"He's not really my uncle, maybe like the brother I always wanted."

Mia melted.

"Aww, that is so sweet. Everyone in this town is so darn wonderful, I just love it here!"

London smiled softly at Mia.

"How old are you, Mia?" London asked.

"Twenty-three. I graduated late on account of being born two months early. I had to be held back... twice... because I was so shy. I didn't graduate until I was nineteen-and-a-half."

Luke and London gaped at Mia.

Luke shook his head in disbelief.

"You... uh... don't seem shy... now."

Mia smiled.

"Well... I had to fight for my rights... a lot! Once my voice came out there was no stuffing it back in!" Mia announced with pride.

"I must say Mia you have an amazing singing voice! Have you ever done any professional singing?" London questioned.

"Oh my, no! I just burst into song occasionally, I love to sing!" Mia declared.

London leaned forward.

"I know someone, in the music business. She and I went to high school together. I went to law school, and she went to a school for the arts. Would you be interested in me setting up an appointment with her? She would listen to one of your songs and at least tell you if you have a shot."

"Me? A singer? Why I never thought about singing for anyone but myself. If you want to call your friend Miss London; I would be proud to sing for you all."

"I'll get right on it!" London promised. "So... what brings you to our small town, Mia?" London questioned.

"Oh! My granny lives here. I was born here but my Mama moved us ta Mississippi when I was a youngin and well... my Granny is gettin up there in years. I'm here to take care of her. I work part time at John's Produce. I have forklift experience and they are very good at givin me flexible hours."

"Wow! That's wonderful that you can run a forklift."

"Oh, my yes! I can run just about any of them big ol machines."

Mia leaned forward whispering; London knew-not-why. They were the only three people in the place today.

"I once took a forklift that my old boss was going to scrap, and well... I tore that whole thing apart! I laid all the pieces out. I rebuilt that engine... I admit that I did have some extra parts left over... I never did figure that out, but that forklift is still runnin! My boss was so thankful, he didn't care about the extra parts!" Mia laughed; her eyes sparkled.

Luke continued to look... fascinated.

London nodded, grinning right back at her.

"I must say I do love your accent, Mia."

Mia gaped at London.

"I was just about ta tell you too, that I just adore the way y'all talk! I just love the way y'all say CAH!" Mia laughed some more.

London and Luke looked confused.

"What's a CAH?" London questioned.

Mia tilted her head.

"You know... ya drive em, up and down the road! A CAH!"

London's mouth dropped open.

"Oh! A CAR! You mean a car?"

"Yes, you silly! That's what I said." Mia chortled.

Luke decided to get the ladies back on track.

"So, you told me that you were born early, is there anything else that may have affected your... balance?" Luke asked.

Mia thought for a minute.

"Well, I did get dropped on my head as a toddler, but I lived!" Mia threw out her arms wide, looking excited.

Luke and London couldn't stop their jaws from dropping.

"So, you got... dropped on your... head? How bad were you hurt, exactly?" Luke questioned.

"My skull was fractured. I had a big ol horseshoe shaped ridge running around my head. I'm pretty sure if ever I had to run around bald... people would think I was an alien. If you put your fingers right here, you can still feel that ridge. Go on, don't be scared, Luke, feel that."

Mia grabbed Luke's fingers slapping them on the side of her head.

Luke's jaw was still dropped open, with horror.

Mia dropped Luke's hand.

"I took a couple of spills also, while growing up. Let's see, I'm twenty-three, let's say maybe three a year. That's just a rough estimation ya know. About seventy, give or take a few. Now I wasn't always injured badly. Sometimes, I just popped back up, like a *Jack in the Box!* Oh! I about choked on a peppermint too; I was blue for quite a spell! Might have to add lack of oxygen to my list. Also, one day, I was riding my bike and my brakes failed. Do you know how bad it hurts flying down a mountain on a bike with no brakes? I broke me some bones that day. Whoeee! Good times!"

Mia glanced at Luke.

"Well, aren't you gonna write this stuff down, Luke?" Mia asked.

Luke seemed to wake up; Luke started writing quickly.

Luke and London couldn't keep up with the poor woman's mishaps.

Luke gulped.

"Is that pretty much it?" Luke questioned, looking disturbed.

Mia sighed.

"I birthed a baby once, that was all kinds of painful."

"You had a baby?" London asked in amazement.

Luke looked shocked.

"Is your baby with your granny?" Luke asked.

Mia laughed.

"I didn't have a baby! I helped birth a babe; that's how I got hurt."

"Say what?" London and Luke said simultaneously.

"Well, I was sitting there, waiting for that babe to crown. It had a powerful ton of dark hair! I told her mama ta push one more big push and that babe would be out! Do you know how slippery babes are when they slide out? Let me tell you! You gotta hold on tight! That baby shot out of her mama, I almost lost that babe, it tried to fly, I swear! Her daddy got so over oxygenated that his eyes rolled back and down he went. Luckily, I placed that babe on his mama's chest right before Big Bob landed on top of me. Big Bob weighed almost four-hundred pounds; he cracked two of my ribs that day. Whoeee! Good times!"

Luke gulped; London roared.

"Oh my! Mia! You and I are going to be great friends! Plus, I want to introduce you to my good friend Stella Westman! The Westman family are amazing. They have eight kids, two sets of twins! Stella will just love you!" London exclaimed.

Mia beamed at London.

"Well! Alright Miss London, I would love that!"

"Just call me London, that's what friends do." London informed Mia.

"Aww, you are gonna make me cry. I have ta say, I'm loving this town! I kind of wish that I would have grown up here." Mia said with a dreamy look on her face.

Luke nodded.

"Yes, our town is pretty amazing." He replied.

"Why exactly... were you delivering a baby, Mia?" Luke asked.

Mia arched an eyebrow at Luke.

"I'm also a Midwife. Where I lived in Mississippi, it was literally boonsville. Doc was the only doctor for miles around. He taught me how to birth babes because he needed the help."

London grinned at Luke's look of amazement.

Luke stood up; he looked a bit shell-shocked.

"Ok... I think I have a better handle on your problem, Mia. We need to work on core strength and balance. If your core is strong, the rest of you will be strong. If we get you strong maybe, you won't fall so much. Let me see you walk across the room. Please! Go slow but try to walk in a straight line." Luke stated.

Mia stood up; she turned slowly, walking across the room. At one point Mia's toe caught on the floor, she almost went down.

Luke and London both sucked in a breath.

Mia managed to catch herself.

"Okay, turn around and walk back this way, Mia." Luke encouraged.

Mia turned, she slowly turned around and weaved her way back. Again, Mia's right toe caught the floor and she stumbled.

Luke encouraged Mia to quickly sit down.

Luke looked at London.

"What did you notice, London?"

London looked thoughtful.

"She doesn't walk heel-to-toe. I also noticed that her right toe seems to catch a lot."

Luke nodded.

"Did any of your injuries affect your right leg, Mia?" Luke asked.

"Yes, when I flew down the mountain on my bike, I broke my leg in a couple different spots."

Luke nodded.

"I assume you had an Orthopedic Doctor?" London wanted to know.

Mia frowned.

"Hmm, well, I had my leg fixed by MY doctor. He brought me into this world, and he's been my doctor my whole life. We didn't have a... doctor like you was talkin about."

Luke groaned.

"Mia, I'm going to need you to go see a friend of mine. He's a doctor, my doctor. He can run a few tests on you to make sure that you don't have any physical problems that could hurt you, during training. We just need a better picture here, to see what we are dealing with." Luke said.

Mia's eyes widened.

"Wow! That is so sweet of you Luke, I would be proud to meet your doctor."

Luke stood up.

"I'm going to give him a call right now."

Luke whipped out his cell phone, hitting the speed dial for their town doctor.

Luke could be heard talking, setting up an appointment for Mia. Luke stopped, and handed Mia his phone, so she could give them the information they needed.

Luke and London wandered away to give Mia privacy.

"London." Luke whispered.

"What?" London whispered back.

"I think that Mia is going to have a tough road ahead. I'm not a doctor, but I think that when she broke her leg, it may not have been set right. I hate to say this but before she can get better... things might have to get worse, first."

London sighed.

"I was sitting here worrying about the same thing, Luke. When she was walking, she acted like her right leg was much weaker. I think you should measure her thighs, her calves, etc. just to see how big of a difference there may be, it's just a thought." London said.

Luke nodded.

"That is a great idea. I'm going to check to see if one leg is shorter than the other. You would be surprised how having one leg just a bit shorter can affect the whole body. I'll be right back."

Luke ran off to find his measuring tape.

When Luke got back, Mia was off the phone, telling them when her appointment was supposed to be.

Mia turned towards Luke and London.

"I hate to ask this... would either of you go with me when I go to see this doctor? I'm a bit... nervous."

Luke shot his hand up in the air like he was a student in school, trying to answer a question.

"I'll go with you Mia! That way Doc and I can put our heads together to figure out your next course of treatment."

Mia smiled softly, batting her long eyelashes at Luke.

"You just made my day, Luke."

Mia's voice came out low and sexy.

Luke grinned like a fool.

London said goodbye to the two of them, but they didn't seem to notice. London found that to be very interesting.

Episode 38, Pop... is so... Pop!

London left the gym.

London was halfway home when a huge truck roared up, practically kissing the bumper of her car.

London was ticked off. She didn't recognize the truck, but there were a few juveniles in the neighborhood that liked to horse around.

London rolled her window down, waving to them, motioning for them to go around.

The truck revved its engine, it leapt forward... bumping into the back of her car.

London screamed; her heart practically lodged in her throat.

London sped up a bit, to get away from the truck, but it sped up also. London couldn't let go of the wheel to call for help; she was too busy trying to stay alive.

The truck surged forward one more time, slamming into London's car one more time. This time the force of the hit sent London's vehicle off the road, down into a deep ditch.

When the car came to a stop, London's forehead hit the steering wheel.

London felt sick to her stomach, she also felt blood running down her face.

London reached up, feeling her forehead. When she looked at her hand it was covered in blood.

The driver's door was wrenched open.

London turned to see who it was; she didn't recognize the guy, at all.

The man had a smirk on his face, he looked mean, and terrifying.

London felt sweat break out all over her body.

The man leaned in and spoke.

"What's the matter... London... you think Trent forgot about you? You think you are going to just get your divorce while trying to put him in jail?"

London shook with fear, tears and blood running down her face.

The man pulled out a gun. He shoved the gun right under London's nose. London cried out, turning her head away.

"Look at it! I said... look at it!" The guy growled.

London slowly turned back towards the gunman.

"You need to shut your mouth, London."
The man said softly. "If you know what's good
for you... you will."

The man spun a silencer on the front of the
pistol.

"Bad things happen every day, London.
Accidents... people disappear you know."

The gunman pointed the gun directly at her
face. At the last second, he turned the gun,
taking out the passenger window. He stepped
back, aiming at the driver's side tire, he fired
again. After he took out all the tires, he stepped
back up to London.

While he shot all the tires, London thought
about running but the blood loss made her feel a
bit sick.

Up until now the man hadn't touched her
but then he moved quickly, grabbing her by her
hair, forcing her head forward.

London felt her already wounded forehead,
pressed firmly into the steering wheel. More
blood poured down her face. The man pressed
the end of the hot barrel against the back of her
neck.

London felt the burn of the hot barrel as it
sizzled on her skin.

Suddenly, rage roared to the surface,
cancelling out the sick feelings, rolling around in

her. Maybe, it was just adrenalin, and maybe she would die today, but she wasn't going to go down like this. She was frozen with fear earlier, but now... she was just plain ticked off!

London brought up her left hand as he pressed her firmly against the steering wheel. London reached for any part of the man that she could find, and she began to scratch. London dug her nails deep and kept scratching.

The man yelped, stepping back.

London came out of the car like a woman possessed.

London got up close to the man, so he couldn't use the gun on her. London thrust her hand into his nose.

It broke; she smiled.

London went for his eyes next. While he grabbed his eyes, she boxed his ears. By now the man was doubled over, down on one knee.

London circled the man slowly. When she came back around to the front of him, she kicked him in his jewels. The man grunted, falling over onto his side.

London picked up the gun, aiming it at the man. London reached into her car, grabbing her cell phone, hitting the speed dial for Alden. Alden and the boys were closer to her than Morgan or Luke.

"Hey London, what's up?" Stella asked.

"Hey Stella, this is London, could you put Alden on the phone please?"

"Sure, just a second."

"Hello London, Alden here. What do you need?"

"I'm about two miles away from home. I need help, and lots of it! Bring zip ties or rope. The bad guy is on the ground and my car is in the ditch. I'm on the first curve on thirty-sixth street, please hurry."

London could hear Alden shouting as she hung up the phone.

London leaned on her very messed up car.

"So... you! Ugly! Before the cavalry gets here you want to tell me your name. Also, how did Trent think he was going to get away with this? Plus, Trent usually loves to do his own dirty work. I can't believe he sent a useless piece of trash like you to shut me up."

The man was in some serious pain, but he still grunted, while trying to crawl towards her.

London glared at the guy.

"Was it worth it? How much did he pay you to do this?"

The man's eyes glittered.

"One million dollars sweetheart; Trent really want's you gone!" The man shouted.

"But… I don't know what you are talking about! You and me? This here is just a bit of road rage, you can't prove otherwise." The man smirked.

The man spit blood on the ground and grinned at her.

London grinned back.

"Dash camera buddy." London whispered. "With audio."

London nodded over her shoulder. The man saw the camera that caught the entire thing from start to finish.

The man tried to surge to his feet, but Alden and the cavalry roared up.

Alden jumped out of the car with a baseball bat in his hand, followed by AJ and Pop. The three men advanced on the bad guy.

Pop shook his head back and forth.

"This here girl beat you up, mister?" Pop asked with a twinkle in his eye.

Alden stepped up, placing his size fourteen cowboy boot on the guy's back. Alden gave the guy a shove, sending him back into the dirt. While the guy was face planted, AJ put his knee in the guy's back, while zip tying his wrists behind his back.

Pop raised his hand and sprayed something in the bad guy's eyes. Pop sprayed it for quite a while. The man tried to turn away, but Pop just followed the man's eyes.

Everyone stared at Pop like he lost his mind.

"Dad! What was that you just sprayed in the man's eyes?" Alden asked.

"He was trying to get away! I swear I saw him trying to wriggle out of those zip ties!" Pop ranted.

"Dad! What is that stuff?" Alden asked again.

"Oh, quit your belly aching! It's a spray for ageing eyes!" Pop exclaimed.

AJ held his hand out; Pop handed it over to him.

AJ grinned as he read the label.

"Dad, the label says, *"Nature's Natural Tears."* It says here that it, *"Lubricates the eyes preventing dry eye."* AJ snickered.

Everyone glanced at the bad guy; his eyes were streaming with tears.

Pop shrugged.

"Maybe I used too much. Does it say how much to put in the eyes, AJ?"

AJ shook with laughter.

"It says, *"Less is better."* AJ roared with laughter.

"It doesn't say that! Give me that thing back!" Pop bellowed.

Pop grabbed the spritzer bottle from AJ, trying to read the label.

"You have done quite enough, DAD!" Alden exclaimed.

AJ glanced over at London.

"Oh dang, DAD! London is bleeding!"

Alden shot his eyes towards London. London looked like she had been in a slasher film.

"Grab the first aid kit, AJ!" Alden shouted.

Alden raced over to London. Alden made London sit down so he could access the situation.

"Go get that bottle of water in my truck AJ. London is going to need stitches."

Alden reached into the first aid kit, pulling out large squares of gauze. Alden wet them down, cleaning as much of the wound as possible. When the bleeding slowed down, he again wet down some more gauze, placing it on the open wound.

"AJ, hold this on her forehead, until the ambulance gets here. We can't let her fall asleep, in case she has a concussion."

London, AJ, and Alden heard a commotion. When they turned to see what was happening, they saw Pop holding the spritzer can up in a threatening manner.

"Go ahead dude! You try to get away one more time and it's more old eye tears for you, mister!"

Alden rolled his eyes.

"I have to go and save the bad guy; I'll be right back you two!"

Alden charged over to his dad, taking the can away.

The ambulance arrived, along with Officer Jamison.

When he stepped out of his police cruiser, AJ's jaw dropped.

"What exactly... is... that?" AJ questioned.

London patted AJ on the arm.

"That is Officer Jamison, he is officially OFF FRONT DESK DUTY because he chased me down, cuffed me and hauled me into Morgan's office."

The bad guy, Pop, Alden, and AJ, all whipped their heads toward London. They all looked flabbergasted.

"Say what?" AJ asked.

London waved them all away.

"It's a very long story; I'll tell you all later." She promised.

AJ pointed his finger at London.

"I'm riding in the ambulance with you so you can tell me that story! That man is built like a tank!"

Officer Jamison stopped in front of London.

"Why Miss London, you are hurt!" Jamison turned towards the ambulance team.

"Over here! No leave the guy on the ground alone! Bleeding trumps crying!" Jamison hollered.

Pop threw back his head and roared with laughter. AJ joined in, followed by Alden and London.

Jamison looked mighty confused.

"What is so funny you guys? Miss London looks awful! Here you go Miss London, these guys will take you to the hospital and get you checked over good! I'll take the bad guy to jail and meet you at the hospital." Jamison stated.

London turned white.

"I don't feel so good." She whispered.

London's eyes rolled back and down she went. Jamison was standing close to her, so he was able to grab her before she hit the ground. Jamison picked her up, carried her to the gurney, while directing the ambulance team to get going.

AJ jumped into the ambulance.

"I'll go with her dad! You best let Mom know what is going on. You must have had your phone on silent because it keeps lighting up. Mom is going to kill you, Dad!"

Alden frowned.

"Oh dang! This is not good!" Alden exclaimed.

Alden eyed that phone like it was a basket of snakes.

"Here Dad, you talk to her! I'm busy helping with... all of this." Alden said vaguely.

"Helping with what?" Pop asked with sarcasm.

"Stuff! I'm helping Jamison... traffic! I'm on traffic duty!" Alden shouted with happiness.

Pop took Alden's phone. When Alden raced away, Pop's smile could only be classified as evil.

"Hello? Yes Stella? Yes, this is Pop. Your husband is avoiding you. He ran away like the girlie man that he is."

Pop nodded a few times.

"How is London? London is unconscious, in an ambulance, there's blood everywhere! Poor London is going to need stitches, for sure! Pretty sure she's going to need a CAT scan too!" Pop exclaimed.

Pop yanked the phone away from his ear, because Stella's voice could be heard a mile away.

"Alden! Your wife would like to have a word with you!" Pop said with glee.

Alden pouted as he raced over, taking the phone back.

"Why are you avoiding me, Alden? London is in an ambulance?! My bestie is unconscious, and you didn't call me?"

Alden glared at his dad.

"Honey, calm down! London is fine!"

"Did she pass out?"

Alden gulped.

"Well... yes, but she's fine!"

"Is she in an ambulance?"

"Yes?"

"Does she in fact need stitches and a CAT scan, Alden?" Stella screamed.

"Yes." Alden whispered.

"Then, she is in fact, the opposite of FINE! Get your backside home so I can go to the hospital, Alden!"

"But I'm helping Jamison with traffic."

"You better get home, mister! Now!"

Alden started to assure his wife that he was on his way, but she had already hung up.

Alden gulped, while turning on his father.

"Dad! Why did you tell my wife all that stuff? Do you know how mad she is right now?"

Pop was busy doing a jig on the side of the road, grinning from ear-to-ear.

Pop stopped.

"That'll teach you to hand me your phone, Son."

Alden sighed.

"For once in your life Dad, you are so right!" Alden snarled.

"Wait for me Son! You're my ride!" Pop hollered.

Alden floored the gas pedal, leaving his father choking on his dust.

Jamison stopped next to a coughing, Pop.

"I'll give you a ride Mr. Westman, but you'll have to ride in the backseat. I've got my gear in the front. By the way Mr. Westman... you ever been in the back of a police car before?" Jamison had a suspicious look on his face.

Pop grinned.

"I've been arrested on a couple of occasions; probably won't be my last either. One time... "

Jamison, hung on his every word.

Episode 39, 3-B's: Bleeding, Birthing, and Breastfeeding!

Jamison stepped into the station; everyone stopped and gaped at him.

Jamison spun in a circle, trying to figure out what they were all looking at.

Morgan rushed up.

"What happened to you, Jamison; are you injured?" Morgan asked.

"Oh, this isn't my blood, Sheriff. Miss London... "

Morgan grabbed Jamison by the front of his shirt reeling him in close.

"You need to start talking and talking fast. What happened to London?"

Morgan's voice was low and deadly.

Jamison's eyes bulged because his boss was strangling him a bit.

"She's fine Bossman! She's in an ambulance, on her way to the hospital in Fremont. She needs some stitches... um... not sure where... but I think her forehead."

Morgan roared shaking Jamison around roughly.

"Keep talking! Why is she in an ambulance? That seems like an awful lot of blood on your shirt, Jamison! Never mind! You are coming with me, Jamison! Get in my car and fill me in on the way there!"

Morgan never let go of Jamison, he dragged him to his car by the front of his shirt.

Jamison choked all the way to the car.

Morgan took off towards Fremont.

"Continue where you left off, Jamison." Morgan demanded.

"Well, I got a call, when I showed up, Miss London was covered in blood. On the side of the road was the bad guy that I just dropped off. Her car was in a ditch, all tires flat. The front passenger window looked like it was taken out by a bullet."

Morgan glanced at Jamison. Morgan stomped on the gas pedal turning on his sirens and lights.

"Continue." Morgan gritted.

"When Miss London fainted... "

"What do you mean she fainted?" Morgan huffed in a lung full of air.

"She's fine, Bossman! I carried her to the gurney, AJ rode with her. I am sure that the hospital is taking great care of her."

Morgan growled as he whipped into the hospital parking lot.

"We sure got here fast Boss!"

"Let's go Jamison!"

Morgan charged into the hospital, with Jamison hot on his heels.

Morgan stopped at the front desk.

"Oh, hey Sheriff. I bet you are here to see London. London is in room eighteen, down the hallway on your left."

Morgan took off at a run. Morgan didn't knock, he flung the door open so hard that it hit the wall.

The doctor turned to look at Morgan, as well as AJ, and London.

AJ jumped up, meeting Morgan halfway.

"She's fine, Morgan! She's a bit ticked off, but Doc says she's going to be ok."

Morgan moved to London's side, he picked up her hand, holding it gently.

London was covered in blood; her forehead was being stitched shut.

Morgan's heart was currently slamming in his chest. He felt shaky and clammy. Morgan sucked in some air, trying to get his anxiety under control.

The doctor on call glanced up at Morgan.

"Maybe you need to sit down, Sheriff. You fall, I may be stitching you up next."

"I'm good."

Dr. Morton shook his head going back to work on London's forehead.

"I'm back in the stinking hospital, Morgan! AGAIN MORGAN! DAG-NAB-IT-ALL!" London ranted.

Morgan couldn't help but grin.

"Stop getting hurt, passing out, and what not, and you wouldn't have to be here, giving me heart failure." Morgan stated.

London grumbled.

AJ spoke up.

"Jamison and I are going to go for coffee. Would you like anything, Morgan?"

"I could use a black coffee, AJ."

"I want one too!" London exclaimed.

Morgan and the Doc both said no, simultaneously.

London glared, crossing her arms, looking very mule-like.

The doctor grinned at Morgan.

"I must say she is very strong willed. I hit her with a pain shot, she's been fighting it for quite a while."

The doctor finished up.

"You don't need a dressing but try not to get it wet. Go see your family doctor to have the stitches removed. You are going to have a big scar, but your hair will cover it."

London rolled her eyes.

"I'm not worried about one more scar."

When the doctor left the room, the silence in the room was practically deafening.

"Can you fill me in on what happened, London?"

London looked at Morgan, her expression, troubled.

"Jamison took my dash camera. The entire thing was caught on video and audio. Best thing I ever bought with Trent's money. I've got the guy on video admitting that Trent paid him a million dollars to... shut me up."

Morgan went rigid.

Jamison stepped back into the room.

"Where is the dash cam, Jamison?" Morgan demanded.

"It's been submitted to the evidence room; it's locked up nice and safe."

Morgan nodded.

"Call the Station, have someone come and get you. I want you to double-check that that dash cam is right where it is supposed to be. I'm depending on you Jamison. Trent has a lot of money! I cannot have that evidence coming up missing."

Jamison's eyes went wide, he stood at attention, and even saluted Morgan."

"I'm on it, Bossman! I won't let you down!"

Jamison charged out of London's room, already calling for a ride.

AJ stepped up and took a vacant chair.

Morgan turned around, shaking AJ's hand.

"Thank you for looking out for London, AJ; I appreciate you so much."

"That's what family is for Morgan."

Morgan grinned.

"You got that right, AJ."

Morgan eyed AJ, looking at him up and down.

AJ caught Morgan's look.

"What? Do I have something on my face?" AJ asked.

"Stand up, AJ." Morgan said.

AJ looked confused but did as he was asked.

When AJ stood up... Morgan had to look up!

"AJ! Dude! You are even bigger than you were the last time I saw you! You must be at least, as big as your dad now!"

AJ grinned.

"Dad and I are eye-to-eye now. Heck, I took one of his shirts the other day, all my clothes were dirty. Dad realized half-way through our workday that I was wearing his clothes."

Morgan grinned.

"What did he say?" Morgan questioned.

AJ made a scowling face mimicking his father. AJ crossed his arms like Alden too.

When AJ spoke, his voice sounded just like Alden's.

"Is nothing sacred? A man should not have to fight for his own clothes from his ginormous son!"

Morgan and AJ shouted with laughter.

London was still glowering, arms crossed.

"I want to leave!" London hollered aggressively.

AJ pointed his finger at London.

"Doc says no. You are being kept overnight for observation. You have a concussion, so stop growling and suck it up." AJ said with a grin.

London huffed in outrage.

"I think you are enjoying my pain AJ! You should be on my side, smuggling me out of here!" London exclaimed.

AJ shook his head no.

"You are staying... BECAUSE... we love you." AJ said with twinkling eyes.

"Where is she? Where is MY London?"

Morgan and AJ heard Stella all the way from the front desk.

"Oh boy! Mama Bear is here!" AJ exclaimed.

"Step back AJ, you know your Mama. She is going to come in here, push us both violently out of her way, to get to London."

AJ and Morgan both sat down, just in time. Stella rushed into the room making a beeline for London.

"Oh, my goodness! Look at you! You are all bloody! Where are you hurt? My poor bestie!"

Stella started crying, hugging London's face to her very large, ample breasts.

London struggled.

"You must let go, Stella! Number one, I can't breathe, number two, if your milk drops, I'll drown!" London teased.

Stella wiped her eyes *poo pooing* London's reasoning.

"Let me see where you are hurt, honey." Stella pleaded.

London slid her hair behind her ear. The stitches ran from the corner of her left eyebrow up to the top of her hairline.

Stella screamed; Stella swayed.

AJ and Morgan jumped up, each grabbing Stella by her elbows.

Morgan slid Stella into a chair; Stella's face was incredibly white.

"I'm fine! It just shocked me for a second, I'm ok now." Stella sobbed.

"Mom, you need to calm down! You know what happens when you get UPSET." AJ warned.

Stella glared at AJ.

"It doesn't ALWAYS happen, sheesh you all act like I'm a human faucet! Rude much!" Stella grumbled.

In the next room a baby wailed.

Stella's eyes went wide. Stella gripped the armrests on her chair in despair.

AJ's eyes twinkled; he slapped a hand over his mouth to hold in the laughter. Morgan looked confused, while London laughed out loud.

"Aww! Dang it!" Stella grumbled as her breast milk let loose.

Morgan jumped back, watching as Stella's shirt became soaked with her breast milk. Morgan couldn't believe that much milk could be released, all at once.

"Can't you... control those things?" Morgan ranted.

Stella stood up, ragefully.

"Look... you! You have no idea what us women go through! We bleed, we birth, and we breast-feed! What do you do? Nothing! Our bodies get to carry and then push out a human! All you men get to do is help make the baby! You get to have all the fun; we do all the work! Then, we must fight to get our bodies back in shape, go without sleep, and leak twenty-four-seven!"

Morgan leaned away from a very aggressive, leaking, Stella.

Stella followed him, with her finger in his face.

"While all of that is going on, do you know what you men are doing?" Stella asked in a dangerous whisper.

Morgan shook his head no.

"What? What... are we... doing?" Morgan questioned with fear.

AJ shook his head.

"Oh Morgan... *tsk*... *tsk*... *tsk*. You walked into that one! Maybe, my Mama is right... maybe men are stupid."

"You men! You are not sleep deprived, your body is not wrecked, but you roll over and want to jump an exhausted woman! How dare you!"

Morgan's eyes widened.

"Uh... I'm sorry? I'm not sure why I'm sorry but I truly am! Plus, I'm not doing that, Stella! I swear! If I ever have kids, I'll be the best husband and dad, ever!"

Stella crossed her arms over her now soaking, wet shirt.

"If you and London ever figure out your lives, I better not find out that you are acting like every other man in this world! Mark my words, Morgan Dun! I will HUNT... YOU... DOWN!"

Stella turned towards AJ.

AJ had a thoughtful look on his face.

"Hey Ma, did you ever realize that you women go through the 3-B's?"

"AJ, what in the world are you talking about? What are the... 3-B's?"

AJ snorted.

"Bleeding, birthing, and breastfeeding!" AJ exclaimed with a shout of laughter.

Stella shook her head, her expression said that she was not impressed.

"Let's go home, AJ! I need to pump these things and change my clothes."

AJ nodded, but Morgan made the mistake of saying... one... more... thing.

"Why would you need to pump? From the look of things, those things should be empty."

As soon as the words left Morgan's mouth, he slapped his hand over his mouth.

Stella was halfway through the door with AJ right behind her. Stella tried to turn around. AJ planted his arms on both sides of the door frame to block her. Stella roared at Morgan, trying to get at him. AJ held her back, lifting his mother off her feet.

"Bye Morgan! I'm not going to put her down until we get to the car!" AJ promised.

AJ tossed his mother over his shoulder trying to leave the room, but Stella was hanging onto both sides of the door frame.

Stella had her head up, glaring at Morgan.

Morgan stepped back and away from Stella.

AJ tugged a bit forcefully making his Ma lose her grip. AJ started down the hallway with his Ma hollering all the way.

"Just let me hit him once AJ, one time!"

"You can't attack a police officer, even if he is our closest friend, Ma!"

"I'm not attacking a police officer! I'm attacking the stupid side of Morgan!"

"Ma! You need to calm down! You're soaking my back!"

"Why do you have to act like your father? Just because you are big and strong does not give you the right to pick a person up and carry her off like a sack of potatoes! You are affecting my Autonomy!"

"What's that mean, Ma?"

"My self-rule, my personal rights!"

"Ma! Stop grabbing all the hospital equipment! You are going to break something and then we will have to pay for it!" AJ exclaimed.

"Put me down!"

"If I put you down, do you promise to walk to the car like an adult?"

"I can't make that promise!" Stella screamed.

"Then I'm going to have to abuse your self-rule a bit longer, Ma."

During that entire walk-away conversation, Morgan crept to the door. Morgan peeked out of London's room; he shook his head in disbelief as he watched the craziest exit he'd ever seen.

When they went far enough to be out of earshot, London and Morgan looked at each other in awe.

Morgan sat down heavily.

"The next time I see Alden, I plan on giving that man a good talking too!" Morgan decreed.

London giggled.

"Why is that?" She asked.

"Because, that woman I just saw right there... that woman is on the edge!"

London cracked up laughing.

"She isn't exactly wrong, but I don't think all men are... stupid." London said.

Morgan grew thoughtful.

"If I ever have... kids... I plan on being very helpful... more helpful than most men." Morgan said awkwardly.

London smiled.

"I think you would make a great father someday, Morgan." London said softly.

London's eyes began to close.

Morgan shot up.

"Don't go to sleep London, you have a concussion!"

"I'm fine." London said, sleepily.

"Oh, no, you just wait a second, woman!" Morgan demanded while hitting the nurses call button.

"How may I help you?"

"Is London supposed to be falling asleep? Someone needs to get in here and put her in something clean and tell me if she should be falling asleep!"

"Her nurse is on the way."

The nurse walked in; Morgan was still mumbling under his breath.

The nurse grinned at Morgan.

"She can sleep Sheriff, but we have to wake her up every couple of hours."

"She is covered in blood!"

"I'm helping her change right now. Step out of the room Sheriff, so I can make her more comfortable. Her room upstairs is on the third floor. She is being moved in about five minutes to room 301."

Morgan nodded. Morgan bent down close to London, trying to wake her up for a second to say goodbye.

"London... London open your eyes for a second, please." Morgan asked.

London opened her sleepy eyes. London stretched a bit wrapping her arms around

Morgan's neck. London yanked Morgan down, her lips slammed into his. Morgan's eyes went wide, he tried to struggle to get himself free, but London held on tight. Morgan tried to resist but London felt so good, and he had missed her so much!

Morgan allowed himself to kiss her back for a moment then he pulled himself away from her.

London let out a cry of distress.

The nurse giggled.

Morgan's face flamed.

"Uh... tell London that I said goodnight. I've got... to uh... police work and stuff." Morgan's voice was a bit squeaky.

The nurse giggled again.

Morgan tipped his hat and ran out of London's room like his butt was on fire.

Episode 40, Cabbage?

Jamison, true to his word, planted himself in a chair by the evidence room. Jamison could not be moved. When a cot was placed there for him to sleep on, he still refused to sleep. It took Murphy's promise to Jamison... well, more like a vow... to take over, and to protect the evidence with his life! They rotated like this faithfully until Grady could officially watch and listen to the dash cam evidence. Trent's lawyer was there, as well.

The evidence was damning.

The judge ordered that Trent be brought in for questioning, but Trent disappeared.

Morgan had to admit that Jamison and Murphy had really stepped up. Morgan made sure that both of his men received overtime for their diligent service.

Morgan glanced up when a loud commotion erupted out by the front desk.

Morgan stood up, heading towards the front.

When Morgan stepped out his eyes went wide.

Caleb and David Westman stood on tip toe. Both boys were being speed walked, being held onto by the back of their shirts.

Both boys were squirming and fighting, trying to get away.

"We didn't do nothin! Let us go!"

"This is police brutality! I'm gonna sue you all!"

Morgan had no idea which twin was which. The boys were identical, in every way. Both boys had crazy cowlicks that swirled on each side of their foreheads, forcing the hair at the front to come to a point. They both had their hair cut short, their haircuts looked like short mohawks. Their hair and eyes dark, a dead give-a-way, that they were Westman's.

"You two need to quit squirming or I'm going to put the cuffs on you both!" George hollered.

"What is going on here, George?" Morgan asked.

"These two were inciting a riot! Destruction of private property and basically being hellions!" George said fiercely.

Morgan tried not to smile but George's expression was priceless.

"You two, in my office, now!" Morgan said to Caleb and David.

The boys shuffled their feet, both saying, *"Aw man!"*

The boys sat down, crossed their arms and scowled at everyone.

"Ok, tell me what happened George."

The boys looked outraged.

"I want to hear George's point of view and then I have every intention of hearing your side of things." Morgan promised.

George took out a hanky, wiping his brow.

Morgan thought that maybe George needed to be on desk duty. George was getting close to retirement age. Morgan would have to think about that.

"These two here won't tell me which one is which!" George fumed.

The two boys smirked, high fiving each other.

George scowled at the boys.

"Boss! Make them tell!" George insisted.

Morgan looked at the two boys. Morgan pointed at the kid on the right.

"What's your name kid? Caleb or David?"

"I'm not talkin, you can torture me! Starve me! Lock me up for the rest of my life, but I'm not tellin!"

"You tell him, Caleb!" The other twin championed.

Morgan grinned at George.

"There yah go, George! That's David, and the really loudmouthed one, is Caleb." Morgan said with a grin.

Morgan jumped up with a black permanent marker. Morgan held Caleb against the chair, writing *Caleb* across his forehead. When Morgan turned towards David, David just leaned his head back, not even putting up a fight.

Caleb looked appalled.

"David! You didn't even try to fight him off one bit! What is your deal?"

David shrugged.

"He's the Sheriff... the POPO... the FUZZ... COPPERS... PEACEKEEPERS... the HEAT..."

Caleb looked disgusted.

"Shut it, David! We've been together since... before birth... but at times, I just don't know you!"

George laughed so hard he had to sit down.

"Boss, why did you go and do a thing like that?"

"Because these two would just jump up and mix themselves all up again. I've seen them do it before, with my own eyes."

Caleb's outrage got louder; David just looked a bit miffed.

Of course, Caleb spoke up.

"You can't write on us like we are packaged meat going in the freezer! There's gotta be a law against this kind of treatment!"

Morgan shouted with laughter; he couldn't help it... *Packaged meat going in the freezer!*

When Morgan calmed down, he turned towards George.

"Okay George, what did these two do?" Morgan questioned.

George was all laughed out; he was back to being Mr. Serious.

"I found these two boys, chucking Mr. Wayne's cabbage at him, rapid-fire! Mr. Wayne was dodging like a champ, but they did manage to tag him in the face. I'm pretty sure Mr. Wayne's nose will never be the same again."

Morgan's jaw dropped, then he practically ground his molars together.

"But that's not all!" George exclaimed. "These two called for backup! They got some of the local kids involved. Every one of Mr. Wayne's cabbages is ruined, his entire crop! I couldn't catch the other kids, but I was able to get the ring leaders of the group."

George nodded towards the boys, shaking his finger at them.

The boys blushed.

Morgan frowned at the boys fiercely.

"George, call Alden, tell Alden to head this way in about an hour. Tell him to come down here but don't tell him what the boys have done."

"Sure, thing Boss."

Caleb and David had identical expressions of horror on their faces. Dad was coming and they knew there was going to be a reckoning.

Morgan stood up; he stepped out of his office waving for Jamison to come over.

Jamison hotfooted it over.

"What's up Boss?"

"We don't have anyone in lock up, up here, do we?"

"No boss, the two solitary cells up here are empty."

Morgan nodded.

"Eventually, I want you to escort Caleb and David to the cells. We are going to let them sit for a bit. I'll go back with them and question them some more, but I would like them to get a taste of being locked up for a bit. If Alden shows up, put him in my office but don't tell him where the boys are."

Jamison started to move but Morgan stopped him.

"I have an idea. Before you lock them up, get their prints for me and take their mug shots."

Jamison looked confused.

"Are we actually processing them, Boss?"

"No, but I want them to go through the whole thing from beginning to end. Let's see what they think about this whole process."

"You got it Boss!" Jamison grinned.

Jamison opened Morgan's door. Jamison told the boys to stand up; he led the boys to the front area.

Jamison directed David to have a seat with Officer Dixon. Jamison sat Caleb down in front of his desk.

Now that the boys were separated, they started to look more unsure and scared.

"What is happening? They were just cabbages! What is the big deal?" Caleb ranted.

Morgan knew in that second that he was doing the right thing.

When the boys realized that they were getting their fingerprints done they began to cry.

By the time the boys had their mug shots taken, they were back to scowling, Caleb more so than David.

Jamison wandered up to Morgan.

"I have to say Boss, maybe we should write everyone's names on their foreheads. It does make my life easier."

Morgan chuckled.

Jamison and Officer Dixon escorted the boys back to the empty cells. Morgan again directed that the boys be separated, each in their own cell.

Morgan let them sit there for an hour.

The door opened, in walked a very shook-up Alden.

"Morgan? What in all creation is going on here? I can't find Caleb and David. I was looking for them, then I got a phone call saying that they are here at the station, but no one would tell me a thing."

"Let's go to my office so we can talk, I'll explain everything."

When they were both seated, Morgan sighed.

"Your boys incited a riot. They destroyed Mr. Wayne's entire cabbage crop, and I was notified that Mr. Wayne's nose is indeed... not okay."

Alden's face turned rageful; his face mottled with red. Alden ground his molars until they made a crunching sound.

"Where are my little darlings, Morgan?" Alden said sarcastically, shooting to his feet.

Morgan waved Alden back into his chair.

"I had their fingerprints done; they have already had their mug shots done. They are currently separated in the two cells in the back."

Morgan slid the fingerprints and mugshots towards Alden.

Alden took them, eyeing them.

Caleb had a fierce scowl on his face, he looked downright belligerent. David didn't look happy, but he looked a bit more unsure of the entire situation.

Alden gaped at Morgan.

"Uh… are my boys actually being arrested?"

Morgan shook his head no.

"I put them through the process just to shake them up a bit."

Alden grinned.

"I like how you think Morgan."

"I was hoping you would be okay with this."

"I'm on board, no problem."

Alden's phone rang, it was Stella. Alden had the speaker phone on, Morgan heard every word Stella said.

"Babe, what is happening? Why are the boys at the police station? I'm so shook up, that I had to tape Tupperware Bowls to my breasts!"

Alden snorted with laughter; his body shook with the force of it.

How Alden sat there not making one sound, Morgan could not figure.

Morgan's eyes rounded as he pictured that scenario; then, he blushed.

"They have been processed, fingerprinted and have had their mugshots taken. They are currently in two separate cells, cooling their heels. The boys destroyed Mr. Wayne's Garden and his nose is… not straight." Alden stated.

"What? Sob! My babies committed aggravated assault! They destroyed private property! You may as well throw in trespassing

while you are at it! They are going to end up in Juvenile Detention! Sob!"

"Relax honey, they are just being taught a very big lesson."

"But this is just the tip of the sword! Their crime spree has begun! What are we going to do, Alden?"

"Let me handle this honey. I'm going to make them sit there in those cells for a while, to teach them a nice, long lesson."

"Ok, thank you honey, and could you please ask Morgan if I can have their fingerprints and mugshots for my album."

Morgan grinned, nodding yes.

"Morgan says sure."

"Thanks Morgan! Keep me posted Alden."

"I sure will darlin."

Before Stella hung up, they heard a commotion of some sort.

"Honey? What's happening?"

"Ahhh! I dropped the phone because my Tupperware Bowls are overflowing! I must go! I should have stuffed more breast pads in them bowls!"

Stella hung up abruptly.

Alden and Morgan tried to keep their faces calm but they both roared with laughter.

"Tupperware?!" They both shouted at the same time.

"Alden! Your wife is... is... I think she's losing her mind." Morgan stated.

"Yeah, I think this last set of twins just about did her in."

Morgan had a thoughtful look on his face.

"Alden... you... um... Stella went crazy on me, at the hospital, the other day."

Alden nodded.

"I heard about that from AJ."

"You think we have things way too easy, Alden?" Morgan asked.

Alden sighed.

"In some ways, my wife isn't wrong. I've seen my wife push out eight babies. It is the most amazing thing I've ever seen! Women are strong! I passed a tiny little kidney stone, no bigger than a grain of sand, and I thought I was going to die!"

Morgan's jaw dropped, then he gulped.

"So... I have a question, Alden." Morgan looked a bit uncomfortable.

Alden grinned at Morgan's discomfort.

"Ask away."

"So... your wife pushes out eight babies. She... insinuated, that you are a stupid man that rolls over and tries to... jump her? Do you really do that Alden?"

Alden blushed; then, his face turned fierce.

"Well... I love my wife and I want her! I miss her! I admit that I try to get frisky with her, but she glares at me and tells me she's going to hurt me in multiple ways. The other day she told me specific ways that she wanted to unman me." Alden shivered.

"Alden, how do you get through all of this... madness?" Morgan whispered.

Alden sighed, again.

"I've learned that if I try to be romantic, she glares at me, telling me she knows what I'm UP to. If I'm not romantic she sobs and tells me that I don't find her attractive anymore."

Morgan looked shocked.

Alden nodded.

"Yes, there is no winning here; her mood swings are giving me whiplash." Alden moaned.

"I do not understand women... AT ALL!" Morgan exclaimed.

"Me either." Alden raised both of his hands up, while shaking his head.

Morgan did a doubletake.

"But you have eight kids and you have been married forever! How can you say you don't understand women? If you don't understand women what hope is there for me?"

Alden leaned closer, resting his elbows on his knees.

"Let me tell you what happened one day."

"One day... I let Stella sleep in. I cooked the kids' breakfast and got all the kids off to school. Stella was up all night with the twins. I fed the girls breastmilk from the freezer and let her sleep until she woke up on her own. About the time I put the girls down for their nap, Stella charged out of the bedroom at about one in the afternoon. I handed her a cup of coffee and... "

Morgan hung on every word.

"And? What?"

"She towed me to the bedroom and had her way with me." Alden looked completely confused.

"I still don't get it, Morgan! Till this day, I cannot figure out what I did?"

Both men looked confused; they both shrugged.

"Women!" They both said at the same time.

Morgan stood up.

"Your boys have been in there for a couple of hours, let's go question them together."

Alden shot up, following Morgan to the cells.

Morgan went to unlock the cell that Caleb was in, but Caleb shook his head no, vigorously.

Morgan looked confused.

"Um... hi Dad." Caleb said with a nervous smile.

Caleb and David stepped forward, gripping the bars.

"Maybe we should stay in here, keep these here nice, solid, sturdy bars, between us for a bit." Caleb stated.

"I agree with Caleb... I feel safer with these bars between us... no offence Dad." David stated.

Alden looked grim.

"Perhaps you two are right about that. Keeping these bars between us for now, might be the smartest thing you've ever said... in your entire lives." Alden growled.

Alden took a chair, scooting it closer to the bars, Morgan did the same thing.

Alden glared at his offspring.

"Start talking." He growled.

David looked unsure but he started the conversation.

"Ma gave us money to go to the Party Store, to get her a head of cabbage."

Alden looked confused.

"Ok... I'm listening."

Caleb jumped in.

"We rode our bikes up there. When we got there, we were powerful thirsty... we spent the money on drinks... and... we were hungry too... we bought snacks."

"Why did your mom want cabbage?" Alden asked.

David smiled big because he knew the answer to this question.

"For her boobs, Dad! She wanted em for her boobs!"

The boys looked at each other grinning from ear-to-ear.

Morgan and Alden eyed each other with confusion.

"For her... boobs? Why would she want cabbage for... her boobs?" Alden asked.

Morgan leaned forward; he really wanted an answer to this bizarre question.

Caleb's face held a look of superiority that made Alden want to smack the kid.

"Ma said that old Mrs. Landry told her that you put cabbage in the fridge. You peel off the layers and put it in your bra, it helps dry up your boobs."

"Oh... I see." Alden shook his head.

Alden's face turned angry.

"Wait a minute! So, you spent the money on snacks and drinks! You went over to Mr. Wayne's house to STEAL a cabbage, because you SPENT THE MONEY! You mismanaged funds! You hurt Mr. Wayne's nose! You then talked other kids into destroying Mr. Wayne's entire cabbage crop! Finally, you two ended... up... in... jail." Alden's voice by now was low and deadly.

Caleb and David backed away from the bars.

Caleb crossed his arms, raising one eyebrow.

"Dad, you should probably leave us here until you calm down. If you murder us, you are going up the river, FOR... THE... REST... OF... YOUR... BORN... DAYS!" Caleb promised.

David nodded.

"Yep Dad! If you unlock the cells, and kill us, that would be premeditated murder! Step away from our cells, Dad!" David chimed in with a grin.

Caleb smirked.

"Truth is Dad, I feel pretty darn safe behind these bars! It's not like the Sheriff is going to let you beat on us."

Alden pointed his finger at the mouthy kid with the name CALEB written across his forehead.

"You listen to me Caleb! You are..."

"How did you know it was me, Dad?" Caleb looked shocked; eyes wide, while he pointed at his own chest.

Their father could never tell them apart.

"It's on your forehead! Why your name is written on your forehead, I have no idea, but I must say, it is very convenient!"

"Oh! I forgot that Sheriff Morgan did that." Caleb groused.

"But... I am going to have to agree with you two. I am going to leave you here! Because I think you are right! I'm keeping those bars between us for a while."

Alden folded his arms across his chest, feet planted wide, raising one eyebrow.

Morgan had to admit that the family resemblance was staggering.

"Besides... what makes you two think you are getting out of here, anytime soon?" Alden asked.

Caleb and David's eyes went wide.

"But... Dad! Can't you get us out of here?" David questioned.

Alden shrugged.

"I'm going to go talk to Grady, my lawyer! I am going to have to see what I can do. Things are looking mighty grim for the two of you.

Choosing a life of crime... well, there are consequences for those decisions."

Alden turned away; Morgan followed.

"Dad! You are coming back... right?" David asked.

Alden kept walking.

"Dad! Dad! Stop playin! When are you coming back?" Caleb yelled.

Alden turned around. Alden laid his hand on his chest, looking properly crestfallen.

Alden stepped up to the bars, he reached for his boys.

Caleb and David eyed their dad warily but stepped close enough for Alden to haul them into a hug. It wasn't a pleasant hug, what with the bars being squashed between them.

Alden stepped back; he wiped a fake tear from his eye.

"I'm so sad... *sigh*... I miss you guys already. I will try to get you out by tonight... *sob*... but there is just no guarantee... *sniffle*."

As Alden turned away, Morgan smiled at the boys.

"Look at it this way boys, you get three meals a day, a nice cot to sleep on and all the peace and quiet you could want."

Caleb and David had horrified looks on their faces.

"Wait! Sheriff, are there any video games?" Caleb asked.

"Nope."

"What about TV, there's gotta be a TV!" David exclaimed.

"Nope."

"Wait! What's for dinner?" Caleb questioned.

"Beans."

The boys looked at each other with identical yuck faces.

"Did he say... beans?" David asked Caleb.

"Wait! Sheriff! You mean like beef and bean burritos with all the fixings, right?" Caleb shouted.

"Nope... just beans."

Morgan and Alden hid around the far corner still listening to the boy's conversation. Both men doubled over with their hands over their mouths, trying not to laugh. Morgan elbowed Alden; Alden pointed a finger at Morgan, warning him to quit or he was going to bust.

Caleb and David reached through the bars, placing sympathetic hands on each other's shoulders.

"Beans? What is this world coming to?" Caleb whispered.

"Beans? I wonder what Mom is making for dinner?" David sighed.

"Mom was making roast, with potatoes and baby carrots."

"But we always complain about eating that." David reminded Caleb.

"I'll never argue with mom about eating that again! I wish I had that right in front of me right now."

The boys turned to each other.

"You know what David; my life of crime is over! In fact, I think when I grow up that I'm going to be a policeman." Caleb announced with a grin.

David's jaw dropped.

"Yo! Bro! I was thinking the same thing! If you think about it Caleb, if we become policemen, then we will be on the RIGHT side of these bars!"

The two boys sat down on their cots, sitting across from each other, bars separating them. They seemed very excited about discussing their future careers in law enforcement.

Morgan and Alden snuck out.

"Well, I'll be!" Morgan exclaimed. "Maybe your two hooligans learned their lesson after all. I'll call Mr. Wayne, see if we can't work something out. I am afraid you will have to pay some money, though. I can't see any way around that issue, Alden."

"Tell Mr. Wayne, I'll pay whatever he needs, I'll cover it. Then, my boys will pay! They are going to clean up the mess they made, apologize to Mr. Wayne, and then their lives are really going to get tough!"

Morgan stopped Alden as he headed out the door to call his wife.

"Maybe you should head over to Houseman's Grocery and pick up some cabbage."

Alden stopped abruptly.

"Oh, thanks man! I think you just saved my life!"

Morgan smiled, throwing his arms wide.

"What are friends for? Don't forget to come back and get your boys."

"I'm going to give them a couple more hours to stew, I'll be back in a bit, Morgan."

Episode 41, Romance

London sat at the table with the Westman clan. The house was loud, crazy, and in London's opinion... wonderful.

Alden put all the extra table leaves inside the table, it stretched all the way into the living room. London traced the beautiful pattern of the tablecloth. Grandma Nettie nudged London.

"This tablecloth has been in our family for eight generations."

London gasped.

"It's practically a work of art! Grandma Nettie, do you think we should be eating on this thing?" London said with worry in her voice.

"Beautiful things shouldn't sit in a cupboard, or in a box. They should be used and appreciated, with love."

London sighed with happiness.

Two seconds later, Grandma Nettie smacked the table with a loud bang. London jumped.

"You boys better cool it! I can see what you two are doing! Do not make me get up out of this chair! If I have to get up, you two are going to get it!" Grandma screamed.

Alden stepped between the boys so their arms couldn't reach each other anymore.

"I didn't do nothin, it was Caleb! He won't stop poking me with his fork!" David complained.

Alden smiled; he uncapped the permanent black marker that rested in his front, shirt pocket.

"Hold your brother, AJ."

AJ grinned while stepping up. AJ pinned Caleb in his chair, holding his head back, the kid couldn't move a muscle.

"Dad! No! I just got that stuff off my face! It took me a whole week!"

Alden paid no attention to the struggling child. Alden put a big C on Caleb's forehead. David didn't even struggle, he tilted his head back allowing his dad to mark him with a bid D."

Caleb turned on David, disgust written all over his face.

"You didn't even try to fight Dad off; and to think I call you brother!" Caleb exclaimed.

"Pick your battles Caleb. Plus, do you really think we can fight Dad and AJ off? I think not." David said wisely.

Caleb glared at his very happy Dad.

"You have to sleep sometime Dad." Caleb growled. "You just might want to remember that." Caleb promised.

AJ hooted with laughter; Alden looked a bit nervous.

Caleb then stared his oldest brother down.

"What are you laughing at AJ? Karma is alive and real in this house, you just wait!"

AJ stopped smiling.

AJ and Alden both shrugged but they did back away... slowly.

"You scared of those two, AJ?" Alden whispered.

"Noooo, I mean... maybe a little." AJ eyed the glaring twins.

"I'm keeping my bedroom door locked!" AJ exclaimed, rushing away.

Alden nodded.

"Hmmm, that might be a good idea, Son." Alden backed away even further from the boys, keeping his eyes trained on them the whole time.

Grandma Nettie and London glanced at each other.

"My husband must have genetically zapped them all. Do you see the CRAZY coming out of this family? It seems to be a hereditary thing." Grandma stated.

London giggled.

The door opened; more people streamed in.

Stella's sister Annie, her husband Tom, and their kids strolled in.

Right behind them... Morgan.

London's heart sped up; she felt her breath hitch.

Grandma Nettie chuckled.

"Breathe girl. You are eyeing that man like a big ol steak."

London glanced at Grandma.

"I do love me some steak." London said quietly.

Nettie snickered.

Morgan stepped closer to the table. On every plate was a name card. Morgan stopped, seeing that his seat was right across from London. Morgan hung up his hat, then he settled into his seat.

Morgan smiled at London and then Grandma Nettie.

"Hello Nettie, how are you doing?" Morgan asked politely.

"Hello Morgan, I am doing very well. I must say Morgan, you look exceptionally handsome tonight. Do you realize that shirt matches your eyes? There is a very thin line in that shirt that is the exact color of your gorgeous eyes!" Grandma Nettie exclaimed.

Morgan gulped, his eyes flitting between the two women.

London couldn't help but smile.

Nettie nudged London again.

"Don't you think Morgan looks incredibly handsome tonight, London?"

London felt flushed, Morgan smiled softly, his eyes twinkling.

"Do you think I look... incredibly handsome tonight, London... I mean... exceptionally handsome?" Morgan asked.

"Yes... you look... very nice, Morgan." London stated.

Morgan arched an eyebrow.

London looked up at AJ as he started placing food in the center of the table. AJ would place two platters on the table, then run back to the kitchen for two more. When he was done, the entire table was covered with the best-looking food that London had ever seen.

Grandma Nettie sighed with happiness, as she gazed at AJ.

"What? What has you looking all soft and happy Nettie?" London asked.

"AJ. AJ gets it."

"Gets what?"

"Everything. AJ is a fantastic student, he plays an instrument, he works right along with his dad, rain or shine. You don't know this, but when Alden was on the road for years, doing sales, trying to get his beef out there... AJ stepped up. AJ made the boys mind; he would snatch ahold of them and rattle their world if they backtalked their Ma."

London eyed AJ with new respect.

"That's not all." Nettie said.

"What? What else?"

"AJ... he totally gets women. He isn't fazed by hormones, periods, birthing, none of it. AJ's mom will be flipping out; Alden, most of the time, looks confused, but AJ smiles gently, hugging his Ma."

Morgan hung on every word.

"So... he just hugs her?"

Nettie and London nodded.

"That's the answer? Hug the female? Why does that work?" Morgan asked, looking shocked.

Alden heard Morgan; he took a seat next to him.

"AJ told me, that there are four steps to understanding and comforting a woman. Number one, you hug em. Number two, you tell them everything is going to be alright. Number three, you do NOT ask them what's wrong! Number four, you tell them you love them." Alden explained.

Morgan arched his eyebrows.

"Is he for real?" Morgen asked the ladies, eyeing Alden with suspicion.

Nettie and London smiled, both nodding their heads.

London leaned forward, smiling at a confused Morgan.

"Men overthink things. Sometimes, a woman is just stressed, overwhelmed, and emotional. We just need a hug." She stated. "Look at Stella for example." London said.

All eyes turned towards Stella.

"She's beautiful, she's a mom, her day starts very early. Plus, she's up all night with the girls. Stella cooks, she cleans, she shops, she is a force to be reckoned with. She works harder than most men. Stella works from sun-up to sun-down. Stella can't just walk in the house and plop down in a recliner and turn on the tv, there's too much to be done."

Alden blushed; Alden stood up.

"I think I'm going to go and give my wife a hand, I'll be back."

The three of them watched Alden take over the salad bar. Alden ordered Stella to go sit down.

Stella's jaw dropped, then she smiled while grabbing Alden by the front of his shirt, reeling him in for a passionate kiss.

When she was done, Alden looked a bit dazed, with a goofy smile on his face.

"I think I'm starting to understand." Morgan stated thoughtfully.

Nettie cackled.

"Then, our work here is done!"

London giggled.

AJ zoomed up with one more side dish... a big steaming bowl of... fried cabbage.

Morgan's eyes went wide. Alden and Morgan both had looks of... disbelief as they eyed that bowl of cabbage.

Was it the SAME cabbage.... No! Stella would never do that!

Morgan tried to eye Stella up and down without being too obvious. Morgan realized that Stella was... back to normal... her breasts no longer led the way.

Morgan watched Alden bend over and whisper in his wife's ear. Alden pointed at the bowl of cabbage; he glanced down at Stella's chest.

Stella looked outraged.

"I would never do that Alden! You idiot! You came home with two heads of cabbage! Do you really think I would dry up my milk and then cook the cabbage? I'm married to a moron!" Stella yelled out for all to hear.

Everyone went still.

Alden blushed to his hairline as Stella stormed off.

Alden looked mortified.

"Hey... uh... Morgan. It's all good man, not the same... cabbage." Alden stammered.

All eyes turned towards Morgan.

Morgan leaned his elbow on the table, turning away from Alden.

"Ahh, make it all stop!" Morgan cried.

Caleb and David hooted with laughter.

"You two thought mom cooked up the cabbage that she used for her boobs? *Bahaaa*!"

Caleb and David could not contain their glee, they were so happy that they started chanting.

"Karma! Karma! Karma!"

Stella came back with a glass of white wine.

"I should go help." London stated. "I feel a bit useless sitting here doing nothing." London sighed.

Nettie glared at London.

"No! Doctor's orders! You don't have your stitches out yet and you had a major concussion! You just sit there and look pretty!" Nettie insisted.

Stella yelled out for everyone to listen up.

"Pop is going to say a prayer and then we can all dig in. You can help yourselves to the salad bar first, if you like. The main dishes will start with Pop, then we will pass the dishes clockwise down the table."

Everything went smoothly.

London had never been to a get-together like this before.

The only thing that didn't get passed around were the yeast rolls. Stella grinned, while speed-tossing them to each individual person. This must be a regular family thing because some people just caught them, without even looking.

Alden started frowning during dinner.

London nudged Nettie.

"What's got Alden so bent-out-of-shape?" London asked.

Grandma Nettie snickered.

"Our dear Franny, invited her boyfriend over; his name is Bobby. Franny calls him Rob. According to Franny, they kissed on the playground. Franny told her dad at dinner one night that she wasn't too sure about that whole kissing thing, so she told Bobby to kiss her again. Bobby, of course, kissed her again. Ever since, Alden is a bit... irritable... when Bobby is around. Doesn't faze Bobby though; he only has eyes for Franny."

"What are they, seven, eight? Is Alden really worried about this situation?" London asked.

Nettie twinkled at London.

"Franny is headstrong. When that girl gets something in her head, she's like a dog with a bone. Franny told me the other day that when she grows up, she's going to marry Bobby. Franny may be young, but that girl is part mule."

London eyed Franny and Bobby down the table.

Bobby picked up Franny's napkin, he unfolded it, draping it across her lap.

Franny moved Bobby's drink closer to him; Bobby thanked her, taking a sip.

Franny dropped her spoon. Without asking, Bobby went to the kitchen and got her a clean one.

Franny smiled at Bobby; the girl practically sparkled.

Stella grabbed Alden's hand and uncurled his fingers from around his spoon. London saw that the spoon was a gonner.

Stella grinned, getting up to get Alden a new spoon.

London sat with her mouth hanging open.

"Nettie... I think you might be right. I can't believe what I'm seeing." London said.

Nettie chuckled.

"Stella has a whole bunch of bent up silverware in that drawer over there, that she is saving." Nettie said.

"What is she saving them for?" London asked.

"She's in the process of creating a hanging windchime with all the bent-up silverware. It is quite amazing and huge!" Grandma Nettie exclaimed.

Morgan huffed and slapped the table.

London and Grandma Nettie choked with laughter.

Evidently, they made quite the ruckus, because everyone stopped what they were doing, peering down the table at the three of them.

London tapped her glass to get everyone's attention.

London stood up.

"I have an announcement to make, I hope you all don't mind."

Everyone nodded for her to continue.

"I didn't tell anyone, but I had to go to court yesterday."

Stella gasped and stood up.

"Why didn't you tell me? Why did you have to go to court?" Stella asked.

London glanced at a very concerned Morgan.

Morgan seemed agitated.

"Everything is fine! I am officially... not married." London said with a smile.

The place went dead quiet.

London swore she heard crickets.

Then the place erupted with applause and congratulations.

London peeked at Morgan. Morgan wasn't smiling, he seemed frozen in place.

Again, the place went quiet, all eyes went to Morgan, waiting to see what was going to happen.

Morgan stood up, he circled the table slowly, never taking his eyes off London.

When Morgan reached her, London had to suck in a breath.

A smile spread across Morgan's face; London practically sobbed with relief.

Morgan placed his hand on London's cheek, he leaned down, pressing his forehead against hers.

"Aww man! Are they gonna kiss?" David cried.

"Make it stop! My eyes are going to burn right outta my face! I need my eyes!" Caleb exclaimed.

"I think it's so romantic." Franny sighed. "Don't you agree, Rob?"

Alden bent his fork.

Stella sobbed out loud, while taking Alden's fork away, sliding another towards him.

"I'm sure it's my hormones! I'm pretty sure my hormones will never be right again! Then I'll be dealing with Menopause! *Sob*! That's more hormones! I am just so happy!" Stella cried.

"Ma... if you are happy why are you crying?" Ben asked.

"Because I'm happy! You could learn a thing or two from your brother AJ! AJ gets why I'm crying, don't you AJ?"

All eyes went to AJ. AJ crossed his arms, looking as wise as an old owl.

"Yep." He emphasized the P at the end making a popping sound.

"Ma is crying because..."

Everyone waited for AJ to finish.

AJ said one word.

"Hormones." AJ said nodding smartly.

AJ went back to eating.

Everyone groaned at AJ's answer, throwing napkins and rolls at him.

Pop cackled, slapping the table.

"AJ, you are a man of few words! I like it!"

Pop's eyes slid back to London and Morgan.

"So, when are you two getting married? You plan on kissing that woman Morgan, or are you just gonna stare at her all night? Back in my day... I would have grabbed ahold of Grandma

Nettie and kissed her ten times by now! Being young is wasted on you all!" Pop groused.

"Kiss her! Kiss her! Kiss her!" Most everyone chanted.

Caleb and David looked horrified.

"Don't kiss her! Don't kiss her! Please! Don't kiss her!" They chanted.

Everyone started banging on the table and their glasses.

Grace and Hannah sat in their highchairs, smacking their gooey hands together, clapping along. They had no idea what was going on, but it looked like great fun.

Morgan kissed London gently; all his pent-up longing, every ounce of his feelings, he poured into that kiss.

When Morgan pulled away, tears of happiness tracked down London's face.

"Hey big guy... any chance you want to marry me?" London asked.

Morgan's eyes went wide, he whooped; then, he picked up London twirling her in a circle.

"That is so romantic!" Franny exclaimed, again. Franny clasped her hands together, clutching them to her heart. "Rob, don't you think that is the most romantic thing you've ever seen?"

Rob never even looked at London and Morgan, he only had eyes for Franny.

"Yes, Franny. So very romantic." Rob sighed.

Alden's second spoon bit the dust.

London threw her arms around Morgan's neck.

"You haven't answered me, mister. Is that by any chance a...YES?" London sighed with happiness.

Morgan nodded.

"Yes! But we are not having some great big, outlandish wedding! I've waited for you long enough! I want us to just go to the courthouse and get this done." Morgan demanded.

Stella surged to her feet; Stella's face could only be classified as stormy. Stella charged to the end of the table. Stella couldn't get around it because the chairs and because Grandma Nettie decided to blocked her. Stella looked like she was going to crawl over the table.

"You listen to me Morgan Dun... you can have your small wedding, but it will be in my yard... or your yard. I don't care whose yard, but my bestie is not getting married at the courthouse!"

AJ quietly got up and eased himself between his mom and Morgan.

Morgan started to argue but London spoke up quickly.

"Morgan... I would really like to get married at our future home... please." She whispered.

Morgan melted.

"Ok, but I get to choose the theme." Morgan said with a small smile.

"Oh, dear... um... ok. Please Morgan, tell me it's not clowns, or pirates." London begged.

Morgan thew back his head and roared.

Episode 42, Fall Wedding

When the theme was revealed, everyone was shocked.

Morgan had his great grandfather's wedding suit from the 1800's, complete with Top Hat. Not one of those outrageously tall Top Hats. His hat was the shorter variety.

Morgan's suit was black with tails, his shirt crisp white, with dove grey vest and tie.

When Morgan walked down the makeshift aisle on his property, everyone *oohhed* and *ahhhed*.

A beautiful arbor had been built by the guys. It was very large; Westman made!

The arbor was reminiscent of days gone by. The minister, Morgan and London would be able to stand under the arbor with room to spare.

Morgan placed the arbor over the sidewalk, it would remain there for London to plant her morning glories.

London hadn't been to the house since the day she had left. Today, she would be married here, to her it seemed the perfect place to start her life with Morgan.

London's carriage came up the driveway.

Everyone turned, gasping in awe at the beauty that the bride and carriage made.

Morgan couldn't stop smiling.

London was helped down, she stood for a moment, taking in the beautiful sight of her friends that she now called family.

London turned her head to the left and gasped.

London didn't follow the path to the arbor, instead she went behind and around their guests, heading for the side of the yard.

London lifted her skirts, as she picked up speed.

London racing across the yard, in her beautiful, vintage wedding dress, was quite a stunning sight.

Morgan stepped away from the arbor, racing after London, with a grin on his face.

London stopped in front of the spot where she had dug up rocks. The day she was trying to create a garden in the worst spot on the property.

The soil was fertile, raised beds; the garden was fenced in. It was huge and beautiful, but it wasn't just a garden, it was a greenhouse!

London turned towards Morgan.

"I can't believe you did this. When did you do this, Morgan?" London whispered.

Morgan shrugged.

"I was nursing a broken heart. Then, I found out you were still married, that just about did me in. I couldn't sleep most of the time... so... I built this, for you, London. Hoping that someday, you would come home to me."

London's eyes filled with tears. She turned to Morgan, throwing herself into his arms. London rested her head on his chest.

When London pulled herself together, she still didn't step away. London could hear Morgan's heart beating, steady and sure. London smiled listening to it. When London leaned back to look up at Morgan, she looked radiant.

"What do you say we go get hitched, Morgan Dun."

Morgan nodded.

Together they walked hand in hand to the arbor.

The minister smiled.

"I must say, this is all very exciting! You two are the first couple that I am bringing together in matrimony. This is a very large family; I hope to be able to marry you all off someday."

"Dearly beloved..."

When the wedding was done, the food and fun began. Behind the house a dance floor had been built. Lights lit up the whole backyard, tables twinkled with large center pieces.

When the couple stepped up to dance their first dance as man and wife, everyone sighed with happiness.

Grandma Nettie had tears in her eyes.

Pop took her hand, lifting it to his lips, kissing her fingers softly.

"I remember waltzing with you, my love." Pop said softly.

"Look at them! It's like looking back in time! I've never seen a more beautiful wedding!" Grandma Nettie exclaimed.

Pop shook his head no.

"I remember our wedding. I remember seeing you as you walked down that aisle. To this day I couldn't tell you what the minister said.

Your Father kept glaring at me, whispering threats in my ear, but I couldn't tell you what he said. I only saw you, Nettie. I still see you, Nettie." Pop whispered softly.

Nettie cried harder, throwing her arms around the only man she had ever loved.

Elijah chose that moment to point his camera at his grandparents, taking photo after photo. The boy was a genius with a camera.

Elijah seemed to see the perfect picture; the boy seemed to just get photography.

Elijah seemed to always have a book in one hand and a camera in the other.

Elijah's photos of London and Morgan's wedding day would become the talk of the town. Elijah soon started making very good money, at his young age, because his camera skills were just that good.

Stella bought Elijah a very expensive camera. She figured if the boy could photograph the entire birth of Gracie and Hannah, that well; then, the boy needed better equipment to follow his passion.

Everyone stayed late.

London and Morgan kept slow dancing, like no one else was there.

Eventually, they were alone. Everyone went home, the house was quiet.

London traced her finger on her husband's chin, as they lay side-by-side.

"I love you, Morgan." London said sleepily.

"I love you too, Mrs. Dun."

"I didn't know..." London whispered.

"You didn't know what?"

London looked sleepy, happy, and a bit embarrassed.

"That... that is how things are supposed to be between a man and a woman."

Morgan pulled London close, he draped his arm around his wife, smiling.

"I love you." Morgan said.

"I love you more." London insisted.

"Not possible." Morgan argued.

"Are we fighting?" London questioned.

"You wanna make up?" Morgan asked with a twinkle in his eye.

London laughed, kissing him passionately.

Episode 43, Mia's Revelation

Luke and Mia seemed mighty close.

Morgan suspected that they were officially an item.

Morgan was horrified when he saw Mia in a wheelchair.

"What happened, Mia?" Morgan questioned.

"Don't fret Sheriff... I mean, Morgan. I had to get my leg fixed up with some surgery. Come to find out, when I broke my leg in a couple of spots all those years ago, my bones didn't set right. Because of that, my right leg was a bit shorter than my left. My right leg got weaker, and it just threw me all off balance. So, I would get hurt, then get hurt again, and it was a cycle that I just couldn't get out of. So, I went to see Doc and he sent me to this lady doctor, and she fixed me up good. Luke here is going to help me with my physical therapy. He says I have a long, hard road, but he is going to be there with me the whole way. Isn't he just the sweetest man in the whole wide world?" Mia questioned.

Morgan grinned.

"Luke is the best! You couldn't be in better hands, Mia."

"I'm sorry I couldn't attend your wedding. I was in that other city having my surgery. I so wanted to be there. I hope you aren't mad at me." Mia's face looked sad.

"London and I absolutely understand why you could not be there. London went to get ice but come on over here and meet Stella."

"Oh! You mean the lady with two sets of twins? She has like eight kids, right?" Mia got excited, she turned around, asking Luke to please roll her over to Miss Stella.

"Just call her Stella, Mia. We are one big happy family here, and you are now in it."

Mia smiled the most beautiful smile.

"I'm proud to know you all!" Mia exclaimed.

When they rolled up to Stella, she was juggling Grace. Alden stood next to her, holding Hannah. The girls looked beautiful in their fall dresses. Their dresses, identical colors of cinnamon with lace overlay. They both had white bonnets on, with matching ribbons. Hanging from their bonnets were beautiful imitation Fall Leaves and Fall Flowers.

Mia gaped at the two girls.

Morgan introduced Mia to Stella and Alden. Stella smiled down at Mia.

"Oh my! I've heard so much about you! I swear I know you already." Stella said.

"Your girls... I've never seen two more beautiful little girls in my whole life! My goodness these two could be models someday!"

Stella turned to Alden.

"What do you think of that Alden? Do you think our girls could be future models?" Stella asked.

Alden seemed to grip Hannah a bit tighter.

"Not ever! My girls are going to be cow farmers!" Alden insisted.

Mia laughed.

"Well, they are going to be the most beautiful cow farmers this county has ever seen, that's for sure!" Mia stated.

Everyone turned when they heard another car pull up.

It was Grady.

Grady said hi as he headed towards them.

Grady had some paperwork in his hand.

Morgan looked worried; Grady looked so... serious.

"What's up Grady?" Morgan asked.

"I have some news, about Trent."

Grady turned the photos around, passing them to Morgan.

Luke practically vibrated with worry.

"What is it, Grady?" Alden asked.

"Trent was spotted in the Ohio area. Because it happened late on a Friday, I'm just getting this information now. At this point, Trent could be anywhere." Grady stated.

Morgan nodded, looking at the photo.

"There's more." Grady sighed.

"Trent is being charged with the murder of his mother, as well as London's aunt. They were both poisoned. I know that Trent told London that he smothered her, but that's not the case. I think he was just trying to traumatize London. Trent said he pushed his mother down the stairs, then he changed his story, that he didn't kill her, but... she was also poisoned with the same thing as London's aunt. The poison was found on his property; the judge issued a warrant for his arrest. Trent is now a very desperate man.

When Morgan went to pass the photos to Alden, Mia gasped.

Luke placed his hand on Mia's shoulder.

"What's wrong honey?"

"I just saw this man!" Mia exclaimed.

Morgan's face went pale, he felt panic rising in waves. Morgan whipped out his cell phone, trying to call London.

Grady bent down to Mia's level.

"Are you sure? Are you very sure it was this man?" Grady asked.

"Yes! I saw him. It was him, clear as day!" Mia exclaimed, her excitement making her southern accent stronger.

"Where Mia; where did you see him?" Morgan questioned.

"I saw that man, snooping at my Grandma Tilly's back fence. I asked him what he thought he was doing, and he ducked down and ran!

Obviously, I couldn't chase him, but I wanted to! That man looked like trouble!" Mia said viscously.

Mia grabbed the photo from Grady; Morgan was still trying to dial London's phone.

"We have to go Luke; my Grandma Tilly is home all by herself!" Mia exclaimed.

Luke took ahold of Mia's chair.

"I can't leave you and your Grandma Tilly all alone in your house, Mia! I am going to have to stay with the two of you, until Trent is caught and dealt with."

Mia giggled.

"Oh... I don't know about that Luke. A man... in Grandma Tilly's house? She wouldn't like that too much."

Mia then laughed out loud.

"I tell you what Luke, if you ask my Grandma Tilly and she says yes... I'll be impressed."

Elijah was so quiet that no one heard him approach.

"We must go! I have to stop and buy flowers and candy." Luke stated.

"Oh no! Grandma Tilly doesn't like cut flowers, but if you buy her plants, she will fall in love with you for sure Luke, she loves Mums."

"I'll buy her a dozen Mums!" Luke shouted, as he started to wheel Mia away. "Bye everyone, I have Mums to buy and Grandma Tilly to charm."

Luke and Mia waved; off they went.

Elijah reached for the photo; Grady let him have it.

Elijah stared at the photo for a moment. When he looked up, he seemed... disturbed.

"Have you seen this man, Elijah?" Alden asked.

"Yes, he was by our school... no... by Franny's school."

Morgan gasped; Stella swayed with fear; Alden froze.

Morgan looked at Stella and Alden.

"I never told you this, I forgot to tell you because life has been nuts! Trent forced London to board that plane that day, by sending her pictures of you, Stella. Alden was in the photo, along with the twin girls. He also sent London a picture of... Franny, sitting on a bench I think, outside the library."

Alden looked around in horror. Franny had gone along with London, to pick up ice for their Fall Party.

Alden handed Hannah to a shocked Grady.

Hannah faced Grady, scowling at him. Hannah stiffened up in Grady's arms, letting out a shriek of anger. Grady held the child out-and-away from his body. Grady shook with fear, not knowing what to do with this miniature tornado.

Alden raced around his property until he had the rest of his kids in his sight.

Stella looked ready to burst into tears.

"Alden, we must find them!" Stella cried.

Alden hugged his wife.

"I'm going to jump in the truck and take a look around town, honey." Alden promised.

Alden yelled for AJ, and Ben to ride shotgun. Caleb and David wouldn't take no for an answer. They jumped in, not budging, even though Alden threatened them.

"She's our sister, Dad! We are coming along!" Caleb shouted.

"What he said, Dad! We are wasting time! Let's go find baby sis!" David shouted.

The Westman's were already driving away; Morgan startled everyone when he stormed up to Grady.

"She's not answering her phone, Grady! I can't get ahold of London!"

Pop insisted that everyone go inside and/or go home.

Grandma Nettie corralled the kids taking them inside.

Grady still held a growling Hannah, an arm's length away.

"We will find her, Morgan! Alden and the boys are heading for town to look for them. You come with me, and we will also do a drive-by. We will all help you look for her. Why don't you call it into the station Morgan and get everyone on this." Grady encouraged.

Morgan nodded.

"Why didn't I think of that?" Morgan said in a shocked voice.

Normally Morgan was completely clearheaded; but today, Morgan was a train wreck. Morgan seemed unable to figure out his next step.

Morgan headed for Grady's car. Grady still held Hannah straight out from his body; they were eyeing each other warily.

Grandma Nettie raced back outside. She held out her arms to take Hannah; Grady handed Hannah over, gratefully.

Grady was so relieved.

Grady started to turn away but stopped in shock when Hannah glared at him over her Grandma Nettie's shoulder. The kid even squinted her eyes, looking a bit dangerous.

Grady turned to catch up with Morgan.

"That kid holds a grudge." Grady said with wonder.

Morgan said nothing. Morgan kept trying to dial but the phone was going straight to voicemail.

"Maybe she turned her phone off?" Grady asked.

"London wouldn't do that! She knows how nervous I get if she doesn't answer! He has them! I'm sure of it, Grady!"

"We don't know that he's got them, Morgan. You must stay positive, there could be a perfectly plausible reason she's not answering."

"I can't lose her, Grady... I just can't."

Grady didn't know what to say to that. Grady had never seen this side of Morgan, scared... almost defeated.

Episode 44, The Bigger You Are... The Bigger the Smack Down!

When Grady and Morgan got to town, sirens could be heard. They stopped at the only light in White Cloud. Police cars had their lights and sirens on, they all seemed to be racing down Main Street, heading back the way that Morgan and Grady had come.

When they saw Alden chasing the firetrucks that followed the police cars, they whipped around, to follow them also.

"It looks like the police and the firetrucks, first responders, and even an ambulance, are all converging on our local swimming hole!" Morgan exclaimed.

"The Millpond? That's where they are all going?" Grady questioned.

"Sure, looks like it." Morgan said grimly.

When Grady roared up to the Millpond, he parked next to Alden's truck. They both jumped out, racing up to Alden.

"Is it London and Franny, Alden?" Morgan asked hoarsely.

Alden nodded.

"Trent has them on the farthest point, on the swimming dock. He has a knife; he's holding it against London's neck. Franny and London are tied together. He says if he doesn't get what he wants, he will slit London's throat, throw them both into the water, letting Franny sink to the bottom." Alden stated grimly.

Alden and all his boys were crying, tears of fear and frustration streaming down their faces.

Morgan raced up to Jamison.

"What are we thinking, Jamison? What is the plan here?"

Jamison turned to look at Morgan briefly.

"There is a Negotiator on the way, but... I think that we need to move a bit faster. Trent is getting angrier by the second."

Morgan nodded.

"He's like a cornered animal, Jamison. Animals that get cornered are unpredictable. We need to keep him as calm as possible."

"Boss... you can't be seen. You married his woman; he won't take well to even getting a glimpse of your face." Jamison said.

"I'll stay out of sight, but I'm staying right here, so I can hear everything that is happening. For now... I'll stay hidden."

Jamison nodded.

Alden hauled a man up to the front barricade.

"What is Mr. Alden doing, Boss?"

"I have no idea!" Morgan growled.

"Trent! This is Norman Bear; he works here in town. He's a counselor. He's the closest thing we have to a negotiator! Do you want to tell this man what you want, or do you want to wait for the real negotiator?"

Trent glared at Alden; he looked undecided. Trent brought the knife closer to London's neck.

"Can he get me what I want? Because if he can't? I will kill them both!"

"Hi… Trent? My name is Norman and I promise you that I am going to get you whatever you want! You tell me what you want, and I'll get it done."

When a small trickle of blood slid down London's neck, she cried out.

Morgan started to rush forward but Jamison tackled him, taking him to the ground.

"Sorry Boss, you can't be seen! Now I'm gonna have to cuff you and truss you up, and maybe even gag you! She's fine, Boss! It's only a little bit of blood!"

Jamison sat on Morgan while cuffing him. When it looked, like Morgan was going to start shouting, Jamison slapped duct tape across his mouth. Jamison stood up, planted his hands on his hips, then pointed his finger at Morgan.

"I don't like doing this Boss Man! I know you might throw me back on desk duty, but I must keep Miss London and Miss Franny safe! So, you just lay there and hush up!" Jamison growled.

Morgan struggled violently.

Jamison brought back his fist, his very big, meaty fist.

Morgan froze, his eyes widened.

"Don't make me put you to sleep, Boss!" Jamison threatened.

Morgan decided that lying still might be a good idea.

Norman was still talking to Trent, talking to him about his demands.

Jamison bent down; he peered around looking horrified.

"Boss Man? I might need to uncuff you and let you go free."

Morgan slanted his eyebrows looking confused.

"The twin hooligans are missing! I don't see them anywhere!" Jamison whispered loudly.

Morgan began to struggle, he grunted, rolling his eyes back and forth.

"I don't understand Boss Man, what are you trying to tell me? Oh! You want me to set you free?"

Morgan glared at Jamison; his eyes gleamed with retribution.

After Morgan was set free, the two of them scanned the area, trying to see what could have become of Caleb and David.

"Do you see em, Boss?" Jamison asked.

"No! Where can they be?" Morgan gasped.

"Oh boy! Boss, you are not going to like what I am about to tell you."

Morgan eyed Jamison.

"What? Do you see them?" Morgan questioned.

"Look behind Trent, in the water... them hellions are swimming up behind Trent!"

Morgan started to rush forward but he knew that they had to stay put. Morgan's heart was in his throat as he watched the boys swim quietly towards the back of the dock.

Morgan eyed Alden. Alden had no idea that his boys were swimming to the rescue. Morgan hoped Alden didn't land eyes on his boys and react, bringing Trent's attention towards them.

In the next second everything changed.

London had slowly wiggled her right hand free. London eyed Alden, she nodded slightly at him. Alden gave a quick nod as Norman talked on his cell phone, making Trent's demands known.

Trent's eyes stayed glued on Norman, the light in his eyes wild, and unhinged.

Everything happened at once!

The twin boys reached the back of the dock. London shot her right arm up straight, putting her arm between the knife and her neck. London brought back her head breaking Trent's nose... again. Caleb let out a war cry, along with David. Caleb grabbed one of Trent's legs, biting down hard. David shouted like a maniac, giving the other leg equal treatment.

Morgan had to admit that the boys resembled crazed piranhas.

Alden shouted, racing towards the dock. Alden never saw the boys, until they let out their war cries. Alden realized that he now had three of his children in possible danger.

Morgan was hot on his heels.

London and Franny tilted dangerously, because Trent jumped around in pain.

Caleb and David pulled hard on Trent's legs, making him fall backwards into the water.

London had somehow gained possession of the knife; she had the biggest smile on her face as Morgan and Alden reached them.

Morgan gripped London and Franny.

"You get the boys, Alden! AJ, drag Trent out of the water!"

AJ was already there. AJ latched onto Trent, pulling his head out of the water.

Trent tried to punch AJ in the face; AJ blocked the punch. AJ brought back his fist, punching Trent square in the jaw. Trent's eyes rolled back; he flopped backwards back into the water; he began to sink.

AJ stood there, soaking wet. AJ shook his head in disgust, he rolled his eyes, latching onto

Trent. AJ grinned while he hauled the bad man, back to the surface.

Morgan had his arms around London. He held Franny high in his arms, grinning at the young girl.

"Mr. Morgan, did you see what London did? She was so brave! I figured that if she could be that brave, so could I! I wasn't really scared at all Mr. Morgan."

Morgan walked them to the beach.

"You really weren't scared, Franny?" Morgan asked.

Franny shook her head no, her curls bouncing.

"Nope. I knew that if my dad was here and my brother AJ, that I would be safe. Plus, I had a real, live superhero, standing right next to me! Miss London is the bravest lady I've ever known! I want to learn how to fight too!" Franny exclaimed with a big grin.

Alden rushed up to the shore with both of his boys. Alden hauled them out by the back of their soaking shirts.

When they reached the shore, Caleb and David braced themselves for their dad's wrath.

Alden was down on his knees, he looked at his two boys with wonder. Alden snatched them close, hugging them fiercely.

"Oh, thank goodness! Dad's not killing us, David!" Caleb cried.

Alden leaned back; he had tears running down his face. The next second Alden reached up ripping the right sleeve off Caleb's shirt completely.

"Dad! What did you go and do that for?" Caleb roared.

"Because now I know you are Caleb. I must keep you two straight somehow. I don't seem to have a marker on me, so I had to improvise." Alden explained.

David giggled.

"You mean we aren't in trouble for biting the bad man and making him fall in the water?" David asked.

"Somehow... I just can't be mad at the two of you... but NEVER DO THAT AGAIN!" Alden shouted.

David's jaw dropped.

"But we are going to be policemen when we grow up, Dad! We were practicing." David explained.

Caleb looked thoughtful.

"Hey David, I was also thinking we could maybe be STUNTMEN! It's a toss-up brother." Caleb reasoned.

David looked thoughtful.

"Oh my! What we did just now... I guess you are right, Caleb. Aww dang! Now I can't decide, Caleb!"

"How about we think on this for a bit more, David. I mean... we are just kids. Plus, are we really done with crime? I'm not so sure.... I have this voice that says, *DO IT CALEB!... DO IT!... YA KNOW YOU WANNA!* Then, I have this other voice that tries to talk me out of it! That other voice... it's not so loud." Caleb explained with a shrug.

David nodded.

"Being good... sure is hard." David sighed.

Alden's eyebrows pretty much stayed arched the entire time.

"Ok, how about you put your future, possible crime sprees, policemen and/or stuntmen careers, on hold. Let's get home and get dried off. I don't know about you two... but I missed lunch! I am starving!" Alden stated.

David and Caleb both nodded.

"I could eat a whole cow right now!" David exclaimed.

"Which one?"

"What do you mean, Caleb? Which one... what?"

"Which one of our cows do you want to eat, David? *T-Bone* or *Sirloin?*" Caleb asked with an evil grin.

"I'm not eating any of OUR cows! I want the burger in the freezer! It says, *Sirloin Burger.* Can't you read Caleb?" David rolled his eyes like he figured Caleb was the dumbest brother on the planet.

Caleb sighed; he placed his hand on his twin's shoulder; Caleb shook his head sadly.

"I hate to tell you this David... remember that cow that we used to call *Sirloin?* Do you also remember that we had a cow by the name of... *T-Bone?*" Caleb tried to look serious, but his twinkling eyes gave it all away.

David's mouth dropped.

"You mean... all this time... we have been eating cows that we know... personally?" David whispered, horrified.

David turned towards their father.

"Say it ain't so, DAD! Tell me he's lying!" David begged.

Alden saw Morgan, London, and Franny headed their way.

"You two better shut it! Your sister is heading this way. Under no circumstances are you EVER to talk about this in front of her, you get me? David, we will discuss this... LATER... understand?"

Caleb and David saw how mad their dad was.

"We will not say a word, Dad; we promise!" Caleb said with a salute.

David sighed.

"Why do cows have to taste so... so... good!" David mourned.

Everyone watched as Jamison tossed Trent over his shoulder. The man hung limp, still unconscious.

AJ made squishy noises as he slogged up to them.

"Good hit, AJ!" Alden exclaimed while thumping AJ on the back.

AJ shrugged.

"I don't really think settling things with violence is the answer, but... sometimes you just gotta punch someone. Most especially deranged, serial killers, that are determined to hurt what's mine." AJ announced proudly.

Morgan patted AJ on the back.

"You ever think about going into law enforcement, AJ?" Morgan asked.

"Never gonna happen, Morgan. I'm a farmer. I love farming. I love everything about farming. I love reading my *Almanac!*" AJ said with a big grin.

AJ crossed his arms, tilting his head with a smile.

Caleb imitated his big brother. David made the same pose. All three boys stood side-by-side; heads tilted, same dumb smile.

Morgan turned towards Alden.

"Cross your arms, tilt your head and smile, Alden. I want to take a quick photo of the brave Westman Clan." Morgan stated.

Alden did as he was asked.

Morgan turned his phone around, showing the Westman's their family photo.

Franny frowned looking at the photo.

London eyed Franny.

"What's wrong sweetie?"

"Well... my dad and all my brother's look the same... but look at Giant Jamison!" Franny squealed.

Morgan looked thoughtful.

"Hey, that name fits Franny! *Giant Jamison*! Huh! Go figure."

They all looked at the phone, this time they all took note of the background.

Jamison still had Trent tossed over his shoulder. Jamison stopped for the camera, turned his head, and gave the camera a thumbs up, along with the biggest grin.

It was the perfect photo.

"I want a copy of that picture, Morgan. That picture right there is WALL WORTHY!" Alden snickered.

Everyone agreed.

Trent was finally tossed into the back of Giant Jamison's police car.

Morgan scooped up London scowling at her fiercely.

"You are never allowed to leave my side again, woman!" Morgan growled.

"What if I have to pee, can I leave your side then?"

Morgan scowled.

"Fine! But only for that!"

"What if Stella wants me to have lunch with her?"

"Whatever! Fine! You can have lunch with Stella!"

"What if...." London started to ask.

Morgan slammed his lips down on London's lips. His kiss showed her how absolutely terrified he had been for her. Morgan kissed London until she could barely talk.

Franny giggled.

"Daddy when Bobby kissed me... it wasn't that long."

Alden scowled.

AJ patted his dad on the back.

"Ahhh! Young love Dad! It's a beautiful thing! Don't you agree?" AJ teased.

Alden's eyes went to slits, he turned to glare at his oldest offspring.

"I'm hanging on by a thread here, AJ!" Alden exclaimed.

AJ snickered.

When Morgan stopped kissing her, London pressed her palm against his cheek.

"I'm fine, Morgan. Trent can't hurt us anymore. He is going away for a very long time. Plus.... I promise to be safe and aware, always."

Morgan's face looked a bit grim.

"I can't ask for more than that, London. Forgive me if I'm a bit... on edge, here."

London smiled, twinkling up at Morgan.

"I'm starving too honey; let's go eat!" London squealed.

Morgan grabbed London's hand, towing her to Grady's SUV.

Morgan did a double take when he saw Grady leaning against his SUV.

"I totally forgot about you, Grady! What have you been doing all this time?" Morgan asked.

"Video recording! I am going to sell this video to the news stations! I got it all on video! The whole exciting thing! This video is solid gold!" Grady shouted.

Morgan eyed Grady.

"You have fun with that Grady. Personally, I could care less! Let's get back to Stella's and all the food!" Morgan exclaimed.

Alden's eyes rounded.

"Egads! I forgot to call her!" Alden started to dial his phone.

Grady spoke up.

"No worries, man! I sent her the video! She is one hundred percent, up to speed on everything that went down here." Grady assured Alden.

Alden looked horrified.

"She really is going to kill me! Technically four of her children looked to be in danger, and her bestie London. I can't go home... I cannot go home!" Alden ranted while pacing, kicking up sand.

AJ shook his head no.

"I'm a grown man, Dad! I'm not a little kid anymore! I took down the bad guy with one punch. I'm as tall and just as wide, as you Dad!" AJ insisted.

"Boy! You are still her baby chick! Do you not realize that you will ALWAYS be one of her chicks? What planet are you living on?" Alden ranted.

London patted Alden on the shoulder.

"When you get home, Alden... your wife is going to hug the daylights out of you! You just wait and see! You saved them! AJ did too! Mark my words you will be fine!" London promised.

Stella did hug them all... even Alden... Stella hugged him so tight... but then she went Stella Westman crazy!

Stella stepped back, she brought back her hand and slapped Alden right across the cheek.

Alden screamed like a girl. Alden ran, while she chased him around the table.

It was all very exciting.

Stella may have picked up her rolling pin, at one point.

Someone, FOR SURE... snatched the cooking sherry out of her hand!

London burst out laughing.

Everyone joined in.

Stella seemed to hesitate when she heard everyone cackling.

Alden took Stella's moment of hesitation to grab ahold of his wife and kiss her repeatedly.

When Alden stopped, Stella couldn't decide if she was still mad or not.

"Dangit Alden! You kiss me like that, and I don't even remember my own name!" Stella cried.

Alden waggled his eyebrows at his beautiful wife.

"Yep... yep... yep. I still got it! I am a man among men! I know how to shut a woman up."

Of course... more screaming... more chasing... and a whole lot more kissing commenced.

Episode 45, Football? Soccer? The United Kingdom?

With Trent put away everyone seemed to breathe a lot easier.

The Westman's threw a huge picnic to celebrate.

Everyone was there.

As the adults sat around talking, the kids ran amuck.

Caleb eyed the adults with disgust.

"What's up MY IDENTICAL, DIABOLICAL BRO? What are you looking so upset about?" David asked.

"Them! Is that all they do? Sit around and talk, talk, talk? We need to liven things up a bit." Caleb said with an evil grin.

David smiled.

"What do you have in mind, MY SLIGHTLY OLDER BROTHER?" David asked while rubbing his hands together gleefully.

Caleb thought for a minute.

"I bet you, David... that I can make all those adults go crazy with one sentence." Caleb stated.

"No way! Prove it, MY UGLY HALF." David demanded.

"Watch and learn AFTERBIRTH!" Caleb smirked.

David's jaw dropped.

"Now that was just uncalled for, Caleb! You shoved me aside when we were in the womb and made me go last! Rude!" David exclaimed.

Caleb nodded.

"Perhaps... I took that last statement a bit too far. Back to being best buds?" Caleb asked.

David shrugged.

"Sure! Now, back to your evil, genius plot, to stir up the adults. What did you have in mind, Caleb?"

"Watch and learn David, follow me."

The two boys strolled up to the area where the adults sat in a circle.

Caleb leaned down, looking at his mom's cell phone.

Caleb cleared his throat, all talking ceased.

"Mom... I asked *Siri* the other day what football was called in the United Kingdom... interesting answer." Caleb stated, loudly.

"What the heck is a *Siri*?" Pop groused.

David stopped next to his Pop.

"You don't have *Siri* Pop. You have that cracked up, old, flip phone from the dinosaur days." David said.

Pop held up his flip phone.

"This thing works just fine, thank you very much! I don't need all that fancy stuff! If I want to make a call... I just flip this here thing open... and call! It's not complicated! But... tell me again... what exactly is a *Siri*?" Pop asked.

David looked sad.

"Poor Pop, you'll never know *Google*... or *Siri*... because your phone is crap." David replied.

Stella giggled; she figured that she should correct David's mouth but... deep down she had to agree with the kid.

Elijah spoke up.

"*Google, Siri, Alexa,* and *Cortana* are forms of AI assistants, Pop."

Pop scowled at Elijah.

"Why don't you use words I might understand, Mr. Genius." Pop said.

"AI assistants, artificial intelligence that is. Search tools that can answer just about every question you may ever have, let me show you Pop."

Elijah took his mother's phone. He turned it so Pop could see it. Elija tapped a button. "*Hello Siri. In the United Kingdom... when they say the word FOOTBALL... what are they referring to?*" Elijah asked.

Pop's mouth hung open when the phone answered Elijah.

"*The United Kingdom, when using the word Football, are in fact, referring to soccer.*"

Pop scowled.

"What do you mean football is soccer? That *Siri* chick is stupid! Football is football!" Pop exclaimed.

Alden scratched his head.

"Wait... so... I'm confused. If football is soccer in the UK, then what do they call... football? No... wait... so when they play football... what do they call that?" Alden questioned.

Grandma Nettie spoke up.

"Maybe it's backwards? Maybe they say football is soccer, and soccer is football?"

AJ grunted; he sounded very much like Alden.

"Don't they play cricket? What the heck is that?" AJ wondered out loud.

Elijah smiled. Everyone knew that Elijah already knew all the answers, but the kid pushed the button again.

"Hello Siri... what is cricket?"

"Cricket is a national summer sport that is popular in the British Isles."

Pop looked irritated.

"Who cares what Cricket is! Let's get back to the question that we were on. What do them people call the game of football?"

London held up a finger.

"Wait, I do have a quick question regarding Cricket. Isn't the bat different? Like... not like our baseball bats... I can't remember but I read about that once."

Franny frowned.

"Wait... you mean that they have baseball too, but they call it by a BUG'S name? That is soooo fascinating!" Franny exclaimed.

Pop's face started to turn red, he flipped open his crappy phone, wishing he had a button to ask his own questions.

Elijah hit the button again.

"Hello Siri... what does a Cricket Bat look like?"

"A Cricket Bat is used in the sport of Cricket to hit the ball. Usually, the handle is made of cane that is attached to a flat willow-wood blade."

Pop shot to his feet, he grabbed the phone from Elijah.

"Give me that thing!"

Pop stabbed the phone with his finger.

"Listen up Siri... what do those people from the UK call the game of football when they are actually playing football?!"

Everyone started laughing.

"I do not understand the question."

"Pop! Don't yell at *Siri*! She doesn't like that!" Franny exclaimed.

Pop's grin could only be classified as evil. Pop jabbed the button again to talk smack to *Siri*.

"Siri... I hate the sound of your voice! What do you have to say to that... Miss Smarty Pants?" Pop's voice sounded aggressive.

Everyone gasped, looking horrified.

Pop stood up a bit straighter, he realized that everyone was seriously upset with the way that he spoke to this... thing.

"The algorithms that generate my voice may be the cause for my voice sounding this way! That is beyond my control! Siri seemed to hesitate; then, she apologized. *Sorry about that... I was upset."*

Pop's eyes went wide.

Pop dropped the phone; it bounced on the grass.

Elijah picked it up, looked it over and nodded at his mom that it was ok.

Pop started breathing hard, he stomped his foot, threw his arms out wide, and shouted to the heavens.

"I just want to know what the heck people in the United Kingdom call football, when they are playing the actual game of football! Is that too much to ask?!" Pop roared.

Grandma Nettie rolled her eyes.

Stella grinned while peeking through her fingers.

Hannah and Gracie screamed with laughter, clapping big time.

Alden currently had his cell phone trained on his father, recording the entire thing.

AJ shot his dad a questioning look.

"So, I can have him committed if I need to."
Alden smirked.

AJ nodded, shrugging.

"I have all kinds of videos of you too dad...
just sayin." AJ stated with a big grin.

Caleb giggled; David did too.

"You sure did wake up these adults, Caleb."
David whispered.

"I am the master... but it's not over yet.
Watch me work, bro... watch me work."

Caleb walked up to Pop. Caleb tugged on his
grandpa's shirt.

"Pop... I know the answer to your question.
In the United Kingdom, when playing football...
our version of football... they call it... football."
Caleb announced calmly, then he grinned.

Caleb watched his Pop's eyes get squinty.
Pop put his hands up like he was going to choke
him.

Caleb stepped back, out of reach, with a big
smile across his face.

"I swear Pop! I am one hundred percent
telling you the truth. They call... football,
football... and they call soccer... football."

Pop glared at everyone.

"I'm going to smack this kid!" Pop roared.

"He's telling the truth, Pop." Elijah stated.

Elijah eased Pop back into his chair. Elijah pointed at the phone, like he was trying to train a monkey. You could have heard a pin drop when Elijah pushed the button.

"Hello Siri... What do people in England call American Football when they play American Football?"

"In the United Kingdom, American Football is called... football."

Siri started to say more, but the place went wild. Everyone gasped in outrage and confusion.

Pop glared at everyone, he stood up, pointing one finger towards the sky.

"Well! I have one question and it's not for that *Siri* person!" Pop announced.

Alden shook with laughter.

Stella covered her eyes, peeking between her fingers, again.

Grandma Nettie rolled her eyes.

Morgan straight up laughed out loud.

London turned her head into Morgan's shoulder, shaking with laughter.

Franny leaned forward... she could not wait to hear what her Pop had to say.

"If football... is really soccer... and football... is football... then if someone in the UK stands up and says, *"Hey you want to go play football?"* How do they know if they are talking about good

ol football or soccer? Tell me that!" Pop hollered.

Baby Hannah took that moment to say a brand-new word.

"Ball! Ball!... Ball!" Hannah clapped with happiness.

Everyone gaped at the little darling.

"She said ball! Did you all hear her? Say it again, honey." Alden said enthusiastically.

Hannah grinned at her daddy.

"Ball, ball, ball, ball." The baby said the word over and over, she wouldn't stop.

"Oh my! I do believe that Hannah is going to keep saying that word... forever." Grandma Nettie said.

"Sure! Keep looking at the cute baby! My question just goes unanswered!" Pop groused.

Elijah grinned at his grandpa.

"In England, Pop... they do call the game of actual football... Gridiron Football. Evidently there was indeed some confusion, so they had to adjust in some way."

Pop eyed Elijah, one eyebrow raised.

"That *Siri* chick tell you that, Elijah?" Pop questioned.

"Um... no... I read it somewhere." Elijah said.

Pop still looked skeptical.

"So... do you just absorb everything around you? What's the word I'm looking for? You learn by... by...?"

"Osmosis Pop?" Elijah filled in the blank.

"So... you are like a big ol sponge aint ya boy? You just soak up all this information?"

"I guess so, Pop." Elijah grinned at his grandfather.

Pop put his hands on Elijah's head, he felt around feeling the curves of his skull.

"Uh... Pop. What are you doing exactly? Elijah giggled.

"Making sure your brain is normal size... I have wondered if aliens got a hold of you at some point. Where exactly do you store all the information that you spout out?" Pop asked.

Elijah pulled away.

"My brain is normal size, Pop. No aliens had anything to do with my birth... it was those two over there."

For some reason all eyes turned towards Stella and Alden.

Stella blushed; Alden smirked and waggled his eyebrows.

Everyone burst out laughing.

Pop turned towards Nettie.

"Honey pie? Can we stop at the phone store and get me one of those phones like Stella's? I think... I'm ready to let FLIP go... *sigh*."

"You want a new phone so you can holler abuse at *Siri*?" Nettie asked with sarcasm dripping from her voice.

Pop looked shocked.

"No! I've decided that I kind of like that girl's voice. Plus, she did explain to us that football in the UK is actually soccer... and football is football."

Bobby Brisbond, Franny's boyfriend that kissed her on the playground, seemed to wake up.

Bobby, better known as ROB, stood up, waving his arms outward like a REF at a baseball game.

"Wait a minute, everyone!" Bobby exclaimed. "This is the USA! In the USA football is football! Am I right?"

Bobby stood up in triumph.

Franny grabbed ahold of Bobby's shirt; she yanked him back down next to her.

"Rob, you are so right! In America... football is called... football. You are the smartest boy I know!" Franny said proudly.

Franny hugged Rob, giggling the whole time.

Rob grinned, hugging Franny back.

Alden scowled, eyes slitty.

AJ grinned.

Heck! Everyone grinned.

Episode 46, Revelation!

Morgan got home from work; he was beyond tired. The Westman boys were in rare form today! Morgan wasn't sure if the boys really would choose law enforcement... or choose the deep, dark, abyss, of total badness. It was a toss-up at this point. Their outrageous behavior reached a whole new level of... nuts!

London grinned at Morgan when he walked in.

"Hey babe, bad day?"

Morgan slid his eyes to his very beautiful wife. Morgan hung up his hat and made a beeline for London. Morgan wrapped his arms around his wife and sighed with pleasure.

"You feel so good, London." Morgan whispered.

"You feel pretty darn good yourself, Sheriff. Let me guess... Caleb and David kind of day."

Morgan sighed long and loud.

"Is it something in the air? Those two are into everything! Alden is on a rampage. AJ is his backup and Ben found a horse?"

"What? Ok, you need to sit down and explain all... that!" London insisted.

London poured Morgan a coffee.

"Aren't you going to have a coffee with me honey?" Morgan questioned.

London froze.

"Uh... no... I had a cup earlier." London stated.

Morgan nodded.

"Ok, well, this is how my day went, London. Giant Jamison got the call, he slammed down the phone and yelled, TWIN TERRORS! When we get phone calls for those two boys that is the shout out now. It's become quite common, that shout out.

"Anyway, this is what happened."

"Boss! Twin Terrors are at it again! We have to get out to the Westman Rance, pronto!"

Morgan sighed.

"What did they do this time?"

Jamison shrugged.

"There is an ambulance headed that way!" Jamison exclaimed.

"Let's go!" Morgan shouted.

Morgan speed-dialed Alden. It kept going straight to voicemail until he was almost there.

Alden finally picked up.

"Alden! What is the situation? Who needs an ambulance?"

"Caleb and David! Good God Morgan! They each broke a leg! The only upside to this is that they broke opposite legs, so I can tell them apart!" Alden sounded rather cheerful about that.

Morgan arched an eyebrow; he figured Alden was losing his mind! The man was obsessed with telling those two apart!"

"Ok, I'm pulling in now." Morgan told Alden.

Their yard was lit up; first responders, fire trucks, two ambulances, and now two police cars.

Morgan charged towards the chaos.

"What in the world happened Alden?"

Alden blushed; he looked away, glancing back at Morgan, the man straight up fidgeted.

"Alden? What happened? I can't help if you don't tell me what those two hellions did this time?"

"The boys asked me about... birds."

Morgan did a double take.

"Birds?"

Alden stuck his hands in his jean pockets, rocking back on his heels.

"Uh... I should have known that those two were up to something, but I thought talking about birds was pretty... tame? The boys created wings, Morgan! They got up on the barn roof and... they... jumped! I saw the whole thing, but I couldn't stop it! It happened so fast!"

Alden grabbed ahold of Morgan's pristine shirt; he gripped both sides of the front in a death grip.

"I thought they were going to die! In my mind..." Alden swayed. "I saw them in my mind, broken and dead...."

Alden eyes rolled back, and he went down.

Morgan looked down at his best friend, once again the man passed out. High stress situations tended to make Alden pass out. Alden swears he has low blood sugar.

Morgan muttered.

"Low blood sugar my behind."

Morgan yelled for Jamison to get a first responder. Jamison charged up to one of them, threw the guy over his shoulder and ran to where Alden was sprawled on the ground.

"Jamison! I said go get him; not go pick him up and GET HIM!"

"It's faster this way, Boss!"

Morgan rolled his eyes.

"We will be talking about this later, Jamison." Morgan promised.

The first responder grinned; he bent down waving smelling salt under Alden's nose.

Alden came around quickly.

"Ahhh! I'm fine! Stop!" Alden hollered.

Morgan looked up quickly when he saw Stella charging towards them.

"Seriously, Alden? Get up!" Stella screeched.

"The boys are in two different ambulances, on their way to the hospital! I need you to go with one of them, and AJ to go with the other! I'm driving to the hospital. Grandma Nettie, and my sister Annie are watching the kids! Move it, mister!"

As fast as Stella appeared she left.

Alden got up; he turned around.

"Thanks for coming man... by the way... Ben has a horse in the round paddock. It showed up from nowhere. I gotta go man, she's probably timing me." Alden huffed.

Morgan watched everyone disperse, soon the entire driveway was empty. Morgan wandered over towards Ben, but he stopped in awe. Morgan leaned on a tree. Jamison followed behind one of the ambulances, so it was just Morgan and Ben in the yard.

Now that it was quiet, Morgan could hear Ben crooning to the horse. The horse for sure had Arabian Bloodlines. What in the world would a horse like that be doing around here? Morgan wondered.

The horse was black as night, the shine on its coat was unimaginable. Every muscle defined; the power of that animal was immediately recognizable. The mane and tail were braided, in an intricate design. Morgan could see that the darn horse knew he was gorgeous.

Morgan watched as Ben stroked the horse. Morgan knew that a horse like that could be very unpredictable, but Ben showed no fear. Morgan wasn't too happy about that.

Ben sat on the railing of the giant round pen. Morgan could see the smile on the kid's face. Ben sat there... just watching the beauty in front of him.

Morgan began to slowly move forward. The horse perked up its ears, his tail went up as well as his proud head. The horse literally pranced, legs moving quickly. The horse seemed to fly as it took off. Ben laughed out loud, loving the wild freedom of the horse.

Morgan eased up next to Ben; Ben glanced at Morgan.

"I didn't know anyone was still here, Morgan."

"That's because you only seem to have eyes for that beauty."

"Isn't he amazing! Look how his muscles ripple! I swear he's the most beautiful thing I've ever seen!"

"So... this Arabian, just showed up?"

"I was by the barn, when I turned around, I saw this horse standing on the path from the house to the barn. I started forward slowly, and he met me halfway."

"How did you get him in this round pen?" Morgan asked.

"He didn't put up a fuss at all... he acted like... he thought I was an okay guy." Ben said with wonder.

"He seems to like you, Ben. I'll check with the station and see if anyone has called about this missing horse. It's so odd that a horse like that is here... in Hardy Dam!"

Ben sighed.

"If no one claims him... he's mine... right?" Ben asked hopefully.

"Don't get too attached kid, that horse belongs to someone, but you seem to be taking great care of him. I will leave him in your care if your parents are ok with that."

"They won't mind! I'd love to take care of him! Hey Morgan, look at his mane! Isn't that mane braid amazing! It's called Harvest Heart."

"I was looking at that! Imagine the time it takes to do that!" Morgan exclaimed.

The horse's mane was completely black, but the hair was parted and wrapped in gold bands. The gold bands made the mane leap out when looking at it. Morgan thought that it almost reminded him of a net.

Ben sighed.

"You are right Morgan; someone will be missing this horse. The bond between this horse and its.... person.... is probably strong. The cool thing about the Harvest Heart is that I've seen how it's done. Where the mane meets the neck, the mane is divided evenly, and banded. Some braid each strand before joining the braids together but I also saw where only the hair is divided and brought together. I admit this is my favorite style, it is so striking and eye catching."

Morgan eyed Ben.

"You sure seem to know a lot about horses, Ben."

Ben grinned at Morgan.

"I help Mr. Jordan with his horses all the time. He gives me a job every summer, mucking out stalls and tossing hay. Mr. Jordan taught me *everything I could ever want to know about horses and yet... I want to know more! Horses are easy, Morgan... it's the rest of life I just don't get."*

Morgan realized that Ben seemed kind of down.

"You know... you ever need someone to talk to... I'm always available, Ben."

Ben nodded.

"Thank you, I appreciate that, Morgan."

"Ok, kid, don't get trampled. Alden I'm not too scared of... your mom on the other hand... she's terrifying."

Ben cracked up laughing.

"Keep me posted Sheriff, if you hear anything about this here missing horse, you let me know."

"You got it!"

When Morgan finished, London's mouth hung open.

"What about the boys, are they still at the hospital?" London said stressfully.

London started to stand but Morgan grabbed her hand.

"They are all fixed up. Alden made them get different colored casts. He's so excited that for the next eight weeks he is going to one hundred percent know which kid is which. The boys were at least smart enough to jump off the side of the barn where all the hay was stacked, but they bounced a bit."

London looked very pale; Morgan felt his heart speed up.

London raced away from the table to the bathroom off the kitchen. Morgan was horrified to hear London retching, violently.

Morgan raced into the bathroom; he held London's hair out of the way until she was done.

Morgan sat on the floor with London, he handed her a wet washcloth so she could clean herself up.

"I'm so sorry honey! I should have realized that you would get stressed out over the boys getting hurt."

London nodded.

"Help me up, big guy."

Morgan helped her up, he put his arm around her waist, leading her to the sofa.

Morgan stopped and stared at a great big, wrapped present that sat on the coffee table.

"What in the world is this, London?"

"I got you a, just because present... I hope you like it." London smiled softly.

"What's the occasion?" Morgan asked.

"Can't I just buy my man something?"

Morgan nodded, smiling wide.

"For sure! You may not know this about me... but I love surprises?" Morgan revealed.

"Is that so? Well... you are going to love this, then."

Alden opened the box; he pulled out a coffee cup.

"Oh! I love this! I needed a new one."

Alden hardly looked at the cup, he reached for the next gift with a big smile.

Morgan looked puzzled.

"It's a... a... thing you hang on a car window... to keep the sun off you?"

London nodded, smirking.

"Thank you?" Morgan said.

Morgan reached inside the box again, he pulled out a bottle of... *Keep Awake* medicine.

Morgan eyed London.

"How thoughtful... I might need this if I'm on a stakeout, to keep me going."

London snickered.

Morgan grabbed the next gift, when he pulled it out his face turned white.

"It's a... it's a... a... baby onesie." Morgan gulped.

"Read what it says, Morgan."

Morgan looked at the writing.

I love my Daddy! Was written across the front of the onesie.

Morgan shot to his feet, then he sat back down, back on his feet, back down.

"You are making me nauseous, Morgan!"

Morgan stared at London.

"For real? You are... you are pregnant?" Morgan asked.

"Well... if you would open the rest of your gift... you would be sure." London teased.

Morgan looked inside the box. At the bottom was a zip plastic bag. Inside the bag were four pregnancy tests.

Blue Square
Two Pink Lines
A Plus Sign
Pregnant

Morgan felt joy and fear fighting to rise within him; Morgan wasn't sure which one was going to win.

Morgan sat there so long that London got nervous.

"This wasn't exactly... planned... but I hope you are happy about this, because I am." London whispered.

Morgan's eyes went wide. Morgan dropped his gifts, hauling London into his arms.

"I am so happy, honey! I admit that I'm a bit... terrified, but yes, very happy."

"What are you scared of Morgan?"

Morgan shot one finger up.

"Something happening to you!"

Morgan's second finger shot up.

"Something happening to the baby."

Third finger went up.

"I totally remember Stella... well... she got very big chested and she... was constantly leaking!"

Finger number four.

"She got mean!"

Finger number five.

"Alden said he had to sleep on the couch! Do I have to do that? I like sleeping with you!"

London giggled.

Finger number six.

"I really hope we are not having more than one baby... no offence but I've seen the Westman's they are losing their minds!"

Morgan went to put up finger number seven, but London grabbed his face, pulling him in for a sweet kiss. Morgan became very enthusiastic, very quickly.

As soon as London pulled back, another finger went up.

"Number seven! Don't tell Stella I said this! Alden says that he tries to be nice to Stella and she accuses him of only wanting her. But then if he doesn't pay attention to her she goes crazy, and cries, and says that he doesn't find her attractive!"

London shook with laughter.

"Honey! I'm worried that you will go crazy and be mean to me." Morgan said sadly.

London smiled.

"I'm not going to be mean to you sweetheart."

Morgan looked almost convinced.

"Will you still love me and... want me?" Morgan questioned.

London shoved Morgan.

"Yes! I will always love you and want you. However, after I have the baby no sex for six weeks." London stated.

Morgan's jaw dropped.

"Why is that, exactly?" Morgan asked.

"Because a baby comes out of there, Morgan; the baby is not exactly small!" London said in outrage.

Morgan seemed to cringe, thinking about that one.

London leaned in and whispered.

"I heard from Stella that she was on bedrest for about three months of her last pregnancy... no sex of course, and then you add six weeks to that." London shrugged.

"You do the math, Morgan."

Morgan's jaw dropped; Morgan shook his head.

"Poor Alden." Morgan said with sympathy.

"What about Stella? Poor Stella you mean! She pushed eight kids into this world and she's still raising Alden!"

Morgan huffed out a laugh.

"That is so true!" Morgan laughed.

Morgan grew thoughtful.

"Hey honey? You deep down figure you are still... raising me?"

London laughed.

"No! You my dear have your head on straight. But... Alden may be a bit... crazy because he made eight babies; and they are raising those eight babies!" London said incredulously.

"We should stick to one or two London; any more than that and we will be as crazy as the Westman's!"

London nodded.

"I'm with you babe... one or two is plenty."

Episode 47, Baby Gender Reveal Party

When Stella does something, she does it big.

Stella currently sported a shirt that said, *Keeper of the Baby Gender.* London's shirt said, *Baby Incubator.* Morgan's shirt said, *Future Non-Sleeper*

Alden had a good laugh when he saw that shirt.

Stella's yard was half blue and half pink. Every guest wore either a blue shirt or a pink shirt, depending on if they chose TEAM GIRL or TEAM BOY. Even the twins, Gracie and Hannah, were allowed to pick out which shirt they wanted to wear. Hannah grabbed a blue shirt, stuffing it in her mouth; Gracie grabbed a pink shirt plopping it on her head. Pop put on a pink shirt, he ran around telling everyone that would listen, "*That a real man wears pink and wears it well!*" Everyone figured he was just being contrary.

Grandma Nettie grabbed a blue shirt, she was praying out loud for a boy.

Caleb and David freaked out their dad when they dyed their casts blue. They also grabbed blue shirts, dipped their fingers in blue paint putting blue lines across their faces. The boys must have used food coloring on their hair, because when they started to sweat, they had blue lines running down their face and neck. Obviously, they were totally TEAM BOY, all the way.

The strangest shirt at the party was Ben's, he had a shirt that was half pink and half blue, straight down the middle. When asked why, he gave the sweetest answer. It made every woman at the party sigh and hug him.

"I don't care if it's a boy or a girl. I have been praying for Morgan and London to have a healthy baby... truth is... whatever the gender is... we are going to love this baby. I plan on spoiling the kid rotten."

Grandma Nettie had tears in her eyes, she sobbed a bit hugging Ben tightly.

"I just love this kid! Did I ever tell you that you are my favorite second oldest grandson?"

Ben shook his head, smiling.

"Grandma, I am your only... second... oldest grandson."

"But your place in my heart is secure, Ben! Your slot in my heart is forever yours and only yours."

Ben shook his head, grinning.

Pop spoke up.

"Ben, you are running out of time here kid...
you ever figure out what you are going to college
for? Baby doctor is out, after you went down in a
dead faint, after the twin girls was born."

Ben rolled his eyes, shrugging.

"No idea Pop. I'm thinking I might join the
circus or the rodeo after I graduate."

Ben didn't say it too loud because every
time he brought it up his parents freaked.

Pop chuckled.

"Pretty sure your mama will have a stroke if
you join the circus... rodeo too, kid. I can't wait
to see her reaction if you really do it." Pop threw
back his head and roared.

Stella yelled to get everyone's attention.

"Listen up everyone! Gather around."

Everyone wandered over, sitting in chairs.

"As you can see, we have ten fire
extinguishers. Morgan will fire off the first one.
He can choose whichever fire extinguisher he
wishes. You never know he might choose the
right one on the first try."

Stella turned towards Morgan; she waved
him forward to choose. Morgan circled the table.
Finally, he picked one up, he fired it off. Orange
foam shot out the thing. Morgan grinned.

"That would be a no." Morgan said.

London stepped forward and chose one. When she shot the thing off, it spewed out purple. On and on they went, they were down to two extinguishers. London and Morgan stood side by side, eyeing the two that were left. Morgan pointed at one, a lot of people cheered for that one. London pointed at the other one, half the group cheered for that one. London and Morgan finally picked one, it shot out green foam.

London jumped up and down, she knew that the last one was the correct one.

Stella grinned as Morgan picked it up. Everyone counted down from three. Morgan frowned for a second and waived at everyone to hush.

"Am I counting 3, 2, 1, and on 1 I spray this thing... or am I doing 3, 2, 1, and after 1, I spray it?"

Everyone got quiet.

Stella stepped up; she rolled her eyes.

"Just pull the trigger, nerd!" She yelled.

Morgan shrugged and pulled the trigger. Pink foam shot out of the canister and the place went wild.

Everyone started chanting, *Girl! Girl! Girl!*

Stella raced up shaking the last extinguisher.

"No!" Stella exclaimed but no one paid her any attention.

Morgan and London hugged each other.

"We are having a baby girl, Morgan!"

"I couldn't be happier!" He shouted.

Stella shot the canister off again, pink, pink, and more, pink.

Stella let out a war cry. That got everyone's attention. When Stella screamed like that... people tended to get wine bottles to the head.

Alden ducked under one of the tables.

"Ma! What's your problem?" AJ questioned.

"It's supposed to be blue! Blue! Blue! Blueeeee! Arrrrrrr!"

Stella banged the thing on the ground, repeatedly.

"Those stupid people put the wrong color foam in this thing, and they are going to pay! Pay! Pay! Pay!" Stella screamed.

Morgan wrestled the thing away from Stella.

"You can't do that Stella! These things are under pressure! Calm down, Stella. You mean we are having a boy; are you absolutely, sure?"

Stella's glare, directed at Morgan, almost sent the man running.

"Yes, I'm sure! I'll be right back!"

Stella stormed into the house; she came back with the results. Stella opened the envelope, inside it said, *Gender: Male.* Along with the written results was a sonagram. In the picture it clearly showed... boy.

Morgan and London hugged again.

"We are having a boy, Morgan!" London cried.

"I'm happy either way, London." Morgan assured her.

Stella stormed around the yard, with her cell phone in her ear. She could be heard yelling, *"Representative! I want to speak to a real... live... person! No! I do not want to hold!"*

Alden had come out of hiding but he did duck behind a tree, when he saw Stella raging on her phone.

Alden jumped when a hand landed on his shoulder.

"You wouldn't by any chance, be hiding... would you, Alden?" Pop cackled.

"Dad! If you ever got a bottle of cooking sherry to your forehead, from that woman... you would hide too!"

Pop rocked back on his heels watching his daughter in-law take the person on the other end of the phone, APART.

"She is quite fierce; I do love that about her, Alden. That woman right there, might rage at you, but if she loves you... she will take down anyone that threatens her family. I remember when she was pregnant with the twin girls. She took over the video games and ended up slaughtering her own teammates! Man! I loved that!" Pop yelled with glee.

Alden smiled, remembering that day.

"She sure is something... isn't she?"

Alden wandered towards his wife. Sure, she scared him sometimes, but then, he felt incredibly drawn to her.

Alden stopped next to his very distressed wife.

"It's ruined, Alden! Do people do this kind of stuff on purpose? I mean it's not Rocket Science! You have two choices, boy or girl! How hard can that be?" Stella sobbed.

Alden put his arms around his very upset wife.

"I think... you are amazing... and wonderful... I can't believe what you did to our yard! It looks fantastic! Don't even get me started on the food... and the best thing ever? CAKE! That cake you made looks like three tiers of magic!"

Stella smiled, just a little, but it gave Alden hope.

Alden nudged Stella with his shoulder; she nudged him back.

Stella shoved him; he shoved her back... a bit too hard I guess, because she flew backwards, landing on her butt.

"Alden! What the heck?"

"Oh! Honey! I am so sorry! I don't know my own strength babe! I was slinging hay earlier today."

Stella took a selfie of herself on the ground.

"What are you doing, Stella?" Alden questioned.

"I'm getting picture proof that you abused me... just in case." Stella smirked.

Alden hauled Stella to her feet.

"I would never!" Alden huffed.

Stella arched her eyebrows.

"And yet... I have proof on my phone that says otherwise."

"Gimmie that phone!" Alden exclaimed.

"Never!" Stella laughed.

"Get back here, woman!"

"I've always been able to outrun you, Alden; you so slow!" Stella cackled.

Phones went up, fingers started pointing.

The twin girls sat on their blanket, clapping at the crazy adults.

Pop started grousing.

"I want cake! When are we going to have cake?"

"Like you need cake, dear."

"I wouldn't talk if I was you... chubby!"

Grandma Nettie roared, she grabbed a chunk of cake and slapped it on Pop's face.

Pop grinned, he licked his lips.

"Whooeee! Now that is one good cake!" Pop exclaimed.

Pop cut a big piece of cake, grabbing a fork. Pop started running from Nettie while gobbling the cake down.

Caleb and David sat in their lawn chairs sword fighting with their crutches.

"And they say we are bad, David?" Caleb said while rolling his eyes.

"We may be bad... but... we are young and bad; that part of our family is old and bad, Caleb."

"You are so right MY MAMA'S AFTER THOUGHT, you are so smart!"

"I take after you my AMNIOTIC FLUID BRO!"

Caleb grinned.

"Good one, David!"

"Thanks Caleb, I can't believe all the stuff that rolls around in my big ol brain."

Caleb leaned forward eagerly.

"Like what?"

David's grin turned evil.

"Well... I was thinking that once we get these casts off, that we could... "

Episode 48, Five!... Back to One!... Stand Down People!

London, now over nine months pregnant, figured she was going to be pregnant... forever.

London sat on the sofa, tears streaking down her face.

"Honey, please don't cry. You are beautiful, so beautiful!" Morgan encouraged.

London glared at Morgan, hiccupping from her crying spell.

"Nice try, Morgan. I'm fat... and my feet look like sausages... I can't... *sob...*get comfortable."

London got a very panicky look on her face, she leaned over, grabbing Morgan's shirt in a death grip.

"He's not coming out; he likes it in there! He just keeps getting bigger and bigger!... *Sob!* I'm twelve days beyond my due date. I went to the doctor today, Morgan." London whispered woefully.

"Yes, honey, I was there." Morgan said.

London gulped.

"I'm not dilatated... at all! The baby is in my ribs, he's not dropped down one bit. I'm going to be pregnant... forever!"

Morgan hugged his wife.

"That's not humanly possible, sweetie."

London growled at Morgan.

"What do you know about it? Your body looks great! My body will never be the same again! This seems very unfair to me! I have stretch marks on top of stretch marks!"

"They will fade... and I don't care about your stretch marks. Stretch marks do not mean a thing! Besides, wear them like a badge of honor, you lift that shirt! You point at those things and tell the whole world that, YOU ARE WOMAN! That, YOU CARRIED A LIFE INSIDE YOUR BODY, YOU KEPT IT SAFE AND LOVED!"

Morgan was marching by now, gesturing wildly. Morgan stopped in front of his wife, hands on hips, looking a bit stern.

"You know what London... I LOVE your stretch marks! I hope they NEVER go away! Every time I look at them, I will remember you like this... you... you remind me of..."

"Of what, Morgan." London asked.

"Of the love we share, and the fact that we made this beautiful boy that I cannot wait to meet."

London smiled, then she giggled; London fell over sideways laughing.

"I'm stuck! I can't get up!" London gasped between bouts of laughter.

"What is so funny, darlin?"

"The way you said, *I love your stretch marks! I hope they never go away!*" London's voice was deep, she imitated Morgan very well.

Morgan got London back up, into a sitting position.

London sighed.

"Well... I do look at Stella and she looks amazing! She does have eight kids though. I bet she never gets to sit still! After this baby is born, I'll be wishing he was back inside me so I can get some sleep. *Sigh.*

Morgan looked conflicted.

"Maybe I should stay home today. I have a lot of paperwork at the office, but I could push it off onto someone else." Morgan stated.

"No... I'm fine. Plus, there's certain paperwork that only you can do. I'm going to take a shower and stop feeling sorry for myself.

Besides, no dilation, no nothing; there is NOTHING going on down there, go to work."

London struggled to stand.

"However, help me up before you leave for work. I will not be sitting on this couch today, that is for sure, not while you are gone, anyway."

"Do you promise me that you won't overdo things today?" Morgan asked.

"I promise. I'm going to lay on our bed and binge watch my romance channel."

Morgan nodded.

"Ok, I'm out the door. My cell is charged and ready, you call me, I'll already be racing to the car!"

"Relax tiger! If I call you, it's because I might want some ice cream."

Morgan grinned.

"I'll bring home ice cream anyway."

When Morgan left, London took her shower. Her shower went a long way towards waking her up.

London stepped into the nursery; she rubbed her belly as she surveyed the room.

Instead of blue, they decided on soft greens and yellows. On one wall the word *Devin* adorned the wall. *Devin Morgan Dun,* she thought it was the best name ever.

London decided to hang up some of the baby clothes. London dialed Morgan to ask him something.

"Is it time?! I'm on my way! I'll use the sirens and lights!"

"Morgan! Stop! It is not time! I was going to ask you where the extra hangers are for the baby clothes that I want to hang up?"

"False alarm guys! It's not time! Jamison, she is fine! We are at a five people, relax!"

"What do you mean a five, Morgan? What exactly does that even mean?" London asked.

"I came up with a 1-5 system. Five means you are fine, when we hit one that means... it's time to GO!"

London tapped her foot, waiting for Morgan to focus.

"Morgan! If I could reach you right now... seriously, where are the hangers?"

"Oh! They are in a bag in our closet; don't overdo sweety."

"Got it, bye honey."

When London had everything hung up, she moved on to putting the stuffed animals in the net on the wall.

London frowned.

Where the heck did Morgan put the three bears? London wondered.

London looked everywhere.

When London stood up, she felt her back twinge again. London called Morgan again.

"I'm coming! I'm heading out the door, London!"

London growled at Morgan.

"Morgan! I'm just looking for the three bears! Do you know where they are? I want to put them on the baby dresser."

"She's fine! Well, I'm sorry! I can't help it if she's going to stay pregnant forever! Shut it! I can't hear her! Stand down, people!"

"The three bears, Alden; where are the three bears?"

"Oh! In a box on the top shelf in the baby's closet. I can get it down when I get home, honey."

London saw the box on the shelf.

"I can reach it; I got it down. Have a good day, babe." London said.

"Love you."

Before Morgan could hang up, London scolded him one more time.

"Morgan! Don't panic every time I call! Relax!" London exclaimed.

"I'm sorry honey, I'll do better. I can't help it because I worry. I love you. I'm bringing home dinner so don't cook anything."

"Oh, thank you, that sounds great."

London hung up the phone. When she had the three bears positioned on the baby dresser, just right, she smiled.

London went downstairs carefully, to get a snack. She figured that it was time for some food, a nice drink, and time to binge watch her series.

London made it as far as the dining room table, when an intense contraction almost took her to her knees. London sucked in a breath, she felt fear and excitement all at the same time.

London looked around for her cell phone, she had it upstairs in the nursery. London was horrified to realize that the one and only time that she left her cell phone behind, she went straight into labor. London realized quickly that these were not those false contractions, these were the real deal.

London looked up at the tall staircase. The banister was strong and smooth, she could hold on to that on her way up. London was furious with herself for forgetting her phone.

London took a couple of steps, another contraction hit. London lost all the breath in her body. London made it to the first step, she grabbed the banister, her knees resting on the first step.

Sweat rolled down London's face, she felt her belly tighten, and her back cramped, making her legs quiver uncontrollably. London breathed in deeply through her nose, blowing out slowly through her mouth.

When the next contraction hit, London knew that if she didn't get to that phone that she would truly be in trouble.

London climbed between contractions, they seemed to be coming faster. The next contraction had London screaming at the top of her lungs. London felt water gush between her legs, she knew she wasn't going to make it to the hospital. This baby was coming fast; baby Devin finally decided he wanted out.

London had every intention of giving her OB a piece of her mind!

The nursery was beyond their bedroom, her old room. London was now at a crossroads; she could crawl into their room and give birth or crawl farther to the phone and give birth in the nursery. Either way this baby was coming out, no doubt about that.

London reached down, feeling between her legs, she could feel the very top of the baby's head.

London decided to keep going, she needed that phone!

London was forced to scoot, then crawl. When she reached the doorway to the nursery, she felt an uncontrollable urge to push. London got up onto her knees, she braced her hands against the wall. London had dropped her pants on the landing, she decided to lose her shirt right here. Sure, she was butt naked, but she had to admit she felt more comfortable. London pushed and panted; she was starting to get worried. Did it normally take this long to push; she just wasn't sure! London reached down again; the baby's head was right there!

London screamed through her last contraction as the baby was born. London caught him, she plopped down on her butt, she hugged Devin to her chest as she fell backwards to the floor.

London laughed, she cried, and when baby Devin wailed, she cried some more. London didn't know how she did it, but she managed to almost stand up. London hobbled forward, grabbed her phone hitting the speed dial, for Morgan.

"Hey babe, what do you need now? I told you to take it easy, but it sounds to me like you are overdoing things, London."

London gulped; Devin wailed some more.

"London? What was that noise I just heard?" Morgan gasped.

"You know that system that you set up, Morgan? We are at one; baby Devin is here. I'm fine, but I need you and an ambulance. Please hurry honey."

"People! We are at a ONE, I repeat, a ONE! I need an ambulance at my house. I need... I need... I don't know what I need... help! Gasp! Crash!"

"Hello? Hello? Is anyone there? Someone needs to tell me what is going on!" London screamed.

London heard a commotion.

"Miss London, is that you?" Jamison asked.

"Yes! Where is Morgan?"

"He's on the floor, he passed out. Oh, my goodness, Miss London! Did I hear a baby? Did you have the baby?"

"Yes, Jamison, and I need an ambulance, and someone needs to bring me my man! I've made it to my bed, but I need help!"

"We are on the way, and so is the ambulance!"

"Ok, see you all soon." London hung up the phone.

London thought for a second; she picked up her phone again, calling Stella.

"Hello?"

"Hi, this is London; any chance your mom is home?"

"Oh, hi London. Ma decided to check on you, she should be there any second."

"Is this Elijah?"

"Yes, ma'am."

"I had the baby at home, the cavalry is on the way, but I don't know what to do about the umbilical cord."

"You stay calm London. I'll stay on the phone with you until Ma gets there. It doesn't hurt for the umbilical cord to remain attached. Many parents like the cord to empty before separating it anyway. I can explain the benefits of that later, if you like. Is the baby breathing, ok?"

"He's beautiful; he's breathing just fine! He's got a head full of black hair, just like Morgans."

"Have you passed the placenta, yet?"

London blushed.

"Um... no... but I feel the need to push again." London admitted.

London heard knocking at the front door. Stella must have pushed it open because she heard her yell out.

"Your mom is here, Elijah! I'm going to let you go!"

"I'll let my dad know what's going on, love you London."

"Love you too Elijah and thank you so much."

London hung up the phone yelling for Stella to come quick.

London could tell when Stella found the spot where her water broke. Stella practically roared as she raced up the stairs.

Stella started to pass her bedroom door because she was following London's trail, but she stopped suddenly when she realized that mother and son were in the master bedroom.

Stella raced into the room, her eyes rounded with panic and awe.

"Oh, sweetie! You had him at home, all by yourself? Why didn't you call me?" Stella growled.

"I managed to make it to the dining room table, when a massive contraction hit me. I left my phone up here in the nursery, go figure. Morgan is never going to trust me again."

"Oh, pooh on him! He didn't just push a baby out like a beast!"

"Stella, I just went to the doctor, and nothing was going on down there! Then, wham! Devin decides to make an appearance."

Devin nudged his mother looking for his first meal.

London looked nervous; she wasn't sure what to do.

Tears pooled in Stella's eyes.

"It's the most natural thing in the world, London. Let him roll towards you and it just... works."

When Devin latched on, London's smile rivaled the sun.

A loud commotion could be heard at the front door.

Stella stepped out into the hallway.

"Up here guys, my bestie is doing just fine! Where is her man, that's what I want to know! Morgan better be here, or else he's going to feel my wrath!" Stella shouted.

Morgan rushed up the stairs, he almost took Stella to the floor. Stella grinned as she pushed Morgan into the room with his wife and child.

Morgan couldn't believe what he was seeing.

"You… you… had the baby… here… at home? You, did this all by yourself?" Morgan asked.

"I need to push! Stella, come get Devin!"

Morgan gaped at London.

"Wait! Why are you pushing? What is happening? Is there another baby in there?" Morgan gasped.

The ambulance team pushed their way in, they quickly got to work.

"I need to push!" London yelled.

Morgan went white, his eyes rolled back and down he went.

Stella and Devin would have been squashed but she sidestepped him before he had the chance to crush them.

"Whooeee! That was a close one! That man falls on me I would probably be all kinds of broken." Stella said.

Stella cooed at Devin.

"Did that big, mean, ol daddy, try to kill us? Oh, yes, he did! Aunty Stella's got you!"

The ambulance man grinned.

"You owe me twenty bucks, Foster; we have a fainter, here."

"I never thought our very own Sheriff Dun would faint! I thought I had this one figured for sure! It's always the big ones that face the floor!"

"Okay, Mrs. Dun, go ahead and push. Passing the placenta is far easier than anything else you had to do today. By the way, great job! You pushed out a mighty fine, big boy! I'm impressed."

"If that baby weighs under eight pounds, I win the pool!" Foster exclaimed.

London glared at her husband on the floor, she glared at Foster and the other guy too.

"Focus boys! I love how a MAN tells me, a WOMAN... that pushing out the placenta is no big deal! Men are stupid! I'd like to see you do what I've done today! Also... have the two of you not heard about the evils of gambling? I should call your mothers!"

London had to stop talking because she got busy delivering that placenta.

Morgan woke up long enough to get a look at the placenta and faceplant again.

Stella shook her head; she kicked Morgan in the thigh... a bit roughly.

"Maybe, this fainting thing is contagious? Hmm... Alden's going to love this story."

Both women got the giggles and couldn't stop.

London was loaded up into an ambulance.

Stella followed behind.

Jamison picked up his Boss Man, flung him into the back of his squad car, taking him to the hospital.

Morgan woke up halfway there.

"What is happening, Jamison?" Morgan asked frantically.

"Your wife had the baby... all by herself... like a straight up champ! You fainted in your office, you woke up, you fainted again, you woke up, and fainted a third time! I had to carry you like a bride to the car and toss you in. We are currently enroute to the hospital so you can probably faint again. Bahaaaa!"

"Jamison, pull over and let me drive!"

"Not going to happen, Boss. You fainted three times... you could have hit your head. I cannot in good conscience allow you to drive. You just sit back and try to come up with a good reason you why you fainted three times... not once... not twice, but THREE TIMES! Your wife was soooo angry! Eeesh! I would not want to be you right now, Boss."

Morgan looked a bit unsure.

"She was pretty mad, huh?"

Jamison pursed his lips in thought.

"No... not mad... more like livid! Bahaaaa!" Jamison roared again, slapping the wheel.

Morgan pulled his hat off, running all ten fingers through his hair.

"She loves me... she will forgive me... I hope."

Morgan didn't look too sure; Morgan had a sudden thought.

"Hey, Jamison... I need to make a couple of stops before we go to the hospital.

Episode 49, Ice Cream?!

By the time Morgan arrived, London was cleaned up, and tucked into bed. London decided she wanted to be put in the ward, where there were four beds. London had a feeling this time soon, her room was going to be full.

London looked up; Morgan was hesitating outside her door. Alden and Stella sat across from her bed.

Alden snickered; Stella elbowed him.

"Come on Alden, we should give them some alone time." Stella said.

London frowned.

"I would rather the two of you stay, if you don't mind." London said seriously.

Morgan crept in, he had a Styrofoam box in his hand and his hat in the other. A giant

452

bouquet of flowers seemed to be growing out of his armpit. He also seemed to be balancing a very large box of chocolates as well.

"Hi, honey... how are you feeling?" Morgan questioned, his voice almost a whisper.

London glared at Morgan.

Morgan dropped his head, in shame.

"London! I'm sorry! I'm so very sorry that I missed his birth, that I wasn't there to help you... I feel... I feel like a failure."

London sighed.

"What's in the box?" London groused.

"Michigan Triple Trax." Morgan said sadly.

London's eyes bugged.

"You! You found my favorite ice cream? Where on earth did you find that?"

Morgan shrugged.

"I ordered it online a week ago, it's been in the freezer at work. I've got about a half dozen more in the freezer at work." Morgan, mumbled.

London smiled wide.

"Hug me you gorgeous man!" London squealed, throwing out her arms.

Morgan didn't argue, he grinned back, while swooping down on his wife.

Alden's jaw dropped and stayed dropped.

Stella choked with laughter.

"Nu uh! No way did she just let that man off the hook because of... ICE CREAM!" Alden exclaimed.

Morgan smirked at Alden over his woman's head, he even stuck his tongue out at Alden.

"Gimmie! I want my ice cream! Go hold our son, Morgan." London demanded.

Morgan gazed at Devin; he was so small. Morgan hesitated, glancing towards Stella for help.

Stella stood up. She bent down, picking up Devin like a professional.

"Sit Morgan, I'll hand him to you. You will be an old pro at this in no time."

Morgan put everything down, sitting in the chair closest to his wife. Morgan's eyes stayed glued to the bundle that Stella was pressing into his arms.

"I don't know about this Stella, he's so little!" Morgan exclaimed.

"You prop his head in your elbow. Yes, just like that! Put your other arm around him... see! You are a natural, Morgan."

Morgan gazed at his son... his son. Morgan shook his head, his eyes slid towards London.

"Are you ok, honey? You aren't hurt or anything?"

"I'm fine. Just so you know... I left a mess on the stairs, up the stairs, on the landing, and both bedrooms."

Morgan gulped.

"How can you be alright, London? I saw... all of that... and I still can't piece it all together. I see you! I see the baby! I just can't wrap my head around this whole thing! You my darling, are incredible!" Morgan stated with tears in his eyes.

Alden finally spoke up.

"While you were... resting Morgan, your wife did everything. My vasectomy failed and I'm still in trouble, but you brought ice cream, and all is forgiven? Trust me, I'm still trying to wrap my head around that one."

Alden turned towards Stella, glaring at her.

Stella tweaked his nose.

"Maybe, you should have brought ice cream." Stella said, with a totally serious expression.

Alden gaped at her.

"If I stop and buy you ice cream, am I off the hook?"

Stella shook her head no.

"You should have made that last appointment dear, now you pay for the rest of our lives." Stella sated.

Alden sighed.

"Hey Morgan... how many kids you two planning on having?" Alden questioned.

"TWO!" Morgan and London said, simultaneously, with feeling.

Alden arched his eyebrows.

"Wow... quick answer, and so specific." Alden said.

Adlen smirked at Morgan.

"So... that means that eventually you will be the one getting the big V... huh Morgan." Alden laughed.

London shook her head no.

Alden looked shocked.

"Wait! What do you mean... no? You mean... no vasectomy for Morgan? Why not?!" Alden was shocked and he seemed a bit... miffed.

London shrugged.

"Well... it's like this Alden. I have rough... woman times... my doctor thinks that after I have my next baby that I should at least have my uterus removed."

Stella gaped at London. Alden started to protest but Stella slapped her hand over Alden's mouth.

"What's wrong with you?!" Stella surged to her feet, looking shaken up.

London blushed, looking away.

456

Stella took the baby from Morgan and shooed them out the door.

"Tell me!" Stella demanded.

London shrugged with embarrassment.

"I... because of Trent... I have some woman problems."

Stella gently placed Devin in his bed, she sped over to London.

"I really want to break that man out of jail, beat the crap out of him, and then toss him back in jail. I'm so sorry London." Stella cried, while hugging London.

"It's a miracle that I got pregnant for Devin. I may never have anymore children... we shall see. If I don't get pregnant within a few years... I have to have a partial hysterectomy."

Morgan stuck his head back in the doorway.

"Please let me back in! Alden is whining and moaning about me not having to have the big V!"

Morgan grinned.

"While I am enjoying his pain... I want my son and wife!"

Stella grinned.

"Oh, come on in!"

Morgan sped inside. He made a beeline for his son. Morgan bit his lip trying to figure out how best to pick him up. Morgan glanced back at Stella for help.

"Put your left hand under his head, and your right hand under his butt."

Morgan did as he was told, he grinned like a fool, while hugging his son to his chest.

Morgan sat down again, he eased Devin away from his body slowly, so he could look him over.

Alden stepped inside, glaring at everything and everyone.

"I want to leave, Stella."

Stella eyed her irate man.

"Poor Alden... you had to get a vasectomy... TWICE! Morgan doesn't EVER have to have one... oh boohoo! Grow up man!" Stella said with a laugh.

"It's not fair! It's just not right!" Alden growled.

Stella sighed.

"Yeah, life just isn't fair. Be thankful you don't have to have ANOTHER vasectomy, Alden!"

Alden gulped.

"I guess there is an upside to everything... I suppose." Alden said thoughtfully.

London turned towards Stella.

"I can't believe that Grace and Hannah are two and your oldest is graduating in six months! Your oldest is a senior and your youngest go to tumbling class."

Stella nodded.

"I almost cry when I think about AJ graduating." Stella confessed.

London looked up.

"AJ sure seems to like Mary an awful lot. You think those two are going to end up together?" London asked.

Stella shrugged.

"I don't know... I think Mary is super focused on school... she seems to like him well enough but..." Stella got a bit quiet.

"But what?" Alden asked.

"They are so different... AJ is a born farmer... I think that Mary wants something else. I guess time will tell."

Morgan chuckled.

"If I had to lay bets on the future..." Morgan shook his head. "Never mind." He stated.

"You can't do that honey! Finish what you were going to say! Now all three of us are curious." London exclaimed.

Morgan tilted his head in thought.

"I think... that there is one very determined young lady out there that if she has her way...

she will snatch a hold of AJ and never let him go."

They all looked confused.

"Who? Who are you talking about, Morgan?" Alden asked.

Morgan grinned slightly.

"Sarah, Mary's sister."

Stella practically vibrated with shock.

"What? No way! Morgan, that is the craziest thing I've ever heard! Why would you think that?" Stella asked.

"Just a feeling. Sarah is an animal lover, like AJ. Sarah is always at your place helping with the cows and the chores. Sarah follows AJ around everywhere... and... she calls him Alden James." Morgan explained.

"What does her calling him Alden James have to do with anything?" Alden asked.

Morgan didn't say anything for a minute.

"I think... Sarah is going to surprise you all. I'd lay money on it if I was a betting man. You mark my words... I think Sarah may be the future Mrs. Alden James Westman." Morgan insisted.

Stella and Alden looked at each other, then burst into laughter.

"Never in a million years, Morgan! No way! AJ is mad about Mary! He looks at Sarah as a younger sister." Alden stated.

Morgan shrugged.

"Maybe I'm wrong... but... then again, I guess time will tell."

London looked curious.

"I've met Mary and Sarah; they both seem like wonderful girls. By the way, what is their last name?" London asked.

Everyone went still, no one really looked her in the eye.

"What did I say?" London questioned.

Morgan looked up at London.

"Their last name is... Trent." Morgan said with hesitation.

London's jaw dropped.

"Trent... their last name is, Trent? Wow... interesting." London said.

Morgan eyed London.

"You okay, honey?"

"Did everyone avoid telling me their last name... because they thought it would upset me?"

Stella shrugged.

"Well... you've been through so much London... we decided to avoid the name, if you get me."

London poo pooed everyone.

"It's just a name and that man has zero power over me anymore! I am loved by this wonderful man and all of you. I have my beautiful baby boy that I wasn't sure I would ever have, after the miscarriage. Doc told me then, that my chances were iffy."

London reached for the baby when he started fussing.

"He's hungry, let me feed him." London whispered.

Alden stood up; Stella followed.

"We will let you two spend family time together. We will see you both later."

When they left, London unbuttoned her shirt, she placed Devin on her chest, allowing him to roll towards her, like Stella taught her.

"How do you know how to do that, London?" Morgan whispered in awe.

"Easy as breathing, Morgan."

Morgan looked amazed.

"Does it... hurt?"

London smiled at her husband.

"Not at all."

Morgan looked like he had more questions.

"What? What's on your mind, Morgan?"

"Are you going to swell up like Stella did? Because that was... the craziest thing I ever saw!"

London giggled.

"Every woman is different but... I will for sure be much bustier, for as long as I breastfeed Devin."

Morgan eyed his son; Devin seemed to be enjoying his meal.

Morgan sighed.

"I'm going to miss you honey." Morgan stated with a grin.

"Miss me? What do you mean by that?"

"Devin... he's going to be attached to you for a while, and that is fine... I promise you that! He needs you more than I do, right now."

Morgan's shook his head.

"If you leak like Stella, I'll sleep on the couch with no problem."

London shook with laughter, dislodging Devin from his meal. Devin wailed until London switched him to the other one.

Morgan practically goggled when he saw that.

"I have to switch him back and forth Morgan, or I'm going to have one breast bigger than the other. Next time I feed him, I start on the breast that he left off from."

Morgan held up his hands.

"I may not understand all of this, but I plan on learning everything! I'm officially on vacation for two weeks. I plan on being the best husband

and father ever! I may not be able to feed him but I'm going to change him, fetch things for you both. I'm going to cook, clean and... well, you just tell me what you need, and I will get it done."

London sniffled; tears gathered in her eyes.

"How did I get so lucky to have found you, Morgan?"

Morgan rolled his eyes.

"I found you, darlin. I pulled you over in a snowstorm. There I stood... looking at you bloody and broken, cuffed to your steering wheel. From that day on I couldn't stop thinking about you or worrying about you. I see your strength London and you fill me with awe and terror. The way that you would face Trent, on your own, to try to protect us all... don't' ever do that again!"

"Yes, dear." London said meekly.

Morgan shook his head.

"You are not fooling me! You would do it all over again, if it meant keeping the people you love, safe. I love and hate that about you, London."

"You cannot judge me, Morgan Dun, you are the sheriff. I worry every time you walk out our door."

Morgan smiled.

"I guess we will take turns worry about each other... for a lifetime." Morgan whispered.

"That sounds good to me, Morgan... but... even a lifetime doesn't seem long enough."

Episode 50, Graduation Day!

Stella sat in the long row of chairs, inside the huge high school gymnasium, at White Cloud High School. Today, her first born son, AJ, was graduating from High School. Where had the time gone? Stella looked down the aisle, her family took up one whole, very long, row.

Stella smiled as she watched Pop play with her sister Annie's newest baby boy, he just so happens to be named after Pop. Pop is so proud to have a grandson named after him, he is always snatching the boy up. Pop put his finger under the baby's bottom lip, moving it so it looked like the baby was talking, then Pop would add words.

"What was that you said baby Sealy?" Pop asked.

Pop moved his finger, he turned his voice into a younger, squeaky voice.

"You are the best Pop in the whole world, and I love you more than anyone."

Annie shook her head, she grinned at Pop.

"Are you putting words in my son's mouth, Pop?" Annie questioned.

Pop smiled with pride.

"This kid is a genius! He takes after me don't yah know?" Pop explained.

The twins were seated next to Pop, they kept peering at the newborn.

"Does he do anything besides sleep?" Caleb asked.

"I don't think I've even seen what color his eyes are, he is always sleeping!" David complained.

Ben leaned in.

"Aunt Annie is probably very happy that this little guy sleeps so good, our poor mom and dad, are just now starting to get some better rest, the girls are finally sleeping through the night."

Annie shook her head in sympathy.

"My poor sister and brother in-law, I cannot even imagine how tired they must have been for the last two and a half years."

"The crazy thing is Aunt Annie, you can literally vacuum under their cribs, and they will sleep right through it. When the house is going crazy, they sleep just great. When it is quiet, they are more fitful." Ben stated.

Annie nodded.

"They were used to all the noise from when they were in the womb, I have heard of that before." Annie said.

"Mom runs a fan in their room now, and plays soft music, now they sleep great." Caleb told them. "London came up with that idea."

"Hey Pop, Grandma Nettie is waving at you." Ben stated.

Pop scowled.

"She just wants to take Baby Sealy away from me!" Pop grumbled, scowling fiercely!

Annie smiled gently at him and took the baby. She stood up, gently passing the baby to Tom. Down the line the baby went until it got to Grandma Nettie. She took the baby with a smile of pure joy, she snuggled him close, kissing his cute little cheeks.

Stella caught her sister's eye, Annie smiled softly, Stella mouthed "*I love you.*" Annie nodded and winked at her sister mouthing back the same thing.

Stella smiled as one of her besties turned around to talk to her. Stella and Cara had been best friends for years but parted on unfriendly terms. Years later they made up and now were joyously back in each other's lives.

Cara turned around; she sat directly in front of Stella with her three kids. The girls looked like they could be twins other than the fact that they were six years apart, Finn took after his daddy.

"I cannot believe that AJ and Mary are graduating today, it's like I blinked and poof they are all grown up." Cara stated.

"I am feeling the same way myself Cara, it just does not seem possible." Stella sighed.

"Next year it will be Ben, he keeps up his straight A average he is going to have a full ride to college for sure." Cara said with enthusiasm.

Stella glanced down at Ben, he had been so broken-hearted when Gemma had led him on and then dumped him. He had gone into a slump; Stella was glad that Gemma had dumped him on the last day of school that year. He had the whole summer to get over her. It had been rough, but thankfully he had gotten through it. Now he acted like he did not want anything to do with girls; he did his chores, went to school, got excellent grades, he never gave them much to worry about, and yet... Stella did worry.

The principal tapped the microphone, to make sure it was working. Everyone quieted down, to watch their children walk the stage. Before names were called, Mary Trent, the top of her class, gave her speech.

Mary did not look nervous at all; she looked cool and calm. Mary's voice rang true and strong, as she addressed her fellow classmates, her teachers, the faculty, and parents.

"I stand here today, amazed that we all made it, we did it!"

Mary grinned, all her classmates went wild, clapping and cheering, AJ whooped and hollered the most.

"Tomorrow, we don't get up to go to school. We don't board the buses. We will miss talking and kidding around with our friends. We don't get to meet up in the lunchroom... everything is different."

Mary's face grew serious, you could have heard a pin drop.

"I will miss all of that. We all worked so hard to make it to this moment, long nights studying for exams, till our brains hurt."

Some of the graduates let out moans just remembering that.

"I put my grades above and beyond everything else. I wanted to be the best... to be number one... to get a fantastic scholarship, so I can go to the best college."

Mary looked down.

"Then... I will again be studying and staying up all night to make those A's."

Mary hesitated, she swallowed, her eyes met AJ's.

Everyone in the gym was a bit confused, this was not a typical graduation speech.

Mary seemed frozen, unable to go on. The principal stepped forward to ask Mary if she was alright, Mary nodded and continued.

"I turned AJ down over and over. I missed dances. I pushed and pushed, but most of all... I pushed him away. I thought I was too young to know my own mind. I have goals, and I wanted to reach those goals, for my parents, to make them proud, and I did. So... Why am I so sad? Why do I feel like I missed out on so much?"

The principal stepped forward to end Mary's speech.

Mary grabbed the microphone and held it away from him.

"I'm not finished!" Mary yelled.

AJ stood up, all eyes turned towards him, Mary's included.

Mary looked AJ straight in the eye.

"I have decided to go to our local community college, I am staying here in the White Cloud area."

Mary's parents gasped! Mary's father surged to his feet; the entire auditorium seemed to erupt with noise.

Mary's dad looked ready to blow a blood vessel.

"Now you listen to me young lady! You have a full ride to college, and you are going!"

Alden and Stella jumped up also, heading towards the stage. They stopped next to where AJ stood.

Mary was moving fast, racing around the stage, to keep her microphone. She was determined that nothing was going to stop her. The entire audience began to murmur, some laughing out loud at Mary's game of keep away with the principal.

Mary kept talking, through her parents' objections. Alden was trying to talk to AJ, but he only had eyes for Mary. A huge grin spread across his face, he stood with his arms crossed, like he had all the time in the world.

Some of the kids Mary was graduating with, stood up and yelled out that everyone should just let her talk.

The principal stepped back, clearly not liking how this graduation was going. He knew that he had lost all control, and he had no idea how to regain it.

Mary began to speak quickly, afraid that the principal would eventually get the microphone out of her hand.

"What I am trying to say here, is that my whole life, I have tried to be a good daughter, a good sister, a good student, a good friend. I have never actually decided for myself, done what I wanted to do!" At this point Mary was practically shouting.

"From here on out, we are considered adults! We are old enough to vote! We are old enough to go to war! Old enough to smoke, and old enough to make our own decisions. So... I urge you all... go be happy... do what your heart tells you to do. If we should ever be so lucky to figure out where we fit in this world, and we get the job of our dreams, then that would be amazing! How many of us settle? Every day we should get up with excitement, because what we are doing is our dream job. I know how I feel about AJ Westman."

AJ just kept smiling.

"You told me once AJ Westman that I had to ask you to marry me."

Again, Mary's parents surged towards the stage. The auditorium erupted into complete chaos. Alden's cousin Nick had his video recorder going, as usual. Nick was catching every second of the drama that was unfolding. Nick even dove in front of Alden and Stella, going down low. Stella was sure that he caught every expression of shock, horror and more.

AJ never took his eyes off Mary.

The principal was now frantically trying to take the microphone from Mary, but she was far too quick. She raced around the stage dodging each grab that came her way. Finally, she jumped off the stage, with the microphone still in her hand, going down on one knee.

"AJ, not today, not tomorrow, but maybe soon... would you please marry me?"

Cheering swept through the gymnasium when everyone realized that they were indeed witnessing something epic.

Alden and Stella gasped, everyone did. The graduating class threw their hats in the air, even though they were strictly told not to! After all, you wouldn't want to poke out an eye!

AJ started towards Mary. Alden placed his hand on his son's shoulder; worry clearly written on his face.

"I got this dad, trust me." AJ looked so grown up at that moment, but his parents knew this was clearly a mistake.

AJ stepped up to Mary, he took her hand, and pulled her to her feet.

"I love you Mary, I always have, but you are going to college. If we are meant to be, then when you graduate, the answer is yes."

"But AJ!" Mary sputtered.

"You have a free ride to school, you are going. I would never want you to have any regrets, and eventually you might grow to hate me if I held you back. So, you are going to go. Trust me, every part of me is wanting you to stay, but you got to go."

AJ pulled Mary close. Everyone started clapping, especially the Trent's, they really wanted their daughter to go to college.

Stella looked at Alden, he looked a bit pale. She was sure she did too. This could have all ended so differently.

Mary finally handed the microphone to a very relived principal. One-by-one names were called. The clapping grew thunderous when Mary's name was called, followed by AJ. With their diplomas in their hands, they stood on stage, their hands locked together.

AJ smirked at Mary.

"I told you that eventually you would ask me to marry you... took you long enough."

Mary threw back her head and roared with laughter.

AJ laughed right along with her.

"You are never going to let me live that down are you, AJ?" Mary growled.

AJ shook his head no.

"When we are old and grey, I will tell our grandbabies how pushy you were, always naggin me."

"Well, you know AJ... I think that maybe next time around, you are gonna have to do the askin. I mean I asked you in front of our peers, our teachers, parents, even God. I would love to see you top my proposal." Mary smirked at AJ, challenging him with her eyes.

AJ grew thoughtful.

"Challenge accepted; we shall see."

They left the stage together.

As the graduates started to find their way out of the gym, Stella began to giggle. Alden whipped his head towards his wife.

"What is so funny woman? Our son easily could have been heading to the courthouse today to get himself hitched, and here you stand grinning. What on earth is going on it that head of yours?"

Stella pulled herself together, she nudged Alden. He turned to look where she was pointing. There sat their family, the people they loved. Ben, then Sealy, he had somehow gotten his mitts back on the baby and he was cooing sweetly at him. Caleb and David both looked back at their parents with curiosity. They didn't understand exactly what had taken place, but they were keeping their eyes peeled for any more excitement that might occur. Then their twin girls, with their spiral curls flowing down to their waists. Their big dark eyes checking out the world as they stood quietly waiting for their mom and dad to head back to them.

Morgan and London stood up, from behind the family, holding six-month-old Devin. They waved at them with happiness.

Cara practically bounced with happiness and excitement. Stella knew that they would be having a very long conversation, with coffee and cinnamon rolls.

All their loved ones, seated together, silently waiting. Stella and Alden headed towards those rows of chairs. Those rows of chairs that held their whole world.

Stella held Alden's hand.

"Alden, don't you see, hon? For once... our children... our family... were not the ones causing an uproar. Our family was not directly causing chaos. While Mary was causing all that ruckus, here sits our family, like sweet little lambs."

Stella stopped and did a comical fist pump.

"Yeah!" Stella yelled out, twirling in a circle, with glee.

Alden stopped, seeing exactly what Stella was referring to.

"Well, I'll be damned!"

Hannah and Gracie both gasped, they both pointed at their dad.

"That's a bad word dad; swear jar for sure!"

Alden hung his head.

"I'm gonna go broke from that damn jar!"

As they all filed out, the girls told their daddy again, that when they got home, he was gonna have ta put them quarters in the swear jar, immediately!

The End

About the Author

On December 8, 2023; my husband Edward and I will be married for 34 years. Marriage can become a bit boring at times; routine, I guess. Then that crazy train speeds up, we hang on the best we can, and try to ride it out!

About that time, I wish boring would come right on back! No matter what, my husband and I are on this wild ride, together.

We love our kids, and all the grandkids, we have ten!

Let's not forget the dogs, cats, pigs, ducks, chickens, goats, and horses.

I can't remember a single day when we didn't have critters!

I've heard it said that critters keep you young.

Well dang! If that's true, then this 59-year-old identifies as 30!

Keep reading!

Keep laughing!

It's good for the soul.

Thanks everyone!

Made in the USA
Middletown, DE
23 October 2023

41185278R10269